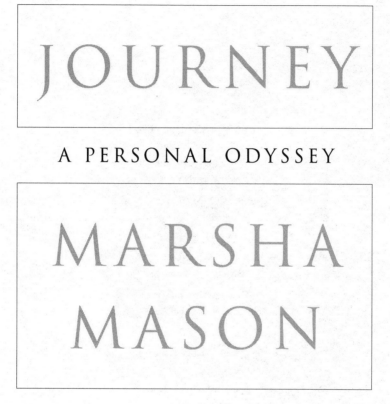

JOURNEY

A PERSONAL ODYSSEY

MARSHA MASON

SIMON & SCHUSTER

NEW YORK LONDON TORONTO SYDNEY SINGAPORE

SIMON & SCHUSTER
Rockefeller Center
1230 Avenue of the Americas
New York, NY 10020

SIMON & SCHUSTER and colophon are registered trademarks of
Simon & Schuster, Inc.

Designed by Chris Welch
Manufactured in the United States of America

1   3   5   7   9   10   8   6   4   2

Library of Congress Cataloging-in-Publication Data
Mason, Marsha.
Journey : a personal odyssey / Marsha Mason.
p. cm.
1. Mason, Marsha. 2. Actors—United States—Biography. I. Title.
PN2287.M5425 A3 2000
791.43'028'092—dc21   00-044048   [B]
ISBN 0-684-81524-9

For permission to reprint pictures in this book, grateful acknowledgment is made to the following sources. Any omission is accidental and will be corrected upon notification in writing to the
publisher. Pictures not otherwise credited are courtesy of Marsha
Mason. 11: American Conservatory Theater. 12: Rothschild Photo.
13: © Martha Swope/Time, Inc. 15: *Blume in Love* © 1973 Warner
Bros. Inc. All rights reserved. 17: Mel Traxel. 18: Hollywood Foreign
Press Association. 19: Friedman-Abeles. 21: Lee Salem/ABSI. 23:
Derek Photographers. 28: Alan Berliner. 29: Carolyn Wright.

ACKNOWLEDGMENTS

Some four years ago I had a conversation with my friend Shirley MacLaine and told her I had been approached to write a memoir. Thinking they just wanted me to write about my ex-husband, Neil Simon, I declined. Shirley, in her energized and charming way, said, "Do it! I'd love to read about your life! Besides, it's probably the most important thing you'll ever do." So, I wrote some thirty longhand pages and handed them to literary agent and wonder woman Esther Newberg at ICM. She read them immediately and called me before I got home. "I think you can write. Now, please type the pages from now on. My eyes aren't what they used to be."

When Michael Korda, my editor, read those typed pages, he said, "I want to publish this. Now, please double space your pages. My eyes aren't what they used to be."

My heart is full of thanks and gratitude to Shirley, Esther, and Michael Korda for giving me the push, support, and opportunity to tell my story. I do apologize for causing eye strain, but Shirley is right. The benefit of writing your story is immeasurable. I encourage everyone to do it. The rewards are not dependent on publication. I am forever grateful to Michael for allowing me to write at my own speed and use a somewhat unorthodox structure. If the reader is at all confused or disoriented, Michael is not to blame. Neither is Chuck Adams, co-editor, whose intelligence and concern kept my thoughts hopefully clear and my "voices" distinct.

And finally I wish to acknowledge Hal Stone, Blanche Saia, Roger Gould, and Marilyn Hershenson for their talent, support, love, and guidance. I am grateful to have known and worked with each of them.

For my mother,
Ellen and Nancy,
Baba Muktananda,
and
Gurumayi.

CONTENTS

JOURNEY

FOREWORD

"Titles are important. Very important." That's what my ex-husband Neil Simon always told me. Michael Korda and Chuck Adams, my editors at Simon & Schuster, said the same thing. These three men are extremely successful at what they do, so if they feel a title is important, it must be important. I tried to think of one before I even started writing this journey . . . this memoir. At first I thought it was important that the title of the book be catchy, the way some play titles are. For example: *There's a Playwright in My Soup, I've Been Down So Long It Doesn't Look That Bad to Me,* or *I've Been Down So Long It's Starting to Look Up to Me,* or *I've Been Down So Long Low Is Looking Up to Me.* What about *I Got My Act Together but It's Too Heavy to Take on The Road?* Or *My Arm's Too Short to Box with a Divorce Attorney* or *Long Day's Journey into Santa Fe?* How about *Same Time Next Century* or *There's a Playwright in My Suite?*

Then it occurred to me that the title of this memoir might be a takeoff on one of Neil's titles: *The Odd Person* or *Last of the Red Hot Divorces* or *Barebreasted in the Park* or *Retirement Bound; Sunshine Girl* or *Prisoner of Bellagio Road; Mason Suite: A Life in Three Acts; Chapter Three: Last and Final.* Ah! I have it: *The Goodbye Girl Does Santa Fe!*

Hmmm. After some thought and conversations with friends it was decided I should take into consideration the foreign sales of the book: *Marsha of the Spirits* (Italy); *A Tale of Two Marshas* (England); *Lower Expectations* (England again); *The Madness of Queen Marsha* (England still again); *Looking through the Glass Lightly* (Sweden); *Marsha's Ashes* (Ireland).

Hmmmmm. After some more conversation and thought, the potential of a movie sale was discussed (what hubris, but I was beginning to feel a bit desperate): *Dial M for Mason; I'll Cry Tomorrow, Laugh the Next Day: Cry, Laugh, Cry, Etc.* or *I'll Scream Tomorrow; Journey to the Center of Marsha; The Bride Came Federal Express; An Affair to Forget; Crimes and Bad Demeanors; Being There (But Not Knowing It); Gone With the Breeze; Playwright Spotting; Lady in the Dark, with a Flashlight; Love Is a Many Splendid Settlement,* which led me mindlessly to think of song tie-ins: "Me and My Many Shadows" or "Me and My Voices"; "The Way We Weren't"; "What Are You Doing the Rest of Your Divorce?"; "I Like You Just the Way You *Were*"; "I Concentrate on Me"; "The Sound of Static"; or "Fly Me to the Moon, One Way."

But what about the New York intelligentsia? I queried my manager and friend Mr. Michael Black, who then suggested: *Marsha's Ashes* (again) or *Mason's Complaint; Withering Heights; A Woman of Dependent Means; Brunch with Your Agent in the Garden of Good and Evil.* I particularly liked that one. *Marsha of Sunnybrook Farm; A Life More Ordinary; From Here to Internally; The Lady* Thinks *the Blues;* or *Restless Spirits.*

Michael, not one to mince words, asked, "By the way, how many 'voices' are there?" Oh, nine or so . . . I think. I didn't count.

"Well," he drawled, "how 'bout *A Majority of Nine* or *Around the World on 80 Couches* by Marsha Mason, a tip-off to the book? Or *Give Me Librium or Give Me Meth*?

But what about the "Self-help" market? I wondered out loud, changing the subject, slightly. Maybe *How to Be Your Own Best Friend and Find Out You Don't Like You* or *Getting to Know Your Inner Child and Realizing You Can't Stand Her. Playwrights Are from Mars, Actresses Are from Venus?* Michael countered.

You're O.K. but I'm . . . (the F word) or *I'm O.K. but . . .* No, that won't do at all. Out of desperation I considered *See the Foreword* and *Titles Are Important.*

I decided to start writing without a title. After completing my first draft some three years later, I sent it to Michael Korda and Chuck Adams with a tentative title, *That Was Then, This Is Now.* Only "This Is Now" wasn't "now" at all (now was now three years old), so I then suggested just *That Was Then* and waited.

Michael sent me his notes with suggestions and cuts almost immediately.

"Explain, with an introduction of some kind, how the book is structured as a journey, so the reader understands, otherwise it's going to be confusing. By the way, I like *Journey* as the title."

Aha! The title. *Journey.* Now to the more knotty problem, the book.

INTRODUCTION: THE CAST OF INTERIOR CHARACTERS

Before trying to explain the structure of this journey I think I should explain that I didn't take it alone. There were real people and animals involved and "other" people, interior people who exist only in my mind. My interior friends are "selves," or aspects of my personality. They have very strong personalities with strong opinions and seem quite independent of me, even to me, as you will see. I'd like to introduce:

G.A.: My guardian angel, hence her name, G.A. She's full of pizazz. Smart, fast talking, stylish in a forties kind of way. When she first appeared some ten years ago she wore a tailored maroon suit, nipped at the waist; shoulder pads; narrow skirt; and to top it all off a jaunty hat perched rakishly on her pretty head. Think Rosalind Russell in *His Girl Friday* and you've got the picture.

The Collapser: Her name's Gloria. Not a bad gal but not a winner. She whines a lot. Doesn't like making the effort. Always complaining about something. Cute but dumb. Well meaning but not someone you want in the trenches comes the revolution. Think Gloria Grahame in any of her B movies.

The Pusher: His name, Chuck Moses. Great guy but can be very irritating. Booming voice that sounds as if he travels with his own echo chamber. He feels responsible for getting the job done. Any job. Think Charlton Heston in *The Ten Commandments;* hence his name, Chuck Moses.

The Critic: No name, not even a face. But a voice and attitude that can kill, literally. Sometimes it's a woman's voice, sometimes a man. Always hard, berating, sarcastic, demeaning, shrill, abusive. Take your pick. A real nightmare.

The Sisters Eccentric: Two distinct voices with separate personalities. Sometimes they appear separately, sometimes together. Think Billie Burke as the good witch Glinda in *The Wizard of Oz* and Martita Hunt as Miss Havisham in the original *Great Expectations.*

The Inner Child: In my case, inner children. Anna and Ed. Anna's around six and Ed's nine going on twenty. Ed showed up a couple of years ago when I was doing a play in New York. I met Anna formally in 1974. I've been in touch with my inner kids practically all my life. Most creative people are, I think, in one form or another.

The Patriarch: On good days he's a great guy. Soft, wise, caring, protective, smart. On bad days he's controlling, demanding, withholding, and very tough. Sometimes he looks like Andy Hardy's dad in those Mickey Rooney pictures. Sometimes he looks and sounds like Edward Arnold in *Meet John Doe* and sometimes like Lionel Barrymore as the wealthy villain Mr. Potter in *It's a Wonderful Life.*

The Warrior: My favorite fella. He's a relatively recent addition to the family, brought to life one afternoon walking on the beach in Malibu. He was a real manifestation. I saw him out of the corner of my eye. Think Daniel Day-Lewis as the intrepid last of the Mohican scouts and you get the picture.

Mr. Olympus: Every gal should be in touch with this gentleman. He's my "strictly business" self. A smart man with a head on his shoulders who understands what it takes to be truly successful in business. If only I'd met him sooner.

The Rebel: She's got blue hair, rings in every orifice, including her tongue; wears black and thinks of herself as a misunderstood artist.

Abused, a loner; loves racing, motorcycles, cars, and misunderstood men. She's in her early twenties going on sixty. But cute, definitely cute.

Sister Mary: She's a nun. More accurately, a novice. She loves being a nun. So much so she's willing to become a monk!

Grace: Ahhhh, Grace. She's a voice. A soft, understanding presence without judgment but filled with discrimination, compassion, commitment, who holds that service to one's fellowman and all sentient beings is our true and ultimate role in life. She is who I want to be all the time. I sometimes think of her as my "divine blue pillow."

I hope you enjoy meeting everyone (real and interior) as they pop up along the way. Now, if you're not already confused, I'll try to explain the structure I chose for my story, my real and personal journey.

My story begins with leaving. Moving from Los Angeles, California, and driving to Santa Fe, New Mexico, in the summer of 1993, a journey of considerable physical distance, defined by the time taken to make it—two days, and the following four days that it took to get my life unpacked and put into a new place, a new time, the beginning of another life. During the course of those six days I went back a much longer distance and time, all the way back to my beginnings in St. Louis, Missouri, some fifty years ago. . . .

CHAPTER ONE

HITTING THE WALL

I t's June 26, 1993. The day is fading and so am I. Twilight is coming on, "Magic Hour," they call it in movie jargon. My favorite time. On this seemingly ordinary California summer evening all is quiet on Turquesa Lane in the Pacific Palisades of West Los Angeles. Standing in the street, a cul-de-sac really, everything appears to be normal, but of course that isn't true at all. Everything is far from normal. I'm packing up my entire life and moving it far from here.

Artwork has been carefully crated and loaded into a temperature-controlled compartment right behind the driver's cab of a very large and very long semi with all my plants squished in there too. Twenty years of a California life packed up in just two days, and the moving men needed a second truck. Finally, just an hour or so ago, the semi and its slightly smaller brother trundled up Turquesa Lane and disappeared from view, already on the road, attempting to beat the torturous high noon heat of the Arizona desert, with the final destination Santa Fe, New Mexico. Everything that screamed chaos for days is packed up and gone. Now, tonight, there is nothing, not a single detail to let anyone know that I'm leaving. I decided not to say good-bye to my neighbors because I'd cry and feel some kind of hellacious pain. I have to spare myself so that everything gets done, this monumental move and everything it symbolizes. Get everything done, without feeling: that's been my mantra these days—one of them anyway.

"Don't let yourself feel. Mustn't feel," commands my inner Critic. She's been on her high horse during these days, functioning in survival mode. So have all my internal voices, my other selves. There are a lot of them. There's G.A., my guardian angel; there's the Collapser, Gloria, named after the actress Gloria Grahame. There's the Pusher, who I've named Chuck Moses. There's lots of others. Every one of them up in arms. Well, why not? This is major change. I listen to my inner Critic tonight. I pay attention. I obey. Of course, I'm full of feeling, almost overrun with a torrent of feelings, but I can't let go right now. Can't unleash. There's too much to do.

The sky is a dusky blue with orange rays fanning a cloudless evening sky. The full, stately Ponderosa pines stand breathlessly still. The birds are silent. The family of deer has daintily made its way back down the hill, gracefully jumping the low back fence, seeking shelter and sleep under those stalwart pines behind the house. God, just thinking of the deer makes my throat constrict. Animals and parades always do that to me—any parade, all animals, especially the ugly ones. I've never been able to figure out why. Some weird kind of identification I have with them, I guess. Go figure. I swallow hard to push the emotions back down, clear my head of the image of a whole family of deer gingerly appearing in the backyard a couple of years ago from far down the steep hill, nibbling here and there, then resting in the late afternoon on the grass, the bigger deer standing guard over the little ones, always alert and cautious. They remind me of a leaded glass scene on an old Russian chandelier that hung over my grandmother's dining table. I wonder if they'll miss me, even know I've gone, and gone for good.

"Don't think about that," comes the silent warning.

Taking a last look around, everything appears spotlessly normal and eerily quiet. No one would know I ever lived here, I muse, standing outside the front of my house, a home I built from plans that were serendipitously dropped into my lap some five years before. I take a last look at my beautiful house. "A proper home for me alone," I used to say. This search for home has been going on for a long time, almost ten years now.

"Hell, longer than that!" This interior voice is another "personality," the cute but irritating wiseass who whines at times, and who reminds me of Gloria Grahame. She always sashayed when she acted, I thought. I don't feel much like sashaying tonight though, as I gaze at my house and the neighborhood around me for the last time, knowing I mustn't hesitate too long for fear of cracking into a million pieces, fragmented forever with no hope of pulling myself back together. I mustn't give in to this swirling emotion roiling in the pit of my stomach. I'm leaving my past and consequently my identity behind, scurrying off to a new, unknown place, like an animal with its tail between its legs, head drooping. Hopefully, in a few days, weeks, whatever, I'll feel that I've found a new home and a new existence, a completely different life that makes sense and brings some kind of sustained peace and enjoyment.

"Lord, girl! You've never really experienced *that,* sustained peace! You're a woman who's known divine discontent most of her life." Right you are, G.A. Well, no, that's not totally true. There were *some* years when my life and career felt good, hopeful, and satisfying.

G.A. is with me most of the time now. She makes me smile. Of course, there have been moments, and years, of happiness. Besides, what does that mean exactly, "divine discontent"? But tonight I'm wired; I'm impatient.

"Divine in that you've always been a seeker, lookin' for the answers. So simple really," G.A. chides, "a seeker of answers to those plaguing questions, 'Why am I here?' 'What is my mission, my true vocation in life?'" G.A. is right, as usual.

My father, James "Jimbo" Joseph Mason of St. Louis, Missouri, used to belittle my philosophical questions. When I'd press him for an answer—"Any answer!"—he'd tell me I was stupid to ask such a question. "What does it matter? Who cares!" he'd snarl or dismiss it altogether getting up to make another drink. I didn't generally ask my mother because when I was a young girl I was sure she wouldn't answer directly anyway. "Go get your dinner, honey. Your Dad and I are relaxing." I didn't understand until later that she was probably trying to smooth things out. I guess I learned that from her, smoothing things out.

When I was much older and a wee bit wiser, I came to understand that my father was a deeply unhappy man who felt that life was against him, that he didn't have a real chance at happiness. He felt his parents hadn't loved him, especially his mother. He was sure she preferred my Uncle Murray, Dad's younger brother. I was eight years old when I first noticed my grandmother's bias. Later I asked my mother if this was true and she told me, "Yes. Nina's a funny bird."

I remember her vaguely, Nina. Her given name was Grace. I don't remember why my sister and I called her Nina. I do remember her dyed hair and powdered skin; and her pretty, manicured nails on slender fingers that shook as she smoked; and her wobbly voice, like someone invisible was always shaking her when she spoke. As a grandmother she was distant, not what you'd call loving or available. That must have been true for Pops as well, I suppose, my father's father, though I don't have *any* memory of him.

My father was a hurting man. He was hurt and he hurt in turn. He felt his father didn't love him or respect him. Pops had wanted my father to go into his printing business, Mason Printing, but he never told him the business was failing. Dad found out after his father died, when nothing could be done about it, when the business was failing, with no hope of recovery. Maybe Pops hadn't realized it. Maybe neither Pops nor Dad were smart businessmen.

"Wonder if that's why being a smart businesswoman is so important to you," G.A. muses.

Small businesses like my Dad's were being eaten up by big ones and the printing unions were making it difficult for him to make ends meet.

"They're taking more money home than I am," Dad bitterly confided about his workers one night over a drink. Everything was changing. Everything that was familiar was dying and a strange new order was taking its place. Just like now. My father felt Pops had set him up for failure in a business he really didn't want to be in. What Dad craved and needed, I believe, was for his father and his mother to love him, and to show that they loved him. What he got instead was failure and it scarred him. I saw it first when I was in high school, but didn't know then how sad he really was. Several years later, on a return trip home while performing in the national company of *Cactus Flower,* I was taken aback. His face was gray and sallow. Too much drinking and way too much smoking were apparent in the hard light of sunshine. His body was caved in, his shoulders stooped. And he wasn't at peace. He was sick and didn't know it. Or perhaps he did, but I didn't want to see it. He was young still, only forty-five or so.

Is that why I'm restless for peace? I wonder. But then, what is peace anyway? I ask myself.

"Who cares about this drivel anyway? What good does it get you!" Gloria Grahame whines. "All this internal stuff!" she huffs, her petulant voice pooh-poohing. I hear Gloria stamping her foot now. I pay her no mind.

Is that what I hope to achieve with this move? Peace? A new life, a new beginning? Or is it simply contentment? Is contentment really simple and is it really a possibility for me? For most of my life, I've felt like an outsider, a loner, a nomad, never truly "at home" wherever I've been. I've never felt as if I really "belonged" anywhere, even Hollywood. Well, maybe the ashram in India, although I haven't really tested that yet, not for longer than a month anyway. And I've certainly not felt truly content, ever.

"Well, that's not totally true, Marsha dear. There was a time when you felt a part of things. You felt like you belonged in New York City when you first went there, and you felt that you belonged in the theater, desperately wanted to belong to that community of struggling, talented actors; and you felt "at home" in the ashram at Baba Muktananda's feet." This voice, another inside my head, momentarily soothes me. She's right, I do feel at home when I think of Baba, my spiritual teacher, my guru. I feel at home with this voice too. I've named her Grace, the Goddess. She's a sound rather than a personality or a face. When she's around she holds all my hopes and dreams for myself as a mature woman.

"That was a long time ago," I say out loud, with a sigh. When? My first trip to India was . . . late 1970 something and the second trip was two years later. Yes, I felt I belonged there too. It's also true I felt I belonged with my first husband, Gary Dale Campbell, at least when we first married, but that changed, of course. And I felt when I married my second husband, Neil Simon, that I belonged with him forever, but that changed as well.

After our separation in 1983, but before moving here to the Pacific Palisades in 1987, I spent an awful lot of time on planes, traveling between New York, Europe, and California; a lot of time living in hotels, buying and renovating a New York apartment; and all the while renting houses in Los Angeles. I needed to be "on the move" following my second separation and divorce. Looking back, I was a whirling dervish, dancing out of control, but at the time I thought I knew what I was doing. However, contentment and peace were nowhere to be found, not around me.

Ten years married, ten years divorced. Married October 25, 1973. Separated April 4, 1983. Amicably divorced (if there is such a thing) April 1984. The thought "ten years married, ten years divorced" skips through my mind like a thrown stone, skimming across a pond. Why, I don't know. Like a mantra, it reverberates, seemingly apt, yet weird, all at the same time.

"Ten years married, ten years divorced." Divorced from a man with whom I thought I was going to spend the rest of my life. Suddenly a sickening wave of emotion starts from deep inside, gaining speed and size. Nope, can't go there, I tell myself. I rub my face brusquely with both hands, shaking the feeling away.

"Oh, you're ever so earnest, Miss Marsha! My, my, my. Ever so. This earnestness of yours is perhaps naively charming, but really now, at fifty? Come now! Some humor, some perspective is called for, don't you think?" Right you are, Miss Eccentricity. She is another voice, my own Billie Burke, the Good Witch Glinda in *The Wizard of Oz*. Thank you for those humbling but sage thoughts, Miss B.!

Honestly, these voices! Some of them are full-blown physical presences in my mind and some are not; some are merely voices from the void. Grace comes to me from this void while Miss Eccentricity, my eccentric self, sometimes appears as two distinct people, sisters if you will. The one that just spoke looks and sounds exactly like Billie Burke but sometimes I hear and see Martita Hunt as she appeared when playing Miss Havisham in *Great Expectations* (the original one), sitting by her wedding cake with all those cobwebs hanging about, living in the dust and the past. They are flip sides of the same coin. One fluttery and a bit of a ditz, the other all rational, to the point, and no nonsense.

What do the *next* ten years hold? I wonder, forcing myself to think ahead. Well, it's certainly going to be different, very, very different. Will the next ten years feel apt and weird too? Will my life ever *not* feel apt and weird? This time nobody speaks up.

I GUESS EVERYTHING always feels apt, weird, scary, and strange to me. My childhood did; grade school and high school did. Certain times in college definitely did. Going to New York and marrying Gary, then divorcing Gary, then marrying Neil. Coming to Los Angeles in the late spring of 1975 as Mrs. Neil Simon was a pretty scary and strange situation. I was a stepmother of one year and some months to two wonderful daughters, Nancy and Ellen, ages twelve and seventeen, and bride to a world-famous husband, some sixteen years older than me. We'd only known each other three weeks before we became a family, yet scary and strange though it was, I soon came to feel ever so settled and stable and secure. We had a formal house all our own in Bel-Air, California, and we had tandem professional careers. I believed we'd live out our lives together and die an old married couple with tons of grandchildren, and maybe even a child of our own. I was *sure* of it. Now it's almost twenty years later and here I am, standing at the curb of my cul-de-sac, taking a last look at my "proper home for me alone," having "hit the wall," my explanation for this life in shards at my feet. And here I am again, starting out on another journey that feels apt and weird and scary and strange, leaving tomorrow for parts unknown just like I did when I married Neil Simon, beginning another journey through uncharted territory, and at fifty years of age no less.

Neil and I never had that child of our own, but the girls are grown and married with children. I haven't remarried. Neil has twice.

"No, three times. Once to you. Twice to Diane." Nevermind, G.A. He swore he'd never divorce again, no matter what, but he did. He still lives in the house that we lived in when we first came here from New York.

"Such is life, dear girl, such is life. It's about time you moved upward and onward!" This from Miss Havisham. I hate when she expounds with her maddening clichés.

"You never know what's around the corner, that's the spice of life!" Glinda the Good Witch warbles in tandem.

I rarely see Neil now, although we're always cordial and warm with each other when we do meet.

"Honey, you are a remarkably different person now, compared to the young woman who married him and came here to live. And that is a mother of a truth. You've come a long way, Baby, and I for one am mighty proud of you." I can't help but smile. Thanks, G.A.

"And while we're at it, let's *not* wallow, shall we?" she continues in her rueful tone.

G.A. got her initialed name during a therapy session several years ago. She appeared in a dream, and Marilyn Hershenson, my therapist at the time, asked me what she looked like, encouraging me to get to know her. Marilyn smiled as I described this guardian angel and asked if this unique voice had a name. "G.A." popped into my head. We're old friends now, and as I said, she always makes me smile. She's been there for me since that first meeting, always. Think of Rosalind Russell straight out of the movie *His Girl Friday,* wearing a tailored suit and jaunty hat, with that quick repartee Ms. Russell was famous for, and you get the picture.

Okay, okay, I sigh as I stretch my sore body, glancing again at the sunset. Those early years on Chalon Road in Bel-Air were heady and happy ones, though. I'd come from New York City with my new family, having already "won" an Oscar nomination for *Cinderella Liberty,* and my first Golden Globe for that movie, although in those days the Golden Globe Awards was a rather amusingly tarnished affair.

"Just like the statue you packed today, honey," G.A. quips. You're right, I think that poor old statue's awfully tarnished.

"Then get on with it!" booms the voice of my internal commander, the Pusher. This sonorous male voice generally gets my attention by issuing declarative statements or forceful commands, like now. I've never asked the Pusher if he has a name, but whenever he announces himself, I invariably envision him as Charlton Heston in *The Ten Commandments,* hence the name Chuck Moses.

There are other voices in my head as well. I suppose they are unique to me, and that other people have voices of their own. Each of mine has a personality, an attitude, even if they don't all have a specific appearance. Some have titles; some have names. They are the various aspects of myself I've come to know through a process called Voice Dialogue.

Some of these selves or aspects of my personality are "primary" selves, and some are or have been "disowned" selves. For example, since my primary self growing up was a Good Girl, the opposite of that was the Rebel. Being born and raised a Catholic in a very strict household, I disowned my Rebel self in order to be a Good Girl. Eventually though, a disowned self will command attention, and left unacknowledged will assert itself, often through relationships. The Rebel then becomes a primary self and the Good Girl probably gets disowned. In my case, I ran away from home in my senior year of college (for a week during Christmas vacation) and began to trade in my Good Girl self for my Rebel self. Of course, way back then I didn't know that was what was happening. I just knew that I had to get out of St. Louis and get to that great city.

When I moved to New York City in the early fall of 1964, after graduation, I quickly married, and in the process "hooked up" with that disowned aspect of myself, the Rebel. The man I chose was Gary Dale Campbell. He was my James Dean, my Rebel self. I loved James Dean, especially in *Rebel Without a Cause,* and I definitely identified with him. Gary, my first husband, reminded me of James Dean—I thought he even *looked* like him. We were both young and scared, hungry for love, and in search of comfort and a sense of security. We married in February 1965, and even though we eventually divorced, we have stayed close—very close as you shall see.

Yes, there are a lot of inner voices running through my mind. Perhaps it's a bit weird if you haven't had the pleasure, but I find it comforting to know that I—the me of me—am much bigger than I thought possible. Getting in touch with these inner voices has helped me to see myself and, consequently, other people with more compassion and has also helped me to understand and appreciate the relationships I have with friends and loved ones. Some of the voices or selves are more dominant than others. Some have appeared for special or limited occasions. Others, like G.A., Chuck Moses the Pusher, the inner Critic, the Sisters Eccentric, and Grace the goddess, stay around fairly frequently. Still others, that you haven't met yet, come and go depending on what is happening in my life. Men are often the catalyst for greater activity amongst them. Life is an ongoing process so there may be new voices that I haven't even met yet.

Disowned or primary, these are my "selves": the Critic; the Patriarch, sometimes benevolent, sometimes insane; the Pusher, Chuck Moses; the Artist/Inner Child, Anna and Ed. Anna is six years old and is me when I was six. She looks exactly like a picture my mother has of me. I was "introduced" to her in an early experience with the Voice Dialogue process. Ed is around nine years old and doesn't look like anybody I know. He just showed up one day during the run of *Night of the Iguana* at the Roundabout Theatre in New York. He's a great kid, my tomboy self, if you will. Then there's Gloria, the Collapser, who you've met, and the Goddess Grace, my integrated and realized self, who I hope will one day be a primary self, and G.A. my guardian angel and protector. There's the Good Girl, the Rebel, oh, and there's a nun self too, Sister Mary. Oh! And there's my Warrior self who showed up one day about six years ago in full tribal regalia prepared both to protect and do battle. I was having a difficult time getting rid of a very narcissistic and negative lover who shall remain nameless. I mentally conjured my Warrior that day while walking on the beach with Mr. Nameless. My Warrior appeared on my left (I actually saw him), walking just a bit away, a tall, beautiful, long-haired scout, with loincloth and spear, feather earrings, and strands of beads adorning his chest and arms. He was barefoot, and bronze in color, with startling blue eyes. Sensitive and strong. Think Daniel Day-Lewis in *The Last of the Mohicans* and you've got the picture.

Now let's see, who else? There's my eccentric selves, Miss Havisham and Billie Burke as she appeared in *The Wizard of Oz* and there's also Mr. Olympus; you haven't met him yet. He's the "strictly business" tycoon who's recently come onboard. He helped me learn how to deal with the authoritative men I've come across in business. He helped me take a "hitting-the-wall" experience in my professional career and transmute that experience into a successful one while racing cars and being my own business manager.

I certainly wish I'd known or owned him sooner. I used to believe that success in business and being an artist were at odds with each other, but there you are. Mr. Olympus also helped me to learn when not to bring my Artist self (Anna and/or Ed) into those important first meetings with producers, or those important, sometimes confrontational discussions with the power boys who are in charge. Sometimes I've brought Mr. Olympus, Grace, *and* my Warrior self to a meeting and it can get pretty exciting. Over the years I've learned to listen to and engage all these voices inside my head. I've learned to own them, respect them, and love them. But it wasn't always that way. I used to be petrified of them.

During childhood, adolescence, and as a young woman in her twenties and thirties, I was afraid there was something seriously wrong with me. I felt high on the list of possible crazies because these voices sounded like whole, separate people from myself. They used to fight each other—and me—for control and for my attention. I used to feel that I was a lot of different people, schizophrenic, like a woman on the verge, so to speak. There was a time when I was frightened to death of abandonment, afraid to be left alone. Now those fears are gone. I love being alone and I'm never lonely. That's because of all the internal work and contemplation and meditation. In fact, I'm grateful for all the voices and for my spiritual teachers. They all taught me not to be afraid to be alone. Baba Muktananda told me that he would always be with me and he is. And how could I feel alone with all these various aspects of myself popping up all the time!

Have I wasted these five years here, I wonder, taking a last look around at my neighborhood? I was trying to cling to my past in this house, a past that doesn't exist anymore, thinking that was my identity, on top of my work being my identity, trying to hold on to that identity and finding myself slamming into those cement or thick brick walls, walls that are obviously saying, "You can't go back there." "You can't get through here." Me not listening, not getting the message, being brain dead or on automatic pilot, like a prizefighter who only knows how to fight the old way, even when he keeps getting beaten down. Trying to jump-start a stalled career, as if it were an obstinate engine and not a dead one. Trying to create a meaningful relationship with the wrong men, men who don't want or can't have a permanent relationship with me or perhaps with anyone else. Or thinking I want to create a meaningful relationship, then not wanting it when it actually presents itself. Foolishly thinking of myself as a thirty-year-old instead of what I am, fifty.

My disowned selves often manifest themselves in the men I'm attracted to or the women I like and admire. This Voice Dialogue process has given me such an interesting way to look at people, especially men. Men often hold what I've disowned. For example, when

Hal Stone, the man who created the Voice Dialogue process, asked me to describe Neil, my second husband, I said, "Successful, funny, shy, patriarchal, demanding, controlling, sexy, intimidating, controlling, patriarchal, successful…" "Well," he interrupted, "then you must have a successful, funny, demanding, shy, patriarchal, controlling self in you." "Oh, no!" I cried, "I'm not at all like that, at all!" There's a reason that opposites attract. And if you find that you are often attracted to men who aren't good for you then it becomes imperative to get in touch with that disowned aspect of yourself they represent and break the destructive tendency of trying to own it through a relationship.

Sometimes I have to stop the voices by yelling "Not now!" although I know that ultimately I'll listen and eventually accept them. It's a bit awkward if I happen to be out in public! Thank God for cars! I do a lot of my screaming in cars.

My selves are sometimes quiet for periods of time, and sometimes vociferous when I'm about to do something important, something major, like now. I used to run from them but now realize they just get louder and more persistent if I don't listen. They sometimes have sent me warnings, that if gone unheeded, would have left me with a painful and humiliating lesson to learn. For example, drinking too much. If I don't stop and pay attention I can get into trouble. I might embarrass myself or embarrass someone else.

One of the best ways to "hear" my voices is to stop and pay attention, to listen for them, to meditate; give them time and some space to come forward. Meditating with mindfulness, that's the key. The voices help me understand myself, and the meditation helps me know my real Self. Even God is me, and the Goddess, and the Inner Child, and all the other selves that are manifest in the other human beings around us.

I think the Inner Child is operating in most of us. She (or he) comes out when I fall in love, when I'm creating, when I'm dreaming, when I'm playing. She or he, as the case may be, is just beneath the surface in all of us, even the most hardened businessman. When I first met Anna, my Inner Child, she wouldn't talk to me. She wouldn't even look at me; that's how shy and scared she was. It was a revelation to me that *I* was that shy and scared when I was a kid but upon reflection I realized it was true. I'd buried those feelings somewhere along the road of growing up. It was difficult recalling my early childhood in therapy. I didn't seem to have many memories.

I do remember being dressed in twin outfits with my sister and hating it. My mother made most of our clothes and made them beautifully. As babies (my sister and I are sixteen months apart) we wore hats and coats of matching wool in wintertime and often dressed in matching outfits for special occasions. I hated being a twin when I really wasn't one.

Another memory that has stayed with me is getting lost. My mother and I were in a very big department store. The aisles went on forever and there were great big bins holding articles to buy in the center of the aisles. I got lost somehow. Fear and panic overtook me. I couldn't find my mother anywhere for what seemed like a very long time. I didn't know what to do. If I kept moving she might never find me. On the other hand it occurred to me that she might leave the store and never come back for me. I started to wail. Somehow we were reunited and I was scolded for wandering off. My mother's solution to this problem was to get a leash with straps that went around the chest and over the shoulders and buckled in back. This was attached to the leash proper, like a dog's leash, with a loop at the end. My sister had one too. We were walked down the street on our white leashes summer and winter.

I don't have any memories of my own when I was a baby. Some people remember things that happened to them when they were two or three. My earliest recollections start around four or five, with one exception. I did have an unusual experience of myself as a baby when I was beginning therapy. Blanche Saia was my first therapist and a terrific woman. I'd been seeing her regularly for a couple of years. One afternoon I didn't think I had much to talk about and told her so. She suggested we try something a little different. "Why don't you lie down on the couch?" I'd never done that before; I always sat in a chair. The couch was against the opposite wall. I suddenly felt awkward getting up and going over there but I didn't say anything. Blanche's chair was behind my head. I was an adult in my mid-twenties, in serious therapy, not liking her couch much. I lay there with my eyes closed and waited. Why was I so nervous, anxious even? I wondered.

"What's happening?" "Nothing," I answered. Silence. "What do you see?" "A farm," I answered, "with a white silo and a white farm house." Silence. "What else?" Slowly an image started to come clear, black bars on a white background. The reflection of bars on a floor. A baby holding on to the bars, trying to stand, and suddenly screaming, but no sound came out and no one came. The next thing I know, I'm sitting up, screaming, "I'm going crazy! I'm going crazy!" Blanche, to my complete surprise, was seated at my side gently rubbing my back, telling me everything's okay. When did she get up from her chair? I wondered. How long had I been "out"? "What happened?" I cried, "what happened? I couldn't scream, nothing came out, but I heard the scream, nobody came, I feel so scared!" The words tumbled out as I sobbed and blew my nose, feeling all jangly and vulnerable. After Blanche calmed me down she suggested I ask my mother if anything unusual happened when I was two or three years old. "What do you mean, unusual?" I asked. "Well, something out of the ordinary . . . something maybe that never happened before?"

I called home one night shortly after that session and queried my mother. Mom thought about it and then said, "I do remember something. I left you with Momsie, your grandmother, to visit your dad before he shipped out." She told me that she had gone to see my father in Quantico, Virginia, where he was in Marine Officer School. He was to be shipped out because of the war. She had never left us before. "How long were you gone?" I asked. "Oh, six or seven weeks. Not long. I remember calling home and Momsie told me that you had been very upset and acting funny so I told her to put you on the phone so I could say hi. But when you heard my voice you became hysterical. I was going to come home but Momsie said not to, that you were all right. When I did get home Momsie brought you to the train station and you acted as if I'd never left. Does that count as unusual?"

My mother, Jacqueline Helena Rakowski Mason, of St. Louis, Missouri, thought I was rather unusual growing up. Perhaps she thought that because I often seemed to frustrate her. Perhaps it was just that she had two babies sixteen months apart to take care of without much help. I do remember feeling alone a lot. I don't know when I first noticed the voices but my mother tells me that as a very little girl, I used to sit on the floor in the living room of our apartment on Clarence Avenue, in North St. Louis, and quietly transfer pennies from one jar to another, pennies that my father "Jimbo" had collected in a big Mason jar that sat on the top of their tall bureau. I do have a recollection that sometimes I would notice a date on a coin and, for some inexplicable reason, I felt better when the dates were very old. While absorbed in this task, my imagination would take off to parts and places unknown. I can't imagine being entertained "for hours" by this activity even though my mother says I was.

My mother, called "Jackie" or "Jake," also told me I lied a great deal when I was young. I did it so much that she took me to a doctor. I used to wonder what she said to the doctor, "Doctor, my child lies! Do something!" I imagine her waving me at him much like a customer returning a defective appliance. When I asked her what the doctor did, she couldn't remember. Where exactly would he begin to examine me? I pondered. Images of fingers in my tush quickly ended my quest to remember.

My mother thought dressing us exactly alike was cute. She enjoyed people stopping her on the street saying, "What cute twins." I hated being presented as a twin when I wasn't. It bothered me enormously as I grew older because I had to suffer for both of us. For example, I wasn't allowed to go on a date with a boy until I was sixteen years old, but when I turned sixteen, my sister got to date too, even though she was only fourteen.

Another big impression I carried into my adult years was the fact that my mother hated to be called Ma. "Call me Sam. Call me Jake. Call me Jackie, just *don't* call me Ma!" "Well, what about Mom?" I asked. "I like Mother better but if you have to . . ." Perhaps this was because my mother was deeply concerned with propriety, with "good breeding." There was a time when she signed all her cards and notes to me, "Love, Philly and Jake" or "Sam and Philly." Philly was a name of a character my father played in one of my college productions. Then after Dad died, she'd sign Jake or Sam. But for the past several years she signs off as Mom and I call her Mom; but I never did call her Ma. My sister also hated her name, Mary Melinda. She insisted her name was Linda or Lin and that we all call her that. I called her Linny when we were young. Now I call her Lin and she has always signed her name as Linda.

I remember that at thirteen I desperately wanted to believe that I was adopted. I was sure of it at times. It mattered a great deal to me. Well, *everything* mattered a great deal to me as a thirteen-year-old and I began the lifelong habit of trying to be like someone else. If I met a new friend while on vacation, and she was from Alabama and spoke with a Southern drawl, then so did I. This habit of being someone else charmed my parents and sometimes came in handy.

My Alabama friend and I were swimming in the Gulf one summer in Sarasota, Florida. She suddenly panicked because she thought we had ventured out too far and couldn't make it back to shore. She was seriously scared. I instantly became calm and started talking to her quietly, telling her to swim on her back watching me the whole time. She did it while I calmly treaded water, gently nudging her feet, inching us back toward shore. When I felt the sand with my toes I told her she was safe, she could stand and bounce up and down till we reached shallow water, cooing to her in my best Alabaman Southern belle drawl that everything was fine. Privately, I surprised myself, feeling very grown-up, in charge. In my mind this feat proved it; I must have been adopted.

On this same trip my father became enraged at my sister and me for following some boys—at a discreet distance, mind you—down the

beach one evening. He came into our room, took off his belt, and
spanked . . .

"BACK TO THE present, old girl," G.A. nudges. It's getting dark.
Sugar! I look at my watch and the shifting sky. Still so much to do.
I'm not going to get any sleep tonight, that's for sure.

Walking to the fountain in front of the house, I start to clean the
small spigots that move water from one bowl to the other. The sky's
reflection paints the water with color—orange, blue, fuchsia, and here
and there, midst the ripples, little trails of clouds.

As I poke the little spigots with a twig and watch the water push
through I notice my hands shaking.

"So what else is new?" I murmur to the fountain. This tremor in
my hands has come and gone over the years, ever since high school, I
am sure, connected somehow to wanting my parents' approval, but always falling short, never quite getting there. Just like James Dean in
Rebel Without a Cause. Sometimes I thought I'd made it; but then
something always happened, and I would lose it. I tried very hard to
become the young lady my parents and teachers wanted me to be, especially my father. I became conscious of a continuous low-voltage
anxiety that hummed in me. I woke up with it; I went to bed with it.
There were some nights when I dreamed I wanted to fly but couldn't
get off the ground, then I would wake up with a start, in a sweat, with
my heart racing and my hands shaking.

These episodes led to private conversations with various saints, the
Blessed Virgin, occasionally Jesus, and once in a while the Holy
Ghost. Sometimes I'd pray out loud, pleading with God to make
everything okay. This situation continued through college. If I was
driving home later than expected and fearful I was in trouble, I'd pray,
plead, and bargain with God, hoping against hope that all would be
well when I got home.

As a young kid I was also expected to hear and heed the social
voice of the late 1950s. "Being a lady of good breeding" was my

mother's Holy Grail. Another favorite was, "What will the neighbors think?" I often found myself believing and saying things I hadn't thought through or even understood. Questioning and arriving at your own opinion wasn't encouraged at all in my house and not at all in the Catholic Church in which I grew up. I was taught I had to take a lot of life on blind faith and do what anyone in authority told me. The catchphrases included: "They know what's best for you." "Because I said so." "We're your parents, we know what's best."

And like the dutiful child my parents wanted, I'd repeat what I'd heard at home or in church without questioning its validity or prejudice. This parroting of unthought-out beliefs and aphorisms often led to my red-faced embarrassment, especially if an attractive boy questioned or called me on something I said and asked me to explain myself. I was totally unprepared, but trying to save my blushing face, I'd blunder my way into an even worse mess, then see derision and rejection light up his face. In those moments I wanted to die. Embarrassment became humiliation and shame.

I also became aware of being unconnected or disconnected to the outside world and to my peers. It felt as if I were born trying to get out of something, out of the confines of my family, the church and its hypocritical morality, out of St. Louis, Missouri. A deep restlessness, a constant uncomfortableness came over me, starting when we moved from North St. Louis to the suburb of Crestwood. I think I was in seventh or eighth grade, although it's difficult to remember exactly, because my sister and I were a grade apart, but treated the same. We were sent and went everywhere together, and I was responsible if anything happened to her.

"TURQUESA LANE, ELMONT Lane. Who cares! Get on with it! You have more important things to do," commands Chuck Moses in his megaphoned voice. Stop pushing! I answer back, but quickly burst out laughing. What do you expect from a pusher? I ask myself; he's just doing his job. Besides I'm prone to identify with petulant

Gloria the Collapser. "Why even try?" she whines. "I can't do it. I'm a failure! Always the bridesmaid, never the bride. A has-been, second best." (She often gets her information from my inner Critic.)

Having finished with the fountain and moving on to my next task, I'm stopped by the fact that I still haven't heard any birds. They usually chatter until its totally dark. The trees are stationary and the colors in the sky are now muted, bleeding into each other like a soft watercolor.

"Maybe they're sad we're going away forever," Anna's soulful six-year-old voice pipes up and surprises me. It isn't often that I hear her, and when I do I pay attention. It's odd that my Inner Child should be so elusive these days.

"I miss the seasons," pipes up Ed, "when the trees are bright red in autumn, and you can play touch football. Then, when the trees are just sticks in the snow, I like watching them sleep. They look cool when they're covered in ice, and the sun comes out and makes them clink and shine."

"I especially like the spring, when you get to go out and play," Anna adds quietly.

I used to play touch football when I was a kid, until I was tackled by a boy and all the pearl buttons on my blouse popped open! When we lived on Elmont Lane, I used to go down to the end of the street to an African-American cemetery, or the "black" cemetery as it was known then. I loved walking there, watching the big trees signal the passing of seasons. There were lots of sunken graves and knocked down markers. It was said the cemetery was once a way station for runaway slaves heading north during the Civil War. After reading the dates on some of the tombstones, that may have been true. Once in a great while I'd see a small funeral gathering there, elderly people dressed in black, the women wearing hats and gloves and the men in suits and ties, and they'd kinda huddle together in the quiet brightly colored autumn, the trees all around the cemetery painted ocher and sunflower yellow and all shades of red.

I loved going there when I felt that familiar Sunday sad restlessness.

I'd tramp around and silently talk to myself or the trees or the dead people. As the years passed I found myself feeling that familiar sadness on days of the week other than Sunday, behaving and thinking in ways that surprised and scared me. This realization made me feel even more "the outsider." By college, I felt like "the outsider" at home.

Deeply affected by the assassination of John F. Kennedy, I hated the fact that my father didn't understand what all the "hoopla was about." He thought it ridiculous that bars should close and that the drama department canceled the remaining performances of the production we were doing. I told him I thought the whole world should stop—everybody, for at least three days. Stop and take notice. How else would his death matter? But my father didn't believe in grieving. Neither did my mother.

Maybe Neil Simon suffered from not grieving the death of Joan, his first wife, at the appropriate time. I know Nancy, my stepdaughter, did. Unexpressed grief can lead to illnesses and depression, which Neil has experienced ever since I've known him. Nancy didn't grieve her mother's death when it happened; she was only nine years old at the time. When Neil and I separated Nancy was devastated, feeling all the unexpressed emotional pain, and grieving all the deaths in her young life, wearing only black for years and smoking way too many cigarettes. With help she learned to share her feelings and not fear losing our love, and I think this helped her to understand herself. She and her sister Ellen helped me to learn and grow as a mother and a woman. They still do. They are wonderful mothers in their own right, and both are gloriously beautiful women. I love them with all my heart and deeply respect their love and affection. I'm proud of the fact that we have maintained our relationship and watched it grow and deepen over the years.

I KNEW I needed to learn about life and relationships early on. In college, that was crystal clear. Life out there in the real world was where I belonged, needing to know why my world felt so foreign, so scary, so unjust. I didn't understand my parents, my sister, and most of all, myself. I desperately wanted to have some palpable sense of security about myself and my life. My emotions felt overwhelming to me, and I knew that my emotions and my actions overwhelmed my family. This need for understanding, for some kind of control, or freedom and security, led me into acting, beginning in high school at Nerinx Hall, and then at Webster College, and finally, thank God, in New York. And just look at me, I laughingly muse, as I study my trembling hands in the faint light of this summer night. I'm a bundle of stress and apprehension.

"Don't be hard on yourself, Marsha. You're much too hard on yourself. You're doing just fine." Grace's soothing voice makes me cry.

"You're crying because you're grieving, mourning the joy and sadness of the past with its accomplishments and mistakes, the pain you caused others, and the pain you experienced. Misunderstandings and misbeliefs. You're also mourning all the dear ones who are gone: Barbara Colby, Baba Muktananda, Fitzy, your father, your childhood, the children you didn't have, and your contemporaries who have died of AIDS. It's good to mourn. It's important." Grace truly is her name.

My daughter Ellen once remarked that I was "into everything," which is true to an extent. I've always searched for answers and explanations, always curious, wondering if I'm missing anything, trying to bring order and sense to my chaotic mind and my crazy life. Thank God for Siddha meditation, Baba, and now Gurumayi.

"But have you made *sense* of anything?" my inner Critic suddenly shrieks. "Who do you think you're kidding! You're a fool! And you're just fooling yourself, as usual!"

"Now," my insidious Patriarch voice intones, "do you honestly believe you've made sense of your life at all?" His question hangs in the air. No, probably not, I say to myself with a sigh. As young women we learn all about the patriarch as God from our mothers, and my Patriarch is often critical of women.

TAKING A LAST look at this beautiful house designed by John Midyette III, a Santa Fe architect, I'm reminded of how life came along and dropped his plans into my lap. The plans of a dream house for a well-known builder in Santa Monica whose wife didn't want to move here. "Here" was then a barren, pie slice of land overlooking the Pacific Ocean, a spot that had miraculously never been built on. All the other houses in the neighborhood were twenty to twenty-five years old.

As my hand moves along the curve of rough stucco, I'm reminded that I didn't want to build this house. I'd never built a house from scratch before. I'd almost bought a couple of other houses but always got cold feet. My frustrated but very understanding friend and real estate maven, Cynthia Marin, patiently asked me, "What *exactly* are you looking for?"

I answered without thinking. "If I'm gonna continue to live in L.A., I want a Santa Fe adobe house with a spectacular view of the ocean." And that was *exactly* what she found for me. It was built in one year for exactly the amount I could afford, built by men who took great pride in their work. They'd never built a traditional Santa Fe home before. The beams and vigas and latillas were brought from New Mexico and so were the men to build the traditional fireplaces in all the rooms. When I made the decision to build here I had hoped that my life would have some of the charm and joy the house possessed, but that was not to be.

Turning the corner, I exclaim "Wow!" There in front of me is the view to end all views, in all its twinkling, twilight glory. To my left, in the distance, is the tail end of the Santa Monica mountains. Behind, and out from them, is Century City and behind that is downtown Los Angeles. Then sweeping to the right, all of the Los Angeles basin spreads itself before me as it meets the Pacific Ocean. Cynthia told me that the coastline is called The Queen's Necklace. It definitely is. The coastline loops in and out in a lacy design that gracefully curves toward Palos Verdes and the horizon, just like a Victorian woman's necklace. The rolling waves lap the shore as if they're attaching millions of seawater pearls to a filigree of platinum and gold. Also in the distance, dead ahead, is Long Beach, and in the sky lined up in perfect order are the planes above LAX as they begin their descent. It amazes me how evenly positioned they are as they wait for their final order to land. It's a clear evening so I can see the lights of Palos Verdes glimmering, and Catalina Island is a gray-blue shadow against the sky. Off in the distance to the far right, I can just make out the outline of the Santa Barbara Islands.

There have been many nights in the past five years that I sat at this edge of this steep hill dangling my feet over the side, with the pool at my back, or in the Jacuzzi with water twirling and steaming around me as I gazed at this sprawling city I've called home for twenty years.

The evening brings on the distant lights as they begin their winking. I watch the headlights of the cars down below as they slowly snake up Bienvenida Avenue going home to family and dinner in this quiet *Leave It to Beaver* refuge. They're going home and I'm leaving, for good. "Please God, make this all okay," I pray. Suddenly tears spring to my eyes and my chest feels heavy and bruised; a stringent-tasting saliva squeezes out from my clenched jaw.

"No wallowing, remember?" Grace gently prods. Yes, no sense to it, I agree.

But *why?* Why *didn't* this work? And when, when *exactly,* did I realize I needed to make such a big change, I wonder, looking out through shimmering tears at Westwood and Brentwood and Bel-Air as I stretch my tense and aching back and shoulders, slowly raising numb, tired arms over my head as I gently look heavenward for stars.

"Penny Marshall and Carrie Fisher's mutual birthday party," Grace quietly answers, "I remember because it took all of us to get you to go, and you almost didn't."

Penny Marshall and Carrie Fisher's mutual birthday parties were famous. I suppose I was invited that year because I was starring in an ABC series for Jim Brooks called *Sibs* that was directed by Ted Bessell. It wasn't a success. We shot twenty-six shows, I think, and the network showed maybe ten of them. I got a residual once from Malaysia. But I'm getting ahead of myself.

Ted Bessell was in partnership with Penny, developing material through their company, Parkway Productions. Carrie Fisher and I had worked on a picture together, *Drop Dead Fred,* starring Phoebe Cates and Rik Mayall, a successful British television comedian. Ten-year-olds loved the picture.

I remember being glued to the seat of my car as I drove up Outpost Road to Penny's home, slowing down to view the house I first rented when Neil and I separated. Penny's street happened to be just to the right. I drove up and down those streets three or four times checking everything out, including the valet parking. There were a lot of cars everywhere. I finally felt I had to at least try to get out of the car. I'd spent hours getting up the courage to come, and hours more trying to decide what to wear. Having promised myself that if it didn't feel right I could leave, I parked where I knew I could get out quickly and walked back up the street to Penny's house. I had come alone, as usual, but tried to appear and feel as cool and sophisticated as possible. This was the kind of moment where trying to be someone else can come in handy. Think of Kathleen Turner, I suggested to myself. I'd met her a couple of times and she seemed enormously self-confident. Penny answered the door in her frazzled kind of way, which was somewhat comforting. I was relieved that she seemed as overwhelmed in her own home as I did. She welcomed me, "Oh, hi Marsha," then proceeded to mumble something about this being the last time she was ever going to do this. I immediately tried to put her at ease by saying something inane, "Don't worry about me, I'll just meander on through." She threw up her hands in a vague gesture of giving up or perhaps welcoming and continued muttering as she went down a hall in search of something or someone. I stood alone.

In the opposite direction of the hall was a large living room teeming with people. Nope. Can't go in there. Suddenly Ted appeared. "You're just getting here? I'm leaving. My girls are sick and Linnell is holding down the fort." With that he kissed me good-bye and whisked out the door. Great. Just great. The only person I know has just left. I stayed attached to the front door wondering if I should just bolt, when bang! from around another hallway came a stunning-looking woman dressed in black, with gorgeous blond hair and a perfectly made-up face and perfectly manicured hands.

"Marsha!" the deep-throated goddess announced, "you're not leaving? Did you just get here? Love the jacket! You know Tom Hanks and his lovely wife, Rita, don't you?" Thank God for my friend Dani Jansen, the Perle Mesta of Hollywood!

"Dani!" I exclaimed while I hugged her. At least I'm unglued from the door, I thought, as I turned to Rita and Tom.

"Of course I know Tom!" I said as I shook his hand. "We all met at your house, Dani! At one of your fabulous parties! Hello Tom, Rita!" I enthused. "I'm a big fan!" Everything I said had the ring of exclamation points with a panicked air. Careful girl, I warned myself, you're a little over the top.

"Of course I know Marsha," Tom gracefully countered. "I've been wanting to tell you for the longest time, I saw your Roxane in the production of *Cyrano de Bergerac* at A.C.T. You were fantastic. I knew I wanted to be an actor that night."

I was dumbfounded. "Oh, well . . . thank you. . . . I don't know. . . . I am a *big* fan of yours. . . ." Great Marsha, just great. Thankfully Dani came to my rescue.

"Come on, I'm going to take you through the party, come on now, say goodnight to Tom and Rita, they're leaving." She took me by the hand, literally, and pulled me into the teeming room and began to introduce me to everyone. Maybe this wouldn't be too hard after all, I decided, hugging and kissing acquaintances, shaking hands with strangers. I perked right up. I'm so easy. Hand in hand, Dani led me to the pool area. It too was teeming with people, people who were hungry. I began to understand why Penny was muttering so much.

"You know Francis, don't you? Francis Ford Coppola?" Dani asked.

"Oh my heavens, of course I know Francis. He directed me in my first show with A.C.T., *Private Lives!*" Slow down girl, too many exclamation points. I hadn't seen Francis since that production in 1971. Francis proceeded to explain to those gathered round that he staged the show in some particular way that hadn't been done before, with a balcony or something facing the audience. Everyone oohed and ahhed. I couldn't for the life of me remember anything about the production design and had nothing to say to add to the conversation. Instead, I glanced to my right and found Gary Oldman looking at me intensely, and I couldn't look away. Staring back, I suddenly felt foolish. Why is he looking at me, that way? I thought. Do I look funny? I looked at Dani as she talked effortlessly with everyone around her. I could ask her if I look all right, I thought, but decided I hadn't the confidence to hear any answer. What if she faltered or spoke haltingly. *Then* what would I do? I mumbled my good-byes to Francis and told Dani I was going to get something to eat and drink. Please God, let me find a drink, fast! I made my way back into the house and asked where the bar was. As I headed in the direction of someone's pointing finger, I glanced up and into a wall mirror. I was stopped cold by what I saw.

Looking back at me was Mercedes McCambridge in *Touch of Evil.* I thought that instantly upon seeing myself with short hair and a black leather jacket with studs. Jesus, I had tried so hard to choose the "right" outfit, but what I saw in the mirror shocked me.

"Who the hell *are* you?" some inner self asked as I furtively looked away. My heart kicked in, but promptly sank to my feet. I *hated* what I saw in the mirror. I was a complete stranger to myself. I couldn't believe what I looked like! Totally panicked, feeling an anxiety attack coming on, I lost my bearing, or whatever you want to call it. I knew I had to bolt, or I'd probably die right there of heart failure and make an even bigger fool of myself. I managed to walk to the front door, inched myself out while no one was looking, and ran to my car. My heart raced right along with me. I buzzed down those Porsche windows and opened the sky window so I could get air and try to calm down. I was driving a 928, speeding through the streets of West Hollywood headed straight for the ocean. It was a miracle I didn't get a ticket. I fervently prayed: If I can just get home, get home, and close the door and never leave again. . . .

I ran into the house and went straight for the wine bottle.

"Darling, isn't that just a teensy melodramatic?" G.A. chided gently. No, I thought; to me it felt tragic. It's not that I went to the party knowing I'd end up crashing!

Just like I hadn't known I'd end up crashing doing the series *Sibs.* When I made the decision to do the series I thought it would be great fun and exciting and the beginning of a whole new direction for my work, because the people involved were talented, powerful, and experienced. Jim Brooks was producing it, a man responsible for the success of *The Mary Tyler Moore Show* and *The Tracey Ullman Show* and *The Simpsons,* for God's sake, as well as writing for other successes in television like *Taxi.* He won Academy Awards for adapting and directing *Terms of Endearment.* He had great people working with him: Polly Platt, Heidi Perlman, Ted Bessell, Sam Simon, and the great staff at Jim's company, Gracie Films.

Heidi Perlman created *Sibs.* She worked on a lot of successful shows of Jim's as well as *Cheers.* Everyone had worked together before. They appeared to be one very happy—if slightly dysfunctional— successful company. This was a great group, for God's sake, mighty talented and extremely successful. Plus, as a producer, Jim was being paid the highest amount of money ever handed out by a network at the time.

What was unique, and a possible weakness, about the series was that we didn't shoot a pilot. The show was about three very different sisters, their sibling rivalries, and how their lives interconnect. I played the oldest sister, married to a very nice Italian guy, played by Alex Rocco, with a son in college, who inherits her boss's company and is suddenly the breadwinner in the family. Margaret Colin played the middle sister, a recovering alcoholic with acerbic wit, no money, no man in her life and hence a stress-filled but funny dame. Jami Gertz played our baby sister, a character who is a complete ditz with no skills at anything and is totally floundering in life. Dan Castellaneta played an accountant who thought he was going to head the company my character inherited and has stepped off the deep end because he didn't. Thus there was a stressful, hopefully comedic world for me to deal with and react to.

We had a guarantee of thirteen episodes on the air from ABC, which is not easy to get. I was told that Jim thought of me for the part after my friend Stockard Channing declined. There may have been others who declined as well. He read a valentine review that Frank Rich, then drama critic for *The New York Times,* had written when I opened in Michael Weller's play *Lake No Bottom* at The Second Stage in New York. Jim was a big supporter of The Second Stage. I'm a huge fan and supporter of Jim because he loves the theater, as well as film and television, and he's immensely talented in everything he does. He's also a hard worker who was involved with two other projects at the time we were working on *Sibs.* He was directing a new play by a young playwright at a theater in L.A., starring Glenn Close, Woody Harrelson, and Laura Dern, as well as writing and preparing a film with music starring Nick Nolte.

Practically everyone from Gracie Films and ICM, our mutual agency, came to woo me, offering a great deal. They told me the script was a work in progress, that we'd all work on it making it even better while we rehearsed. Michael Black, my then agent, now manager, and always dear friend, was supportive yet objective. ABC offered a terrific deal, so there I was, stymied. Something instinctual kept telling me "If it ain't on the page, it ain't on the stage." No, no matter what, I didn't think this was going to work for me. But I needed to work, I thought, and all these good, good people were telling me it was all going to be great. I wanted it to work. I wanted it badly.

Good work with talented people was slow in coming my way. I was a mature woman, doncha know. The parts aren't out there for us. I needed to jump-start my career. The networks—hell, the world—was gearing everything to teenyboppers.

THE NIGHT BEFORE Ted Bessell was to come to this house to make a last pitch to join them, I walked to the edge of this hill and stood where I now stand and remembered my friend Barbara Colby. She and I worked together at A.C.T. (The American Conservatory Theater) in the 1970–71 season and again at Lincoln Center in New York in 1974 in a production of *Richard III*. It was during our run in that show that she introduced me to Siddha meditation and, most important, introduced me to my guru, Swami Muktananda. This woman, always in pursuit of the ideal when it came to her work and her life, was constantly searching for the most creative environment. She finally found it on a television series and couldn't have been more surprised. She appeared in an episode of *The Mary Tyler Moore Show,* playing a prostitute, and they loved her so much that they asked her back. When they were preparing a spin-off show for Cloris Leachman, they asked her to be a regular.

"Can you believe it?! Marsha, I've searched everywhere: Peter Brook, A.C.T., New York, you name it, I've looked. Of all places, I found it doing a half-hour sitcom, a little play every week, like repertory, with a wonderful company!" She was ecstatic. Unfortunately she was shot dead along with her boyfriend by unknown assailants coming out of her acting class one night. But that's another story.

I loved the idea of doing a little play every week too, so why hold back? I asked myself. These people want you. It's a great opportunity. Maybe this show will turn everything around. Maybe it will be a terrific experience. I said yes. By the fourth day of rehearsal I knew I was in trouble.

We were doing a run-through for all the writers and Heidi, Jim, Sam, and other people from Gracie Films. They were sitting or standing about six feet from us and they were talking loudly with each other while we were playing the scene. I was stunned at this behavior. I didn't know what to make of it. How could they possibly get what we were trying to do? How could any of us concentrate? I *was* nervous and tight, but how on earth could they really hear the material and see what we were doing with it if they were already talking about it *and* the set and our costumes? I stopped. They continued to talk. I managed to get their attention and began to speak.

"I know I'm new to this form and you all have been doing it for a long time but I would like to be able to do a scene, I don't mean the whole show, just each scene once, with you all not talking. Just so I can feel what it's like to get a run on these scenes. Perhaps eventually I'll be able to work the way you do, but for now I would just like to do the scene once, without any talking, and then we can do it again, as many times as you want, and you guys can talk." There was complete silence. Everyone looked to Jim. He was pissed. Thank God for the weekend.

On Monday we were all called to Jim's conference room. Lunch was served and we made small talk, then Jim began to speak. He had been giving my request serious thought and although he tried to appear calm, he seemed agitated. "I've worked this way for the last twenty-five years." He may have said thirty-five; I'm not sure, because I was calling on all the years of therapy to keep me calm and strong because anxiety was crawling all over my skin.

"Well, Jim," I ventured as I tried to breathe and appear calm, "I've been working my way for about as long, and I don't want to upset you, but perhaps it would be a good thing to try it my way for just a little while and I will try your way, I promise. But not with the first show." He interrupted with a slightly strident tone saying something like, "No, it's not a problem," but it was clear by the tone of his voice as it climbed higher and higher, that it *was* a problem. I guessed he was used to working in an environment in which the actors did as they were told and didn't give him a hard time, especially not right away. At the run-through that afternoon everyone lined up as usual, but they didn't make a sound the first time through. I thanked everyone for their patience, but the atmosphere was tense.

Several weeks later I managed to get into more trouble. I came to rehearsal one day and Margaret pulled me aside to alert me that Jami was in tears in her dressing room and Ted, our director, was angry. I went to Jami's dressing room and heard her side of the story and then went to Ted. Maybe because I've directed before, maybe because I was "in" my role of Nora, the lioness of the family, maybe because we couldn't talk to the writers and had to go through Ted all the time, maybe because I was scared silly and needed to act like I knew what the hell I was doing, I lectured Ted on what it takes to be a director. Oh my, my, my. Marsha, Marsha, Marsha. It's a credit to Ted that he stood there and listened. A gentle man, in every sense of that word. He loved actors more than anything. Maybe he understood that I felt like the mother of our pack and nobody was messing with my loved ones.

Perhaps the truth for all of us, including Heidi and Jim, was that we weren't sure we could pull it off successfully. Maybe I counted too much on their taking care of me. It occurred to me that perhaps I wasn't any good at that kind of work. I certainly was running scared, unsure and insecure, seriously doubting my ability.

At the filming of the very first show, friends and loved ones came to cheer and root. Danny DeVito and his wife Rhea Perlman, came and cheered us all on. Rhea loved the show and loved us and Danny told me, "This is the best job you'll ever have!" My face froze in a smile as I muttered something idiotic and walked quickly to my dressing room. He couldn't possibly have known that statement was the kiss of death for me. I had been told that exact same thing ten years or so before, on a famous project with very famous and powerful people, and that movie never finished filming!

Despite our first success, as the weeks went by everything—including me—kept unraveling. One week we'd decide that I had raised Jami after our mother died; another week the writers decided that our father and stepmother raised her. I didn't know which end was up and it was maddening not to be able to talk to any of the writers. I asked for a meeting with Jim and Heidi. Quite a to-do was made of my request, which made me feel even more nervous and isolated. I spent several sessions with Marilyn Hershenson, my therapist at that time, preparing for the meeting. We devised several visualizations to help me stay clear, calm, and present. Mr. Olympus hadn't yet made his appearance as one of my voices, so standing toe to toe, or sitting knee to knee for that matter, with a strong patriarchal character like Jim Brooks was not something that came easily to me.

What I hoped would be a small, friendly, low-key meeting turned into something else entirely. It had the look and feel of a summit conference. On the way over to the conference room, Jim and Heidi passed me in Jim's go-cart. He slowed down and told me he'd invited several people in his office to join us and asked if that was okay. I was taken by surprise and mumbled some kind of . . ."Sure, no problem" response. Ted escorted me to the meeting and was very supportive. We got there first and he suggested I sit in a certain chair. So I sat. I wound up facing a minimum of ten or twelve people, all sitting in a semicircle facing me; no one was smiling.

I accomplished an important task in maturation at that meeting. I stayed calm and didn't cry or get shrill. Instead I quietly argued for what I thought was right, keeping a calm voice and a quiet demeanor. At one point Jim raised the issue that I had let it be known that I wanted some funny material. Blushing, I took a breath and calmly said, "Well, yes, if I don't have a clear sense of my character and can't figure out my relationships to my family, then at the very least, I do want to be funny."

The meeting didn't help, unfortunately, because afterward things just got testier. I wish I could say that I handled it all like a grown-up, but I didn't. Being miserably unhappy and very scared, I took to going home after filming ended on Friday night and drinking wine or beer, sometimes in the car, I'm ashamed to say. There were some weekends I just plain checked out, didn't answer the phone, ate or didn't eat, slept or didn't sleep. I was a mess. I vegetated and drank too much, ultimately feeling like I was back in my own dysfunctional family drama. It all reminded me of my childhood, with drinking parents and crazy erratic behavior from everyone. I was scared that I would just succumb, thus letting the Collapser have the last word. I was afraid I'd started drinking seriously just to get through it.

Talking to Marilyn in her office one day, I whined, "Why is this happening to me? I've worked so hard to get clear of alcoholism. I've tried to understand it all. Now, why am I back where I began?" I pleaded and cried, "I don't understand. You've got to help me understand why I brought this painful experience into my life!"

Marilyn thought for a moment while I noisily and self-righteously blew my nose; then she began to speak. Sometimes we find ourselves in these situations so that we can see where we've been and how far we've come, she said. But now, you have the tools to change your old responses; you've learned how not to react in the old way. "Oh yeah?" I countered. "Then how come I drive home with open bottles of beer or wine in the car?!" She asked me to think about the meetings with Jim, how I handled myself, took care of myself, stayed calm, and spoke up for myself. "You couldn't do that with Neil," she said. I told her that it was sad that I was learning all this so late. It wasn't Jim's or Heidi's problem; they had problems of their own. This was my problem, my responsibility. I left her office feeling somewhat mollified with a better perspective. One thing I've learned and accepted over the years is that whatever's happened to me, whatever I'm feeling, it's *my* responsibility and *my* perception—no one else's.

Despite a new resolve, the best of intentions, and a great amount of talent and effort on everyone's part, what was supposed to be the best job I could ever have wasn't. What should have worked didn't. It didn't help us that the network kept changing our timeslot from one week to the next. They tried to bring the series back the following year with Margaret and Jami and Dan but it still didn't fly.

Thinking back tonight on my miserable failure in situation comedy and remembering my inability to cope at Penny Marshall's party, all of it reminds me of why I wanted to flee from this place. No wonder I thought I needed to "get out of town." I felt as though I'd already been tarred and feathered. Now if somebody would just bring in the rail . . . I actually heard G.A. laugh as I took a last look at my gardening endeavors and the glorious view. The lot was totally barren when I built the house, and now, just five years later, it was a verdant landscape of fragrant roses, night blooming jasmine, live Christmas trees planted and growing, the hillside draped in white African daisies with winding, hand-laid pebble paths leading down the steep sloping hill to those statuesque pines the hawks and owls like to nest in. And at the end of one of the paths are the sweet smelling compost piles that helped make everything grow so bountifully. Well, at least I can garden, I think with a sigh.

"Let's please go down to the meditation spot," Anna says quietly. "Yeah, I'd like to go too," says Ed. My inner children's presence is a comfort tonight.

Walking down the path, I see dimly the outline of the wicker chair that's on a small redwood platform, nestled between the heavy, strong trunks of the great pines. I plop down on the platform's edge and look out at the ocean, which is now just a dark space. Looking to the west, the last hint of sunset faintly colors the darkening sky. Magic Hour is waning fast.

"Albert Finney watered this hill on the eve of a Fourth of July, two, or was it three, summers ago." I'm amazed that Anna knows this; why, I don't know, but I am amazed.

The year before *Sibs*, Albert and I were filming *The Image* for HBO, with a great cast of actors including Kathy Baker, John Mahoney, and Swoosie Kurtz. The film was directed by Peter Werner. Albert was playing a Peter Jennings type whose life is all about work and being a star television newscaster. I was playing his long-suffering wife who's fed up with their floundering marriage. We had a scene in the bathroom of our home, in which he discovers me in the shower. I hadn't been nude on film since 1973 in *Cinderella Liberty* and no man had seen my body for over a year because celibacy descended on me after a couple of very unhappy love affairs.

I'd become a couch potato basically, angry and frustrated that all those millions of hours of therapy seemed a waste, at least as far as my love life was concerned. I had "hit the wall" with men that year. It came to me that deciding to go cold turkey on romance was my only option. "Desperate times require desperate measures," was the pronouncement of my growing list of selves. It was time to "clean house." It became a game, counting the days I went without. It was not unlike giving up cigarettes, except giving up cigarettes was much much harder.

In my younger years, I'd always been dependent on a relationship with a man to make me feel complete, and that need continued after my divorce from Neil. I loved physical affection. In the past I managed to fall in love and involve myself in a man's life without taking a good hard look at who I was getting and what I was getting into. Finally, after some disastrous choices, I decided to stop. "Just stop," I commanded myself. "Face it, you don't know what the hell you're doing!" This was a humbling truth. Fortunately, premenopausal symptoms stepped in and my sexual urge took a dive anyway. So there I was, having been celibate for a year and *liking* it, acting up a storm with Albert Finney, naked as a jaybird.

Albert seems to have a great time with life; he's a flawless actor, a kind and terrific man who loves being social. He loves good food and great wine; he's deliciously funny, full of energy, and a great flirt. His joie de vivre became enormously appealing to Marsha, the Couch Potato Celibate. His love of life was charmingly contagious. Dammit, I decided, I want some of that! He made me laugh and I started to feel sexy again.

"I think it's time we try on a new pair of shoes, don't you?" I asked all my selves in the mirror one day. (I'm addicted to shoes too.) Surprisingly everyone was in agreement. He was the perfect person to lose my virginity with. Again. I've sometimes been rather straightforward when it comes to asking for what I want in the romance department. "Would you like to spend the Fourth of July weekend with me?" I asked straightforwardly, smiling all the while. If only I had some of that brazen quality when asking for what I needed in some other areas of my life.

"Why . . . I'd be charmed," he answered charmingly. "You take my breath away," he added, kissing my hand, being Tom Jones all over again. What a great adventure. I was definitely pleased. I told him I planned a big party on the Fourth for the whole cast and a bunch of my friends, that I had everything arranged and he could sit by the pool and relax.

"Nonsense, I'll help," he replied. And help he definitely did.

He brought coffee, juice, and toast to bed in the morning and patiently answered the zillion questions I asked him about his personal and professional life. I was way too earnest, but he was forever gracious. We spent the next day picking up food and drink and setting up tables under the portale by the pool.

Then, mysteriously, even to me, I became withdrawn. Personal growth, hitting walls, celibacy, and sudden intimacy were a bit too much for me, even though men and sex still made me a bit frivolous. Withdrawn, frivolous. Frivolous, withdrawn. Poor guy, I was hard to figure.

We finished all the preparations for the next day's party as the sun was setting and twilight was creating magic. Albert decided he wanted to water the grass and the hill so that everything would look perfect. I came down the hill, where I am now, and cut flowers for the tables. Looking back and seeing him watering everything so intently, I was struck by the domesticity of the scene and thought how nomadic the actor's life is, and how important it is to have some creature comforts in our lives when we're on the road, working hard. He was having as pleasurable a time watering the lawn at twilight as I was having surreptitiously watching him.

The following morning after coffee and more fun in bed, Albert left to return to his hotel, dress, and then come to the party with John Mahoney and a couple of guests. When he arrived we greeted each other as if he'd never been here. It was delicious having this secret together. Albert was the hit of the day, and as twilight darkened the sky, everyone stood at the edge of this hill and watched the various fireworks displays in Malibu, Long Beach, and a huge one right in front of us, at eye level. Watching the colorful explosions, I thought that this celebration was a glorious "stepping out," celebrating the end of celibacy with a grand display of fireworks no less.

"A resurrection after a very long sexual Lent," uttered G.A.

And on *that* note . . . , I chuckled to myself, it definitely was time to go in.

CHAPTER TWO

ROOMS, EMPTY AND FULL

I've lived in lots of places, but I've had very few homes. My first was my parents' apartment on Clarence Avenue in North St. Louis. It was a red brick, four-family apartment house owned by my mother's parents, Bridget and Justyn Rakowski. Justyn came to the United States from St. Petersburg and met Bridget, whose family came from Prussia and settled in Missouri and Illinois. They married in the United States, in Chicago, I think. I've also been told my grandfather was a greengrocer, ran numbers out of his store, and was a successful businessman prior to the stock market crash of 1929. Whatever the story, he had enough money to buy the four-family apartment house on Clarence Avenue and take my mother and Bridget on a tour of Europe when my mother was eight years old.

We lived above them, and I didn't think of it as a "home," although I suppose it was a home. My grandmother's kitchen was big and spare and very, very clean. Everything was pushed against the walls, including the kitchen table covered in colorful oil cloth. Everywhere you looked, all surfaces, including the floor laid with linoleum, was spotless and always shining. I used to creep down the back stairs holding tight to the wooden handrail that connected our kitchen with my grandmother's. I loved going down those back stairs to Momsie's kitchen all by myself. I'd invariably find her at the sink or the stove, scrubbing away. My memory is of fresh baked crab apple pies cooling on the sill of the wide open window between the white porcelain sink and the white enamel stove.

Momsie had frizzy permed gray hair and wore no makeup at all, not even lipstick. My mother always wore lipstick. It was the first thing she put on every morning after brushing her hair, before she even dressed. Momsie always wore a housedress of a print material and an apron that she put over her head in order to tie it in back. It had wide lapels with rickrack on the edges. She had two of them and they always hung on a hook just inside the kitchen. They were always clean too. I never saw her in a nightgown or bathrobe. My mother always wore pretty bathrobes in the morning. Momsie's nylons were rolled and held in place with elastic bands just above her knees, and her shoes were of sturdy black or light beige leather with a chunky heel and tied up the front. "Sensible shoes," she used to say. Momsie was known to have a very sharp tongue, definitely a "no-nonsense" type person. My mother always wore nylons that were held by fasteners just below her hips and her seams were always straight.

Momsie's kitchen was my favorite room in her and Grandpa's apartment, but the dining room was more interesting. Big, thick, heavy furniture dominated the small room. You could hardly get around the table and chairs for the sideboard at one end. There was a beautiful frosted lamp that hung low from the ceiling, casting light on the center of the heavy black table. Around the edge of the lamp there was a pastoral scene in metal in silhouette and the glass was colored in shades of ocher and beige.

Momsie and Grandpa's kitchen was always filled with light. There were no shadows. Everything used to happen there, all kinds of conversations. Mother and Momsie didn't get along and altercations often happened there and by the door leading to those back stairs.

I remember also our backyard, which I loved too. It was totally symmetrical. There were two crab apple trees and two cement walkways that ran parallel from the broad back steps to the identical-looking garages. There were sturdy square wooden poles with laundry lines attached running alongside the walks. The backyard ended with the alley, another favorite place. Every week in the summer a black truck came through the alley with fresh produce from a farm outside the city, and I'd run down the back walk to the gate waiting for it to show up. I liked the farmer who drove it. Momsie and my mother would buy tomatoes, corn, cucumbers, greens, and beans. The best part was that the farmer would give me a big ripe tomato to eat right there. He always kept a salt shaker with him and always knew exactly how much to sprinkle. My mouth watered as I watched his rough hands delicately handle the fruit. They were delicious and juicy, and I remember having tomato all over my face and hands and play clothes and then skipping back to the house to get washed off at the sink in the basement.

I liked the basement too. It was cool in the summer and warm in the winter with rough whitewashed walls of rock and a cement floor, and Grandpa kept it immaculately clean for Momsie. She had a cold storage room there where she kept her pickles in ceramic crocks with blue trim. Her pickles were delicious, and I could hardly wait for them to cure. "Brine" was one of my favorite words, "hot" being my first word. There were also shelves along the wall that held the other canned goodies: glass jars filled with summer carrots, beets, sauerkraut, and pickled tomatoes. I loved going down there and looking at everything. Perhaps it's these early memories that have influenced my decision to have a farm.

Summers were great on Clarence Avenue in North St. Louis. There was so much to do and see. The arrival of the ice man was another big event, and he'd give us cold clear shards to suck on. On those hot summer days Grandpa used to put out Momsie's big tin washing tubs in the backyard—just one at first, because my sister and I were small enough to sit in it together. As we grew, or perhaps because I insisted, he brought out two, one for each of us. He'd hook the hose to the laundry line post and put it on spray. It was heaven running around the post in our underpants, climbing in and out of our metal tubs, feeling the slippery yellow-green grass between my toes. At least, until I fell and hurt my elbow. The doctor scared me because he talked to my mother about the dangers of chipped bones. For weeks I imagined I had this sliver of bone floating around my body, a white fragment from my elbow, traveling here and there all around my body in the dark red blood.

In this same memory, my grandfather is sitting outside in one of his lawn chairs, watching us. He was the night watchman or janitor for the high school across the street and he built the chairs in his spare time, making them sturdy and strong out of thick wood that he painted shiny white. They looked like Adirondack chairs. He'd sit in one of his chairs and I'd sit on his lap and study his right eye very closely. There was a tear in his iris, and a tiny brown drop of something trickled down from the rent, flowing into the white of his eye. He told me his eye was crying a brown tear.

He was Russian and looked it. He had a stocky build with a full face and high cheekbones, curly light brown hair, and hands that showed hard work. I know I loved his voice although I can't hear it anymore. He and Momsie died when I was little. He was sixty-four and my mother tells me he died of a seizure. Momsie died of a seizure as well, six or eight months later. She came up the back stairs one morning with her coat on and berated my mother for not being in church on Sunday. I remember being curious because I knew it wasn't Sunday. She looked funny—gray and sad. My mother seemed frustrated or beleaguered by her but patiently answered, "No Mother, it's Wednesday. Not Sunday." Momsie didn't believe her at first, then suddenly she looked confused and embarrassed and turned and went back down the stairs, head drooping as she slowly lumbered down to her kitchen, holding tightly to the wooden railing with one hand and the opposite wall with the other. I felt sad too. She died shortly after that. I remember my mother saying that Momsie died because she wanted to be with Grandpa.

THERE WAS A schoolteacher who lived down the street from us who reminded me of Momsie because she wore nylons that were rolled above her knees, she had white frizzy hair, and she always seemed to be cleaning something. I don't think she was ever married. One day, while she was scrubbing her front steps, she invited me to visit the school she taught in. I was going to go to school the next year and she thought I might like to see what I was in for. I was very excited to go and insisted I wear my favorite dress with strawberrys stitched across the top. My white shoes were cleaned and polished and I wore them over white socks with a frilly cuff. I thought I looked terrific. My mother had wound my shoulder-length hair in strips of old cloth the night before so that my hair would look pretty.

The school was totally empty when we arrived, like it was waiting for something, and I remember our footsteps echoed down the long hall. The wood floors were shiny yellow and were splashed with yellow light. The desks in her room were made of black wrought iron in an intricate design, with yellow wood tops that lifted. The chair, with a yellow wood seat and back rest, was attached to the desk and there was a special place for pencils and ink. As she watched me investigate a desk, she told me that when I started school my desk might be just a bit smaller, but that I would grow into a desk like this. I fervently hoped that I would have the identical same desk. "I'm a big girl," I told her.

The whole school smelled wonderful, inviting, mysterious. Everything looked and smelled just like I expected, which really made me happy. I remember thinking, I'll fit right in. I only hoped my school, a Catholic school across the street, had these exact same desks.

I loved growing up on Clarence Avenue. I loved walking the eight blocks to school and seeing all my friends who lived within a ten-block radius, my boundaries having been established by my parents.

We played stickball in the street in front of my house in the summertime, and in the winter we built snowmen and had huge snow fortresses and wars with snowballs. I even went on a city bus on Saturdays to the roller rink that was far away from my house. I wore my hair in a ponytail and was dressed in my special skating rink skirt and carried my skates slung over my shoulder. The bus drivers were always nice and told me I looked pretty or asked me if my practice had gone well. Friends going to the rink would get on the bus at various stops and we would compare outfits and hair ribbons and talk about just about anything. There was a candy shop at the bus stop and I loved the penny paper candy. Long strips of shiny white paper with pastel candy dots that you peeled off and ate. I loved the freedom of getting around on my own. That I was young still, somewhere between eight and ten, didn't faze me. Life in North St. Louis was much safer then. Life in our house on Clarence Avenue . . .

THE WORD "HOUSE" sounds empty to me, just like this house now. Walking through these empty rooms now, hearing my heels click on the saltilla tiles, the place sounds and feels empty too.

"Hell, it *is* empty, Girl!" That's right, G.A. "Home" has a much warmer ring, bringing with it a smile. Love is in the word "home." My best girlfriend, when I was little on Clarence Avenue, was Ruth Ann Hogue and she lived in a house that was a home, just a couple of doors from me. Ruth Ann had her very own room on the second floor. Her parents were really nice people, especially her mother. The Hogues had the first TV on the block, and when they first got it I'd go over to her house and watch the test pattern, anxiously waiting for programs to begin. Over that summer I quickly became addicted to television, to the point that I didn't want to go out and play.

Before we were able to afford a television, the radio was my first love. We'd sit at the kitchen table eating dinner and listen to *The Inner Sanctum* and *The Green Hornet* and other wonderful shows with eerie, weird sounds like creaking, squeaking doors that excited me. I remember some performers too, like Fanny Brice, and Amos and Andy but my favorite show was *The Lux Hour.* We'd listen to that show in the living room while my mother rolled my hair in long pieces of old socks in preparation for bed. My father would rarely let us listen to the end of the program though. He'd say it was past our bedtime. It's one of the unfair things parents do: Why on earth start listening to a story only to be told you can't hear the end of it?

When we finally got our first television, I was ecstatic. I was mesmerized. The television was put in the living room against the front wall between two windows. I was still made to go to bed, but I learned that from my bedroom at the other end of the apartment, if I hung over the side of my bed and stretched out a bit, keeping my balance with my hands on the floor, I could still watch TV upside down. I was thrilled with myself for having discovered this feat. The fact that I had to twist in such a way was somewhat frustrating but it beat seeing no television at all. My father caught me one night because I had stretched out too far and couldn't pull back quickly enough. After that my father turned around every five minutes to see if I had disobeyed, so I reluctantly gave up trying to see TV that way, instead straining to hear whatever was being said and imagining what the picture might look like. This tactic quickly became too frustrating though, because they lowered the sound on me.

One night, my sister Lindy and I couldn't sleep, so we devised a game of going back and forth to each other's bed by using the bottom drawer of our very tall dresser. We surreptitiously inched the drawer open, being extra careful not to let the drawer pulls clink when we got it out far enough. We were having a ball going back and forth stepping in and out of the open drawer and landing on each other's bed. We were having such a good time that we didn't notice that the bureau was about to topple over, which it did, with a *huge* crash. My sister and I immediately jumped under our covers and pretended we were asleep. That we thought we could fool our parents into thinking that we were innocently sleeping with this huge piece of furniture lying on its front between our beds makes me chuckle still. Unfortunately, my father didn't chuckle. He was furious and gave us a whipping we didn't forget for a very long time.

SOME FRIENDS IN the neighborhood had parents who were affectionate with each other. They'd listen to the radio or watch television while sitting on their couch holding hands. I was surprised by
this open show of affection. I thought it very unusual, but appealing. I
knew that, in their own way, my parents loved each other, and my sister and me, but I wished that we could have been more physically affectionate with each other. I didn't know back then that my mother
and father grew up in desperate need of love themselves. They didn't
find it with their parents although my mother has always spoken of
Justyn, her father, with great affection. She never spoke of her mother,
Bridget, that way; she didn't like her mother at all, probably because
she thought her mother didn't like her. My father never spoke affectionately about either his parents or his home life, even when I was
small.

When I was to go into eighth grade my parents moved from
Clarence Avenue to the suburbs, to 969 Elmont Lane, Crestwood,
Missouri. It was about as far as you could get from North St. Louis.
They were afraid of what was happening there. A "bad element" had
moved in, and there were gang fights in O'Fallon Park. My life
changed dramatically with that move. I lost my friends. I lost my freedom to get around and had to be driven everywhere. Buses, if there
were any, were few and far between and didn't run very often at all. I
became very depressed.

"Well, Webster was a home to you." Grace gently reminds me.

Oh, my gosh, yes! Webster College, my sanctum sanctorum, my
haven. I thought of Webster College as my emotional home. I loved it
there. I loved staying in an empty room in the dorm during exam
week. We always had tests and finals scheduled during the time of various theatrical productions I worked on so I used that as an excuse to
stay at school. I loved going down the steps to the basement of the
main building where the Drama Department was housed. It was there
that I worked day and night in a state of happiness and excitement. In
order to earn some money and stay even longer, I answered phones
and filed papers for Sister Marita and the other teachers in the depart-

ment. I studied and worked in the scene shop, learning to make flats and model sets and how to paint with various implements and techniques. The sounds and smells made me feel alive, passionate, excited.

"You were probably high from all the paint fumes!" G.A. crackles. Hah, maybe you're right, but I finally had purpose, a commitment, a focus in my life. Everything made sense there. I knew what I wanted to do. I was loved and given support by the teachers and nuns and my classmates. It was there that I headed when I heard that President Kennedy was shot.

I was at home when Walter Cronkite's voice cracked as he issued the stunning sentence, " . . . the president is dead." The words pierced my heart, and I bolted for the door. I had to get to school; I wanted to be there. My mother was worried there would be chaos in the streets. She didn't want me to drive, but I insisted. My refuge, the drama department, was where I belonged. I did expect chaos in the streets and was amazed that everything around me looked totally normal as I drove to school.

We all hugged each other, students and teachers. Sister Marita led us in a prayer for the family and the world. She told us that we would cancel the performances of whatever show we were doing then. We all agreed it was the right thing to do although, truthfully, I had a momentary pang because that meant we wouldn't be working on any production for some time. The small group of us who made up the drama department, maybe twelve of us, not counting the teachers, all held one another's hands and everyone shared their thoughts and emotions. We talked of what we liked about our president and his beautiful and sophisticated wife. Everyone was devastated and grieving. I didn't want to go back home later that day. I wanted to stay at school. When I did return home, my father was still sitting in the kitchen. I told him about the cancellation and the plans at school to acknowledge this terrible thing.

"Life goes on," he responded. "What does it matter anyway. The man's dead."

I felt myself completely shut down, and I went to my room, wishing I could say something to him. But it was a big no-no to be openly angry at my parents. I'd be punished severely for that infraction. To this day my first reaction when I'm angry is to shut down.

As I went to our bedroom, Lindy's and mine, a disturbing feeling came over me. I realized I didn't like my father at that moment. I didn't respect him either. He was prejudiced, mean, cruel, punishing, and heartless. I didn't realize then that he drank too much and was unhappy and probably very depressed. Because of his strict and somewhat weird rules "that separate the men from the boys," it took me years to learn how to express my anger, let alone understand it. I had to learn how to have a fight or a disagreement, to understand that having a fight doesn't mean the other person doesn't love you, and that to feel anger doesn't mean that I don't love him. The rage and hurt for all those belittling comments or reprimands, the hateful beatings, the oh so conditional love, and the realization that both my parents drank too much—none of these would be dealt with for some twenty-five years.

MY FIRST HUSBAND, Gary Campbell, had parents who drank too much too. His mother died young, having drunk herself to death. Amazingly, his father is still alive and looks pretty darn good for a man in his nineties who drank his entire adult life.

"Hell of a constitution!" I'll say, G.A. He's amazing. Buried two wives and still on his third. Gary has told me his life was hell growing up, but he always clung to the hope that his father would one day be a dad who was proud and supportive of him. I didn't feel my father was supportive of me when I was in high school and college, although he performed in shows with me at Webster. He was never enthusiastic about my plans for the future but then he wasn't enthusiastic about anything at all, really. He never forbade my plans; he just didn't seem to really be there. Perhaps he was giving his blessing by not saying much of anything.

My parents hated the fact that I married the first time, especially since it was totally my own decision. I was petrified to tell them because I knew they'd punish me for it somehow. Gary wasn't sure I had the correct perspective on them, but when they finally came to visit us in New York, he met them and understood. We were living on East Eleventh Street in the East Village at the time and they were going to stay with us. The second night they were there my mother and I had an argument and she refused to stay with us any longer; my father went along with her, checking into a hotel instead. I don't think they ever sent a wedding present. It took me a very long time to understand why they were so upset at my marriage.

WHEN GARY'S FATHER, Dale, and his second wife, Diane, came to visit, we proudly showed off what we had purchased with the money they had sent us as a wedding present, but it was hard to tell what Dale was thinking. He started every day with a shot. It was bourbon, I think, and he kept the bottle on the sink with a glass turned down beside it. By nighttime he was drunk. My grandfather Justyn had told me that he started every day with a shot of vodka when the Russian winter came. When Dale wanted a drink the season had nothing to do with it.

"The apartments you and Gary rented while you were married—they were homes to you, old girl." That's true, G.A. I loved our second apartment on Jane Street in the West Village. We had the basement floor of a lovely brownstone that had been renovated by the owners, the Laraines. Harry Laraine was a mind and memory specialist. He and his wife lived in the three floors above. Harry traveled a lot and they decided to rent out the bottom floor so that his wife wouldn't be alone. It was a great apartment, all newly renovated with a slate floor in the hall. Gary and I antiqued the woodwork around the doors and painted the rooms the way we wanted. We had a tiny portion of the backyard, which was screened off with a tall white fence. Yes, those two apartments I shared with Gary were definitely home to me as was the city of New York.

The apartment I rented on West Seventy-second Street after Gary and I separated was a home to me too, my first in the city all by myself. I had a very clear idea of how I wanted to decorate. The bedroom walls and ceiling had plaster detailing so I painted the whole room like Wedgwood china. The walls were a beautiful dusky blue with the plaster detailing left white. The living room had a wall paneled in old barnsiding that Gary stained and put up for me. Being an artist, his sense of color was much better than mine. He was also very sensitive and never said a word about my choices in color. Of all things, I chose wall-to-wall bright orange wool carpeting for the living room. I didn't know at that time that those colors, orange and blue, would have great significance in my life.

"I hope your taste won't regress when we get to cowboy land. Orange carpeting in the living room and blue walls in the bedroom? Some combination!" Well, I had off-white carpeting in the bedroom, G.A. It didn't look as weird as it sounds. I had that apartment for three or four years although I didn't live in it much. My career took off, literally, and I was away a lot.

When I married Neil Simon, he lived in a lovely brownstone on East Sixty-second Street with Ellen and Nancy, and Ponti, their dog. They had lived there as a family with Joan, Neil's first wife, before Nancy was born. It was home to them. I moved in and spent a little over a year there—sleeping in Joan and Neil's bed—before we decided to move to California. I did feel like a stranger in a strange house. There were times when I felt that Joan still lived there, her presence was so palpable. There were times when none of that mattered. My new family was my home.

The house that Neil decided to buy for us in California was on Chalon Road in Bel-Air. That house was my first serious major home and I took a crash course in how to go from a small, one-bedroom, blue and orange New York apartment to an seven-thousand-square-foot house in Bel-Air, California. Fortunately, my pal, Dixie Marguis, was in the interior design business. Together, she and Mimi London, her partner, taught me everything I needed to learn, and they charmed

Neil, which was most important because he was nervous about my taste. He didn't know if I had any either.

Since my second divorce I've lived in . . . six houses, counting this one, all in the space of ten years. Some weren't really homes to me, but each in its own way gave me comfort. This house that I'm leaving, was home to me, although I wish I could have enjoyed myself more while I was here.

"But it was the perfect refuge," Grace intervenes.

That's true, Grace, thank you. Thank you for suddenly making this traumatic move a little easier. And thank you, you beautiful house you, my private home, my sacred sanctum. Perhaps some part of me has died in this house. Perhaps we are capable of living several lives if we choose, giving up the outworn or worn-out cloth or old skin by sloughing off the past. In this house, this home I'm leaving, I've discarded the old worn-out me for a new me, a someone I'm just now beginning to know. Why hold on so fiercely to those old layers? Why do I feel such sadness and pain at letting go of them? Fear of the unknown, I suppose, and a longing for the past.

"Well, what would Baba say, old girl? You sure aren't in the present." That's true, G.A. It's no good living in the past or fearing the future. I have to remember that I have everything in me, that Baba is with me. I Am That; That I Am. My mantra, So'ham. I died and was reborn in this house, this home built for me alone. These walls and ceilings and floors bear witness to the anguish, the despair, the death, and the grieving I went through, a major personal renovation, down to the bare bones. And here I am, a different person, attempting to stand on quivering legs, about to walk into a new life in a new place.

"Oh my God, my body aches," I moan as I check to see that the front doors are locked and finally turn out the lights. In the darkness the view is truly beautiful. Three big picture windows frame the night, the sequined lights shimmering and the distant planes lined up to land. A crescent moon high in the night sky is reflected in the black bottom pool. Three windows, three beautifully distinct night paintings. Look how far I've come! I think. I'm amazed. I've taken care of myself. Each despair, each struggle I've experienced since being on my own, has been painful, but by God (and the guru's grace), I've ultimately provided a safe haven for myself. In fact, I've always tried to take care of me even if it meant running away. Running away from home for a week when I was a senior in college was my first conscious act to get out of a dangerous and painful experience.

"Well, Honey, you're not runnin' this time," snaps G.A. "You are carefully walking to your future. You started with one picture window and now you have three, and in another couple of years, you'll have a whole goddamn wall!"

In a therapy session once, Roger Gould talked to me about running away. "Neil is probably the most important man you'll ever have to deal with because of what he represents to you. It's extremely important that you don't run away. You have to learn to stay in the room, as it were, and stand toe to toe with him, expressing yourself clearly and calmly. Then if you choose to turn and walk away, you can make that decision, knowing you have done your best."

Roger's intelligent advice reverberates as I stare out the three grand windows framing L.A. below.

THE SMALL LIVING room on Elmont Lane in Crestwood, Missouri, had a picture window. Staring out of it, on a gray November day, I saw my father's legs go out from underneath him. He would die on December 17. "The big C's got me, Jackie," he whispered, as we bent to help him. A couple of years before that, one Sunday morning, I was visiting my parents' house and found myself staring out of that same picture window. It was a Sunday morning and my father was reading the newspaper. All was quiet but I was tense.

"Are you being a nice girl?" he asked. I had stopped off in St. Louis after finishing up a summer stock engagement of *Barefoot in the Park* with Ken Kercheval. Ken and I had visited his mother in Indiana and stayed a couple of days. When we left, she gave me a Jenny Lind plate from her glass collection. We slept in Ken's room down the hall from

his mother's, in an old brass bed with worn box springs. I was mortified that the whole bed sang out its plinks and squinks as we made
love. I thought his mother would be furious with us, but Ken said of
course not. After all she's an Indiana farm woman who always knew
exactly what was going on. Besides, we're grown-up, and making love
is what grown-ups do. I was twenty-eight years old and divorced from
Gary, but I knew this behavior wouldn't fly in my parents' home and
told him so. That's okay, he said, I'll sleep on the couch. Wanna bet? I
thought to myself.

When we arrived at 969 Elmont Lane, Ken had to bunk with a
friend because my parents wouldn't let him stay in our house, not
even on the couch in the living room. My father pointedly asked me
that silly question about being a "nice girl" the day Ken was to pick
me up as we made our way east. His churlish attitude and his silly
controlling question made me so angry I could barely speak. I wanted
to yell at him, say something to jar him. Instead, one strained sentence
was all I could muster.

"I am *always* a nice girl," I responded, through clenched teeth.

Some fourteen years earlier, in that same living room, my mother
sat in a chair looking out the picture window. I'd decided to ask her a
most important question. "What was your wedding night like?" My
mother's answer shaped our relationship for years to come.

"It's . . . like . . . a miracle, dear," she answered. I waited for her to continue, but she went back to whatever she was doing. I felt the iron door
of noncommunication slam shut between us. I wanted to scream at
her, "I didn't ask for a metaphor! Who the hell knows what a miracle is
like! I'm not the Virgin Mother! Why can't anybody *talk* in this family?!" In that chilling moment, I swore to myself I would never ask her
another important question. And I didn't, at least not until some fifteen years later when we were in my orange-carpeted New York living
room one night, getting ready for bed. Dad had recently died and she
was visiting.

"Did you and Dad have an active sex life?" I asked straightforwardly.

"Why, yes," she replied, rather hesitantly, "I guess so."

"Well, what do *you* mean by active?" I pressed. "Once a week, once a month?"

"Oh, three times a week?" she answered tentatively.

"Really!?" I gasped.

"He used to call me up at lunchtime sometimes and say he was going to pop in for a little dessert!" I gasped again and then we both began to giggle. I heard the years of hard ice between us crack and break apart. As we sat there on the sofa bed, dressed in our nightgowns, I told her about the "miracle" moment when I was fourteen and what I had promised myself. She was nonplused.

"Why couldn't you talk about this kind of stuff?" I asked. "It would have been so much better to have talked, shared stuff. . . ."

"Oh, I guess it was just the way things were then. Momsie and Grandpa never talked to me about *anything*. . . ." She looked wistful and sad. For the first time we talked to each other, long into the night. I asked her a ton of questions and she answered them as best she could. I couldn't remember Momsie ever talking to my sister or me. Bridget was a stern woman. My mother confided that night that her mother hated her and told her so. I was stunned. She was an only child. She quickly added that she loved Grandpa and that Grandpa loved her. What would that be like, I wondered, to hear your mother telling you she hated you? Was that why she didn't like to be called Ma? Was the need for strict propriety and good breeding all she ever got from Bridget? I knew what it felt like to overhear my sister say that she had no feelings for me, that her heart was as cold as ice toward me—a brick. That hurt a great deal. I felt betrayed somehow and consequently I felt very alone at that moment.

Lin was standing in the kitchen on Elmont Lane talking to my mother. It was my senior year of college. I had just returned after running away from home to New York City the day after Christmas 1963. I was twenty-one years old and feeling hurt and saddened by the whole mess I was in. But what if it was a mother saying that to her only child? No wonder my mother had such mixed emotions about being a woman and a mother.

I didn't know that night that she would never grieve after my father's death. Instead she romanticized Dad and their relationship, forgetting the bad and enhancing the good, never becoming romantically involved with any other man. She was my age when my father died, fifty years of age. Dad was fifty-four when he died. Joan, Neil's first wife—Ellen and Nancy's mother—died when she was forty. Barbara Colby, a dear friend, was thirty-six when she was gunned down by unknown assailants. I haven't any grandparents; they all died by the time I was nine.

Turning from the night view, I suddenly remember my fiftieth birthday party, here in this room. I did have a great birthday party and it was a complete surprise—my first and only surprise party. Chris Clark, my business manager, arranged everything. She even had a delicious cake made in the shape of a race car with my number, 34, in icing. I've been racing cars for seven years now, came in second in my division, and consistently finished in the top five in my GT-3 races, and I've qualified for the Valvoline National SCCA runoffs four years in a row. At the runoffs in Ohio I was the first woman to be initiated into the Chevaliers (racers fifty years young and growing). But what made my fiftieth party so great was my friends and my daughters, Nancy and Ellen. El flew in from Santa Fe where she lived then, just to be here for the surprise. I'll never forget it . . . she was standing right where I am now. . . .

Something shiny on the banquette catches my eye, a Mother's Day gift from Nancy, made by her with great care. This gift is precious to me and I've always kept it close. It consists of a message Nancy had written carefully with a calligraphic pen in red ink. "Dear Marsha, I hope this will be the greatest Mother's Day ever, 'cause you really deserve it!—I love you alot—Love, Nancy." It is decorated with lace and a red and white flowered fabric tied in a bow and pasted on the handmade present. The message is faded a bit now. There's a stuffed heart made from the same red and white fabric to top it all off. The entire thing is boxed in wood with glass to protect it, and it's framed in a shining gilt frame. She must have worked on it forever. Perhaps Ellen helped her. I was so touched that she had taken so much care. This morning I'd carefully wrapped it and was about to give it to the movers. Then I suddenly decided to carry it myself. I didn't want to let it go. I've never wanted to let Ellen and Nancy go either.

I have regretted that I didn't give birth to any children. When I was younger, I was afraid I'd wreak havoc on the poor innocent, believing myself to be a terrible mother. I realized when I was older I would indeed be a good mother, but it was too late. Endometriosis and the subsequent loss of my left ovary, plus the end of an affair, all conspired against it. I did think about adopting and called Mia Farrow for advice and information. I also spoke with other women who were trying various methods in order to have children in their lives. What a funny thing to think about now, I mused.

"Come on, be honest," G.A. interrupts. "You were always ambivalent about having kids."

No, that's not true. There was a time when I wasn't ambivalent at all. But if you are saying, "If you really wanted to have kids you would have had them," then maybe you're right, I don't know. Fortunately, this regret was assuaged by my love and desire for a continuing relationship with Ellen and Nancy. Their love and inclusion of me in their lives is most precious. Just like this Mother's Day gift. And now there are grandchildren. I've learned an enormous amount about family from Ellen and Nancy, and Neil too. I learned a lot about my relationship with my sister while watching Nancy and Ellen and their sibling conflicts.

TURNING OFF THE lights in the office, I run my hand along the empty wall as it curves toward my bedroom. The plaster feels cool and satisfyingly uneven against my palm. My dogs, Dulcie and Buddy, are suddenly padding along with me, their toenails clicking on the cool saltillo tile. There is the slightest echo surrounding us as we head for bed, or rather, sleeping bag.

"What have you been doing, Marsha May?! We have to get up in four hours! I sent the animal search party out to find you!" Gary is standing there, obviously having just come from the bathroom; toothpaste foam circles his mouth and is making its way down his chin and onto his dark green T-shirt.

"Oh, I was just mentally dervishing. Saying good-bye to my roses and the Christmas trees and the view and the empty rooms and their memories. Just the usual. You look cute standing there with toothpaste all over you."

"Shit, I was gonna wear this tomorrow."

"So sleep in it and wear another one tomorrow. How's Max? Where's Max?" I ask about my third dog while carefully packing Nancy's artwork in my gym bag.

"In the bathroom, sleeping. Which is what we should be doing this minute. I set the clock for four A.M." I go into the bathroom to check on Max and brush my teeth. Everything personal is gone, except for my toothbrush by the sink, the last thing to pack. Max looked sad and sick.

"Hell, he is sad and sick. Wouldn't you be too if they operated on you twice in two weeks?" my inner Critic says accusingly. Heavy attitude drips off her shrill words and I feel appropriately guilty. It's automatic with me.

"Hello, big guy," I murmur, crouching next to him and gently stroking his side, "how ya feelin'? I'm sorry you're not feeling good. Get some sleep, won't you? You're gonna be okay, I promise." Max doesn't even raise his head to sniff my face in acknowledgment of my effort. This is so unlike him.

"Everything's gonna be okay, Max, I promise. I'm gonna make sure you get well—that's a promise too. Now go to sleep. You need your strength for the long haul." I talk to plants too.

Max had developed a hard, baseball-size growth on the side of his head by his jaw; it had come on in just two days time. Dr. Didden operated and it went away, only to come back again in exactly the same spot within a week, just as big as before. He operated again and took out some strange line of little blips that looked translucent on the X-ray. He wasn't at all sure what had caused this problem. I don't want Max to travel in this condition, but I have no choice. I also don't have any recommendations for vets in Santa Fe. I closed my eyes and prayed: "Dear God, please help Max make the trip and be all better again . . . and Baba, please look over him and protect him."

Getting up from the hard tile floor took quite an effort, and looking at myself in the large mirror, tears started to well. What else is new? I thought, studying my face in the mirror. I look different. I can't say how exactly, but I definitely look different. I tried to see what was changed while stabbing at my teeth and whisking the toothbrush around without thought or purpose. But as I rinsed what occurred to me was . . . nothing. That's that, I thought with a sigh, turning off the lights.

"Put on your flashlight, Gary, so I don't kill myself tripping over Dulcie or Duddy—I mean Buddy—trying to find my sleeping bag." Gary grunted, fumbling with the flashlight, and I made my way into my sleeping bag next to his.

"This wood floor is hard!" I grumbled as I tried to get comfortable. We were lying on the floor where my bed used to be, side by side in sleeping bags. There were grunts and shuffling and the clicking of animal feet moving around in the dark.

"What's going on?" I asked, peering into the dark. Max had come and was gingerly lowering his bovine one-hundred-pound-plus body down between us, placing his swathed and swollen head on my stomach. Silence and breathing.

"Okay. What's that?" I ask loudly. "What's that sound?"

"Nothing. Go to sleep," Gary answers quietly.

"My God, Gary, what *is* that? I've never heard anything like that before. What is it! Listen carefully now. Don't talk!" We listened to silence. Suddenly there were scratching sounds all around us. They'd stop totally and then suddenly start again.

"Mice," he states. "*What?!*" I reply, bolting. Max whimpers and winces as Dulcie and Buddy bark in the dark. "Calm down you two," I order, "I'm so sorry, Max. I didn't mean to hurt you."

"Yep, mice. Just think of them as charming little creatures. . . ."

"*You* think of them as charming little creatures. Here we are laying on the floor; they could charge right over us. I *never* had that sound in here before! Great! I can listen to them infesting my house and I'm not even gone yet!" I lie back down and gently pat Max's head. Silence follows.

"Maybe they heard you," Gary says with a chuckle. Silence continues.

"Remember the last time we slept on the floor?"

"In San Francisco," Gary murmurs.

"God, Gary, isn't it amazing, the way life twists and turns? That was, what, almost twenty years ago? You and Dontzig came to see me at A.C.T. You saw a matinee of *A Doll's House* . . ."

"And afterward we gave you that book. . . ."

A Mystic in the Theatre by Eva Le Gallienne. It became my acting Bible. I read and reread that book over and over again. I wanted to be just like her on the stage. I still use that St. Thomas Aquinas prayer that Ms. Le Gallienne translated. I hope it's packed in one of those hundreds of boxes; I'll kill myself if I've lost it. Silence.

"The three of us slept on the floor of my apartment on Russian Hill. Remember?"

"Yeah," Gary says as he yawns. "We put the mattresses down on the floor and you slept between us."

I didn't know then that he and Gary Dontzig were lovers and would become partners for the rest of their lives, a twenty-seven-year marriage between men. At one time I was married to one and best friends with the other. And now I'm best friends with both and they are a couple. Family. Gary and Gary. The Garys. They have loved me since the beginning, unconditionally, no matter what. Through all the ups and downs, the crazy boyfriends, the bad relationships, the good relationships, they've been friends with Neil, friends with the girls, and my friends to this day. They've never stopped loving me, never stopped showing and sharing their unconditional love and support. We have supported and loved each other totally and unconditionally, even when Neil didn't know what to make of it. Both Garys are part of my family, along with Ellen and Nancy. And here I am with one of them, trying to get some sleep, about to set off on a terrifying adventure. Gary Dale Campbell, husband number one, my first male friend, my first gay ex-husband friend.

"Gare . . ."

"Hmmm . . ."

"Thanks for helping me with this move. I really appreciate it. I don't think I could've done it without you. Thanks, thanks for . . ."

"Marsha May?"

"Yeah Gare?"

"Go to sleep." Silence. Scratch, scratch.

CHAPTER THREE

HEAD 'EM UP,
MOVE 'EM OUT

G ot everything?" queried Gary as he grabbed the sleeping bags and headed for the cars.

"I can't find the keys to the car!!!" I bellowed back.

"I have them. Let's go!"

"No! The other car! The Mazda! I can't find the keys to the Mazda! Shit, shit, *sugar!*" I screeched as I tore through my purse for the umpteenth time. "So where are you, you . . . ?"

Mantra, Marsha, mantra . . . breathe! I reminded myself. Taking in a deep breath, I sounded the first syllable, "Hum," inside my head. Exhaling, I sounded the second syllable, "sah." Keeping the repetition attached to my breathing, *Hamsa*-ing away, I began to calm down. If I had slept two hours last night I was lucky, and the early morning already had started badly. I woke up with what felt like a vice clamped around my head and neck. I felt both drugged and in pain. Also, my back was in agony after coaxing, pleading, and finally lifting the bandaged one-hundred-ten-pound Max into the Explorer. Max looked even worse than I felt. His big chunky head, swathed in medical gauze, looked as if Lawrence of Arabia had dressed him.

Gary's driving the Ford Explorer and I'm driving the Mazda Rx-7

to our appointed rendezvous, a Chevron station on National Boulevard near the entrance to the freeway. Of course I haven't the vaguest
idea where the station is. I've lived here for twenty years, and I had to
have a map drawn for me. My mind is mush. We're meeting up there
with Chris Clark, my friend and business manager of some fifteen
years, and her husband, Gary Da Silva. Besides being Chris's husband
and the father of two of their three children, he's also one of my
lawyers. Neil's too. Gary Da S . . . my life is *full* of Garys! They'd picked
up my gorgeous black Porsche 911 Cabriolet S4 yesterday afternoon
(I love saying 911 etc.). I've been panicked ever since they picked it up,
fearing that it would be stolen from their driveway in Manhattan
Beach. My original plan was to put the Porsche on the truck with all
my stuff, but there was no room—I have too much stuff!

Chris and Gary volunteered to help drive the cars to New Mexico.
"This isn't business," Chris said, "we want to do this as friends." I cried,
I was so happy . . . and so stressed. Once we are on the road, headed out
of town, Chris is to drive the Mazda and I'll ride with Gary and the
dogs; we agreed I shouldn't try to drive anything. Chris told me that
her husband was unbelievably excited about the trip because he was
getting to drive the Porsche. (It was the S4 part that particularly excited him.) Chris often has to tell me what Gary's feeling. He's a super
lawyer, and one of the most stoic men I have ever met. I'm fascinated
by him. Chris confided that "very still waters run mighty deep."

Driving away, dawn is doing its thing. I don't dare look back. My
throat's so constricted it hurts worse than when I had the mumps. I'd
bought this '91 Mazda Rx-7 model used, from an ex-girlfriend of my
racing partner, Mike "the Champ" Lewis. It was his idea.

Mike Lewis is a god I give thanks to every day. He's in his thirties,
taller than six feet, good body, and wears sexy underwear. Seeing him
in underwear is the only benefit I receive when changing in and out
of race suits in the back of our truck that hauls two race cars and all
the other equipment needed on race weekends. We like each other
enormously and we can talk. We talk about a lot of things: sex, women,
men, relationships, parents, business, cars, and racing. And we both

think the other is cute, definitely cute. Mike's got a great smile and a mischievous glint in his eye. He's a handsome hunk with a kind face that's topped by a full head of jet black hair and he's always fussing with it. He's the only driver on the SCCA circuit who reaches for a hairbrush before he gets out of the car at the end of the race. It's partly because he's usually the winner and his picture's taken for race magazines, and partly because he has a thing about his hair.

David Steele, our crew chief, razzes him about it, but then Dave almost never takes his hat off. On the rare occasions that he does, like at his wedding, the top half of his forehead is lily white while the rest of his face is seasoned by the sun and car grease.

I'm glad Mike and Dave and the rest of the crew aren't here right now. If they heard the way I just shifted gears I'd never hear the end of it. My arms feel like Jell-O after the workout they got trying to get Max and Buddy and Dulcie in the Explorer. I have to start picking smaller dogs.

I'm driving this blue Mazda Rx-7 street car this morning because Mike thought that since my race car is an Rx-7, I should tool around L.A. in the street or stock version of my race car, practicing double-clutch downshifts in traffic. Mike's idea of getting this sporty blue Mazda was a good one because the sound of a rotary engine rev is much different than a piston engine rev. Hearing this car rev in all kinds of traffic taught me to know when to shift by her sound instead of looking at the tach. Of course, this morning the poor car sounds like the early years in my racing career. During the national runoffs one year I managed to grind a tranny into thousands of tiny shards. When the crew took it apart, the inside looked just like a magnet toy I saw on a desk one time.

PAUL NEWMAN AND racing saved my sanity.

"If it weren't for racing, honey, we'd *all* be very depressed. And that includes the shrill goddess herself, Ms. Critic!" Thank you, G.A. That's my first laugh of the day.

Paul and I ran into each other on an American Airlines flight from New York to L.A. I asked him what was bringing him to the West Coast. He said, "racing," and graciously invited me out to the track. He was racing at Riverside Raceway, in Riverside, California. It was the last race that track would have. He told me how to get there and what to wear so that I could hang out in the pits. I hadn't been that happy since I married Neil.

I was reminded of the Sundays back in high school when I would pass out pit passes or walk the pits, watching the local guys with ducktail haircuts and cigarette packs rolled in the cuff of their black T-shirt sleeve carefully unwrap each important piece of machinery for their rails, hot rods, and funny cars. The father of one of my best friends, Jane Lindenbusch, had acquired a track outside St. Louis, and Jane and I, along with another best friend, Sally Dooling, would go to early Mass on Sundays and then head out to the track. I loved handing out the pit passes to the guys who were hauling their cars and rails into the track, and some were driving what they were going to drag. The smell of grease and rubber and the deafening squeal of the competitors racing against the clock and each other was downright sexy to me.

Having the opportunity to hang out with Paul Newman and his racing team was what heaven is surely like. I was feeling mighty low back then, not working much and involved in a relationship with a very nice fella but one that was going absolutely nowhere. That first invitation from Paul led to many others.

It sometimes took two planes and a drive of some distance to get to the tracks. Paul and his co-driver, Jim Fitzgerald, were on the pro Trans-Am Tour, and the tracks are usually out in the boonies, in the middle of cornfields. I stayed out of everyone's way, but watched closely and listened carefully. I did that for a year, I think, traveling to Wisconsin, Minnesota, Atlanta, Detroit, New York, northern California, Ohio—you name it. Paul finally looked at me one day and said, "What on earth have I wrought!" I laughed. I was just one big happy camper, hangin' with the guys. Me and my tomboy self as happy as a lark.

One weekend Tom Cruise showed up. He was heavy into the sport himself and very good at it. A freelance photographer or newspaper guy started following Tom and Paul everywhere we went. Well, they decided to have some fun and escape this guy, who was following us as we left the track. Paul was driving, and by getting far enough ahead of the reporter, we pulled off the road and hid behind an abandoned filling station. The three of us, crouched in the weeds, watched the fellow race by, and Paul and Tom broke up laughing, high-fiving each other, having the best time. I was spellbound, watching how free and playful and comfortable they were, and asking myself why I couldn't tap into that energy and pure sense of fun.

Paul is shy, serious, funny, kind, a little distant, and a lot of fun. Being a handsome movie star there's a big price to pay. You have to search for privacy, and then there's the way men and women go crazy around you. I watched a woman with two small children totally lose it, shaking and screaming, she was so excited to see Paul. As I watched this curious moment, I was reminded of some of the black-and-white footage they show on television of teenyboppers losing it over the Beatles. It was interesting to see a grown woman with two small children do the same thing. I wondered what this woman's husband was thinking as he tried to get her to calm down and move away.

The words "shy, serious, and a little distant" could be applied to me too and probably to most actors I know. I feel that way in public most of the time, even though I don't have anyone losing it over me. Paul and the crew all made me feel welcome and comfortable on those trips, taking me and my love of racing at face value. Paul was kind, thoughtful, funny, serious, and focused about racing too, and majorly in love with his wife and family.

Mostly I was curious about racing, but once in a while I sought Paul's advice or perspective on marriage and relationships, asking how he and his wife, Joanne Woodward, managed to stay together for so many years. I wanted to know how to do that in order to have a sustaining relationship for the rest of *my* life. Only later did I realize how presumptuous my questions were. He's worked hard for everything he's accomplished because as he put it, he wasn't "a natural" at anything. He pretty much told me what other smart, experienced folks have said: Marriage takes work, which he and Joanne are committed to do; but it isn't easy, there are always difficult times as well as good times, and to stay together takes a willingness and an ability to communicate. That, he emphasized, was crucial.

I spent a lot of time thinking about this issue of communication. I had no real talent or skill back then in that area. Oh sure, I had some experience in communicating my feelings to men. I could yell and demand and get frustrated and make them wrong. But really communicate? No. I couldn't really talk to Neil either. Not comfortably. Oh yes, we could talk about the work. But about personal feelings? No, not really. I was too scared of his disapproval, too fearful of his criticism. My favorite way of communicating my feelings with the men I loved was to send balloons and flowers. And to Keith Hernandez I sent over one hundred condoms when he left for spring training. Ohhh, but that's another story altogether.

It's not that I didn't talk. I did—a lot. Men can't always talk to a woman, but frequently they are communicating. Women, those like me anyway, talk a lot but to little effect. I talked but I wasn't really communicating.

I never even talked much with my sister and we shared the same room for twenty years. I still don't talk much with my family, not the way other people do. It doesn't come naturally to me like it does . . . Ellen and Nancy, for example. My sister and I fought a lot as kids. My father used to warn us that he was going to put boxing gloves on us and let us fight it out. As a kid, no expression of anger was allowed, not to anyone really, and especially not to authority figures. As a result, I never learned how to handle my anger appropriately, let alone identify it. When I was a kid you also couldn't be physical with another person, nor did anyone talk about his feelings. Finally, when I married Gary, he suggested therapy. I went. It was a godsend, as was the therapist I met, Blanche Saia.

Acting class helped too, but for me therapy made the difference. Being able to talk to someone about anything and everything and not worry about her liking or approving made living bearable for me. It didn't solve everything in one fell swoop, but when I felt overwhelmed by something or someone, like marrying Neil Simon and becoming an instant mother, I sure was glad Blanche was still around and practicing.

Neil talks a lot, and he can talk about everything, especially when he's mad or upset. He also talks very, very well. He's incredibly articulate. And he's able to talk to a lot of people. He's been known to call people he doesn't really know and express his feelings, sharing intimate details of what he's going through at the time. I'm the opposite. I say nothing. I'm the animal who goes into a dark closet when in pain. There's a lot of pain in Neil and a lot of anger too. Perhaps he doesn't want to control his feelings, because he's a writer. He likes drama. Blanche once said to me, "Where do you think all that comedy comes from? It comes from enormous pain."

Perhaps it's the writer in Neil that needed to "mix it up." Unfortunately I wasn't able to handle "mixing it up." The drama left me exhausted, scared, and unable to put two intelligent sentences together, but once in a great while I'd find the words and say something that was like connecting a bat with a ball and hitting a home run. One such home run is on film, in *Chapter Two*. It's the big speech toward the end of the picture; that scene was taken from life, more or less.

Neil was always in turmoil about my acting. He loved my work and respected it, but didn't want me to be away from home. He felt it was important for me to work but couldn't be happy with me as long as I actually wanted to work, or wanted to do some things on my own, like have an office away from the house, or take a trip with a girlfriend. He tried valiantly to handle my being away, but inevitably I'd come home to a crazed man, or worse, a calm one who wanted a divorce. If I wanted to do someone else's movie and it meant being away, he saw that as a major threat to our relationship. My great failure at that point was that I as yet had no ability to argue or even discuss what mattered to me; my overwhelming concern was his approval.

In those early years, out of his own insecurity and fear, he often said, "We shouldn't be married" or "Maybe we should get a divorce." What I heard was my father telling me, "Marriage and career won't work." I'd collapse and take the guilt of the situation on my shoulders. My inner Critic and Patriarch had a field day.

I realize now Neil was saying he needed reassurance of my love and commitment. His issues started in his childhood, just as mine had. His father abandoned him, as his mother did in some way, and then Joan, in dying, abandoned him as well. But whatever I did to try to assuage this panic and hurt from childhood, it was never enough. It felt as if he wanted me to make everything okay, and then I couldn't do it completely because it would mean giving up myself. I think this was the reason he finally, really, asked for the divorce. He felt abandoned in the first year of our marriage and he felt the same in the eighth. I never was able to convince him of my love. For Neil, abandonment was a big issue.

"That and control." True, G.A., control was a big issue too. At least it was when we were together. I guess actually they go hand in hand. If you feel abandoned you feel your life is out of your control, and it's natural to want to be in control of your life. Losing Joan surely made it all worse. And then I came boppin' along not knowing what was really going on. Neil's need to replace Joan, and to do it so quickly, was probably a big warning flag, but I was in love and looking for safety myself; so there you are. Besides, I understood abandonment because I'd dealt with it in my own life.

Jesus, my mind's nuts today. From racing to Neil, in four seconds flat! Paul Newman was like my guardian angel. Always kind and patient, even when I asked a zillion questions. And he gave me a wonderful gift: racing. One of my favorite memories of those times was watching Paul and Joanne together. She didn't like racing particularly; it scared her, driving that fast. But even though it wasn't fun for her she was a real trouper, showing up at Road America outside Atlanta, cheering Paul and his team.

Bob Sharp, Paul, Fitzy, and I, as well as other men from the team, were all watching Tom Cruise race. Paul said that Tom was an incredible driver, a natural. I asked him how he knew.

"I've been in a car with Tom, in situations that I thought were impossible to save, and the kid saved it. His reflexes are amazing. His only problem is, he says 'Shit!' *after* he's made the mistake." As we watched Cruise race, from a tower high above the track, I listened intently to the men as they ran commentary, hoping to learn something. I was so intent on the race that I didn't hear Joanne come into the tower. Paul had been anxious for her to arrive, and when he turned around and saw her, his face lit up. He put his arms around Joanne and gently embraced her, holding her for a long time, whispering something in her ear, and then kissed her. There was shared history and sweetness in that moment. I thought to myself, I want someone to greet me like that. Bob caught my glance and we both smiled. There's something so beautiful about a couple who makes that kind of connection. I saw it a couple of times between my parents, especially near the end, when my dad was sick.

One afternoon, while flipping his famous hamburgers for the crew, Paul said that if I was really serious, I should go to racing school. He said he'd call Bob Bonderant for me. I had no idea there was such a thing as a racing school. Then Fitzy invited me to his school in Atlanta.

"It's kindergarten next to Bonderants," he said with a smile. Fitzy put me through a slalom course and put me on the wet pad. I didn't know then that in two years I would race there in the national runoffs.

At Fitzy's school the wet pad was a large piece of asphalt with a white circle painted on it. The surface was sprayed with lots of water, and your goal was to keep your inside wheel on the white line while the car skids out. Driving control was what this exercise was all about. Unfortunately, car sickness was what it was all about for me. Fitzy was driving, showing me the exercise, and I was in the passenger seat. As he increased the speed and we went round and round, I suddenly became nauseated and had to open the door and throw up, all around the circle. It was humiliating. Fitzy just laughed, patted me on the back, and told me that there were professional drivers who got carsick and puked their guts out after a race. I felt a little bit better but said, "Yeah, but at least they can hold it until the race is over!" Fitzy was a super teacher. He used to ask me to pet his car for good luck before a race. He said I was his good luck charm. It all started at some race where I spontaneously patted his car, mentally telling it that it was going to win, and he did.

Later that year I was supposed to join the team in Florida for a race but had to cancel at the last minute. Fitzy died during that race. He drove into a wall at full speed. They think he had a heart attack. For about eight months after that I wasn't sure if I wanted to pursue racing. While meditating one day, Fitzy's laughing face came to me. "Get out there!" he said. "Go for it. I'll be watching."

When I started on the adventure of amateur racing I had no idea where it would lead. If I'd been married I wouldn't have been able to explore this new world. Neil once described me as "the White Tornado" because of my energy and various interests. This from a man who's "the Big Twister" himself. I interpreted his remark as a subtle criticism of some kind. Perhaps I was overly sensitive but I'm convinced that most of the time we ascribe to others those traits that are our own. How else would we be able to recognize and label the qualities in another person?

"The Big Twister and the White Tornado? What a convergence!" Exactly, Miss H.

There it is! The Chevron station. Ahh, we're here. The Porsche is nowhere to be seen. They aren't here. Great! Here I am already late, and they aren't here. I pulled into the station and parked next to Gary. As I open the door I can hear the busy traffic whizzing by on the freeway below. My viselike headache has now blossomed into a raging one, war drums pounding my forehead and temples in rhythm with the beating of my heart.

"Gary, I have to find some aspirin and I have to pee."

"Already? We just left the house."

"I have to pee." I ran to the filling station and asked for the key to the ladies' room, went inside, and had a serious talk with myself in the metal mirror. I was nervous about the Da Silvas. They have three small children; something could have happened to them. Maybe they've had an accident. Maybe one of the kids had to be rushed to the hospital. Maybe they overslept. I prayed the Porsche is okay.

Coming out of the john I see the Da Silvas and the Porsche. Everything's okay.

"Hi guys! You're here! I was worried. Everything okay? Kids okay?"

"Marsha, breathe, you're over-revving," Gary Dale says. "I found the aspirins *and* the dogs' pills. Both were in your purse. Now, let's hit the road, shall we?"

"Yes, of course!" I sang out a little too loudly as I hugged Chris and her Gary and immediately sang out again, waving my arms, "Let's gas up the cars and synchronize the maps!"

Gassed up and ready to go, I give the Mazda keys to Chris and gratefully drop into the passenger seat of the Explorer, immediately reaching for a bottle of water to wash down three aspirins.

"Hold it!" I scream out the window at the Da Silvas. "Don't forget: we're drugging the dogs!" I yell at Gary.

Max and Dulcie took their pills without a struggle, but Buddy gave me such a hard time I couldn't get it down his throat. Gary shut off the engine, crawled over his seat, and between the two of us we managed to get the tiny pill down Buddy's throat. I collapsed back into my seat. My arms, shoulders, and neck were aching so badly I wanted to cry. Instead, I closed my eyes hoping to breathe some of the pain away as I mentally began my mantra. Immediately the pounding in my head came crashing into my consciousness.

"I wonder if *humans* could take these pills?" I wondered aloud, looking at the packet of medicine for the dogs. Gary didn't answer. He was watching the road intensely, waiting for a break in the frantic morning traffic. As he drove out, he motioned our cavalcade to follow. Explorer first, then the Porsche, with the Mazda bringing up the rear. We were finally on our way, headed for the freeway entrance. I leaned around to watch the Porsche being maneuvered into the flow of traffic right behind us. Keeping my neck craned to the rear until I was sure Chris was right behind her husband, my vision suddenly doubled. Closing my eyes, I tried to open them to see if the double vision was still there. Buddy chose this moment to slurp my face with his big rough tongue, starting from my chin, across the lips, and straight up to my hair.

"I made the right decision drugging him, Gary. Now, if only the drugs would kick in. And my aspirins." I moaned as I popped another aspirin into my mouth and gulped down the last of the water. "Is four aspirins too much, do ya think?" I asked as I closed my eyes.

"Put some ice water on your head and neck with paper towels. It might help."

"I can't take the chance of being French-kissed by a dog," I mumbled. Gary started to laugh and then so did I, only I couldn't stop. Tears streamed down my face. The movement of my shaking shoulders actually made them feel better, so I shook them all the more. The viselike grip on my body was letting go. Taking a deep breath to ease the laughing cramp in my stomach, I lay my head back and again closed my eyes. Memories of Neil and the girls laughing came to mind.

NEIL USED TO cry too when he laughed hard and he'd double over in pain and come up laughing and coughing. When something was funny to him, he enjoyed it full out, scatological humor especially. We were watching Mel Brooks's film *Blazing Saddles;* the scene around the campfire, where the "cowboys" are farting after eating their beans, brought Neil to his knees, literally. He finally got up and ran up the aisle to the men's room, not being able to contain himself. Afterward he told me that as a kid he watched Charlie Chaplin movies, sometimes sitting on the railing at the back of the theater. He laughed so hard he fell backward onto the floor and got kicked out of the theater for making such a disturbance.

I loved making him laugh. I did it unwittingly, by making a non sequitur, or just responding in a way that seemed normal to me, but which he found extremely funny. When I asked what was so funny, he'd laugh harder as he tried to explain. It became a private game of mine to see if I could make him laugh.

Sometimes Ellen and Nancy were unwittingly funny. One Indian summer afternoon, we were enjoying a walk in Bedford, New York, where Neil had a house on Blue Heron Lake. As we passed by a large window at the back of the house, we saw inside a "mummy" wielding a long, wooden-handled object, attacking something out of sight. The "mummy" was Ellen, wrapped in sheets and quilts that covered her entire body. She was also wearing long rubber gloves. Neil and I crept to the window to see what she was up to. There she was, broom in hand, attempting to sweep up some dog doo that Ponti, their very old and somewhat spastic Tibetan terrier, had obviously deposited. Nancy was standing in a doorway, holding a bucket and giving Ellen suggestions and encouragement between bouts of giggles. El couldn't get herself within range of the foul-smelling object because she was alternately laughing and gagging. Both girls were so engrossed, they didn't notice us standing outside. We knocked on the window and yelled "Boo!" Nancy screamed at the top of her lungs, dropping the metal pail, and Ellen spun around, tripping on her sheets as the broom went flying. Neil was on the ground doubled up with laughter and I had to cross my legs so I wouldn't pee.

Ellen sometimes lost it out of sheer nervousness or embarrassment, but her laugh is so infectious that we'd all laugh with her. One night we entered a restaurant after having seen a show on Broadway. She had brought a date that night, and we were all waiting to be seated when I happened to turn around to her. I gasped and started to laugh. She'd somehow managed to smear something black all over the lower part of her face, including the tip of her nose. I started to apologize for laughing when Neil and Nancy saw it and started to laugh as well. Trying not to giggle, I told her about the black schmootze she had all over her face and pointed the way to the ladies' room. She ran up the stairs just as the maître d'. motioned us to our table. As we were seated this muffled but distinct shriek, followed by hysterical laughter, wafted down to us from the ladies' room. Still laughing, Ellen finally came to the table and gently chastised her date for not saying anything to her. He blushed and apologized, saying that he hadn't wanted to embarrass her, so he decided that he wouldn't say anything; besides, he thought she looked cute. The consensus was that the ink from the *Playbill* cover was the culprit.

So long ago, I think to myself. I miss those warm, familial experiences when we were a happy family. Nancy was so quiet back then. Nancy is very shy and has a quick mind. As a young girl she didn't talk much at all, but sometimes she'd surprise us by an offhanded comment or retort in a conversation. She and Ellen get each other's humor so completely that they seem to speak in shorthand. They'd be walking down a New York City street and find the most fascinating and hysterical things to laugh at, causing each other such merriment that their repartee and consequent laughter were contagious, even if you hadn't a clue what was so funny. Aw, I miss them so much.

CHAPTER FOUR

HELLOS AND GOOD-BYES

omen drivers!" The sun was up and so was Gary's dander. "I'm sorry," he said somewhat guiltily, "but they are the *worst.*" Defiance sparkled in those eyes.

"I know, I know," I said. "It does *seem* that way, but you've watched Asians drive, elderly people, young hotshots, both male and female, and *their* driving makes you crazy too." His constant criticism of other drivers, whether he's right or not, pushes my buttons, but I definitely did *not* want to start off this two-day road trip with an argument about driving!

"Well, I guess so," he grumbled. I smiled at him gratefully, a major source of irritation and tension having been avoided, for the moment.

We're out of the city, following the base of the San Gabriel Mountains, traveling northeast on Interstate 15 toward Barstow.

"I'm glad I'm leaving all the road tension of L.A."

"I wish I was," Gary says with a sigh.

"Well, you will be soon. You'll be out there before you know it. You can come anytime and stay with me, you know that." Gary has been wanting to move to New Mexico for the last fifteen years.

"I know New Mexico has its problems," he continues, "but they'll feel different because New Mexico is different."

"I know what you mean. I'm actually starting to feel positively positive. This is good! Maybe I'd feel this way no matter where I was headed, but now that we're finally on our way out of L.A., I'm a startin' to feel okay. Good-bye La La Land," I exclaim, "Good-bye smog!"

"Good-bye Grover's Corners." Gary's falsetto reading of Emily's famous line from the play *Our Town* made me chuckle.

"Good-bye freeways!" I chimed in, challenging him to play.

"Good-bye . . . crazy . . . drivers!" he responds, grinning his gorgeous grin.

"Good-bye heartache!" I yell.

"Good-bye Hollywood!" he snaps back.

"That's the same thing!" I shout, laughing.

"Good-bye Pacific Palisades," he shouts, picking up the speed of the game.

"Good-bye ocean," I respond wistfully.

"Hello, clean air!" he counters immediately.

"Hello . . . beautiful open spaces!" I shout in response.

"Hello, New Mexico!" he says, smiling.

"Hello . . . you win!" I shout and laugh.

"No, no, no," he says. "Your turn, Marsha May." He is so proud of himself. He loves being right and I love hearing him say "Marsha May."

He started calling me "Marsha May" when we first met—that and "Sweet Pea." He likes double names. Like Barbara Jean—she was one of our many cats. He wanted to call her Norma Jean, because he loved Marilyn Monroe, but I liked Barbara Jean better. He identified with Marilyn. His early experiences in Hollywood left him feeling like he too was a sexual object, especially to male producers.

He has named his latest dog Grace Ellen. She was running loose around the streets of L.A., when Gary Dontzig, his lover and significant other of some twenty-five years, spotted her as he was driving to Warner Bros. Dontzig and his writing partner, Steve Peterman, are successful, Emmy-winning writer/producers in television comedy. Of course, they too started out as actors. Gary Dontzig and I appeared together in the film version of Neil's play *The Good Doctor,* shown as part of the *Great Performances* series on PBS. That was in 1974, twenty-one years ago.

Our director, Jack O'Brien, hired us separately. Jack and I met in 1970, at the American Conservatory Theater. He directed me in *You Can't Take It with You* and we have all been terrific friends ever since. Dontzig is also an excellent photographer, but his passions, in addition to being a loving human being, are Chinese medicine and studying people's tongues (I kid you not). The tongue study started several years ago when he became fascinated with Chinese medicine and Dr. Mao, his physician. He's often said that if he hadn't been interested in the creative disciplines he'd have been a doctor. Meanwhile, studying tongues is his avocation. He has combined his interests in photography and the study of tongues by taking pictures of all our tongues and showing them to Dr. Mao. I got a very good grade!

He and his writing partner met at the gym. Both being frustrated with the acting business, they started writing spec scripts for shows already on the air. They submitted them, landed an agent, and began working their way up, eventually becoming successful in situation comedy and winning several Emmy Awards for their work on *Murphy Brown.*

MY GARY AND J. Gary Dontzig are always saving strays and people. It doesn't matter who or what kind: me, friends, the needy, the sick, dogs, cats, birds, worms, spiders, flies—you name it. They even taught me how to catch flies and release them outside! As a result, I can't kill anything anymore. Not even mosquitoes. Oh, once in a great while, I've lost my patience and smacked one, but I feel so guilty about it later, I wish I'd been bitten. I know it's crazy but what can I say? Between the Garys and Eastern philosophy, I can't kill anything anymore, or if I do, the guilt is strong. Guiltily, I still eat meat once in a while. Siddha Yoga, Hinduism, Jainism, Buddhism, Taoism, all Eastern philosophy, and the Garys raised my consciousness about all living things. They've been strict vegetarians for years now. Going out to dinner with them is quite an adventure.

It all started with some brutally graphic pictures of newborn calves being squished into tiny dark boxes. All that punishment for a veal chop! When they showed me the pictures, I gave up veal too, forever. Because of the way animals are abused, they don't eat any animal products except organic free-range eggs, and Dontzig won't even eat goat cheese. They even gave up all milk and dairy products because of the way the dairy farms abuse their milking cows, forcing them to overproduce. Gary told me the average dairy cow used to live a long and healthy life, like fifteen to twenty years, but nowadays they have the life expectancy of maybe five. Fortunately, both of them are fantastic vegetarian chefs, which I'm not. I've been a vegetarian at times, but on occasion I eat fish and chicken and even meat—no veal though. It depends a lot on what my body tells me. Once in a great while my blood cells yell out for a thick New York steak, which suits me just fine.

Being vegetarians led them to natural medicine, and I naturally followed their example. Dr. Mao is a wonderful Chinese doctor, a Taoist like his father, Master Ni, and his brother, Dao. Some of the herbs we take are the weirdest looking, most awful smelling and tasting stuff I've ever had to deal with. It's a lot like boiling the forest floor, and it tastes exactly like what I'd expect a forest floor to taste like. But we're strong, happy, and healthy, relatively speaking. Our hearts are big and we continually work for an enlightened mind and a lightened spirit.

These men put their beliefs into action every day of their lives. They've given homecare to their friends dying of AIDS and worked in the kitchen at Angel Food, a charity that provides hot meals to AIDS patients and other folks who are homebound with terminal diseases; Gary Dale did it two and three days a week for years, even serving on the board. Losing so many friends to AIDS tested their stamina and emotional well-being, but their faith and beliefs brought them through. We've loved and supported each other unconditionally since the beginning, helping to guide each other through some rough times.

"Gare, you know what I was thinking this morning driving to the gas station? I found myself thinking about all the friends and family who've died. People I haven't thought of in forty years! Isn't that weird? At first I couldn't even remember my Dad's father's name; he died so long ago, 1958 I think."

"Do you remember his name?"

"Yeah, James *H*. Mason. I called him Pops. My father's name was James *J*. Mason. Obviously, I had a senior moment. It scares me what I don't remember sometimes."

"I can't remember anything either . . . but then I never could!"

"I couldn't remember my grandfather's name, but suddenly found myself remembering a boy, whose name I *did* remember—Anthony. He was killed in a car crash in high school. I had a crush on him at the time, but honestly I haven't thought of him in many, many years. Then, just as I remembered him, I remembered one of my best friends, Jane Lindenbusch, who was killed. . . ."

"I know," Gary said with a sigh, "Dontzig and I had to stop counting all the friends and family we used to know. And . . . that guy!" he suddenly bellowed, pointing his finger, "that motorcycle guy over . . . there!" His sudden decibel level caused me to jump.

"What?! Where?! I don't see him. . . . Gary, you scared me to death!"

"I'm sorry," he said. "There! In the far lane, to the right. You probably can't see him 'cause he's weaving in and out of traffic so much, without *signaling!* He's gonna get killed. Or worse, kill somebody else!"

"That's a terrible thing to say!"

"Well, it's true!"

Suddenly I spotted the madman cyclist, darting in and out of lanes as if he were skiing a downhill slalom. He wore camouflage gear and a dark brown leather bomber jacket. On the back of the jacket was a good-size patch. As he darted to the left again I could make out the words, "Vietnam Vet." As I watched him dodge through the traffic ahead, televised images of soldiers visiting the Vietnam Memorial flashed in my mind. The pain and anguish these men and women suffered, the lives lost for politics, big business, and the sheer ego of some of our leaders.

MY FATHER SIGNED up with the marines when he was called up in 1943 and immediately went to officer's school, coming out a second lieutenant. He was only twenty-four years old and Mother was twenty when I was born in 1942. I didn't see him again until the war was over. My mother told me I didn't remember him when he came home, that I was scared of him. But I have a copy of an old picture of him in uniform, taken right before he shipped out. His face looks soft and sweet and his smile was a killer. The war probably changed him. Mom told me that he was a sensitive man with great humor, but those qualities disappeared over the years.

He served in the Pacific; I know that because of the lacquered bowls that still sit on my mother's coffee table, and the white Japanese flag with the red sun in the middle, and the ivory chopsticks that I have in my desk. I wanted to have something of his to remember him by.

I vaguely remember the Korean War. A newspaper, thrown on our steps on Clarence Avenue, had a bold black heading that took up a lot of the front page, announcing something like BLOOD FLOWS IN THE KOREAN WAR. And another sentence under it told the number of men killed. As a young child, that image seared my brain.

As a large "child" in college, I remember my father and me sitting at the kitchen table late one night having a beer, my sister and mother having already gone to bed. On these rare occasions when it was just the two of us, Dad behaved differently toward me, treating me as an equal. Our conversation was honest and straightforward. He shared thoughts and feelings I've never forgotten. I broached the subject of the Marine Corps. He loved the Corps; "separating the men from the boys" was his favorite phrase. He said it was the best time of his life, and later he regretted not making the Corps his career. The money was good, and he could have retired in his forties as a colonel.

Because he seemed so available, talking like a friend, not a father, I asked him why Mother was so harsh and shrill lately, behaving so impatiently, so critical of everything. He looked down at the ashtray and said that she had a difficult time growing up. He was aware of her demanding nature, her impatient tone when she'd say, "Never mind! I'll do it myself!" But it had been hard on her burying Momsie, Grandpa, and Aunt Mamie all in a year's time.

"But that was a long time ago!" I said.

He took another drag off his cigarette and said, "Your mother's a good person who's put up with a lot. You and Lin are lucky to have a good and loving mother." The tone of voice and attitude of his response gave me the impression that his mother, Grace, was not like that at all.

After getting another beer and lighting another cigarette, he confided that he hadn't wanted to go to work for his father.

"Then why did you?"

Leaning back in his chair, sucking in a deep drag on the Kent cigarette, he sighed and blew smoke out of his mouth and nose. "It was expected of me," he said.

"Well, what did you really want to do?" I asked.

"If I couldn't stay in the Corps?" he asked.

I nodded. "I'd rather have been a paper salesman. Selling paper to the other printers. I'd really like that." I thought he'd have been good at it. What flashed through my mind at that moment was a vision of my father at an earlier age when he used to smile a lot and play golf with his buddies and enjoy socializing. How unhappy he seems now, I thought. Dad worked hard for his father and the Mason Printing Company. "And look what I got for it," he said bitterly.

"I liked going to Stan Musial's restaurant," I volunteered, trying to change the tone of the conversation. "It was neat studying the menu because you printed it." He looked down at the ashtray again and quietly replied, "Yeah, your mother liked it too." After a moment, he snubbed out the cigarette and said, "It's late. You better get to bed."

"Here, I'll take that," I said as I picked up the little mountain of ashes and cleared the table of bottles. He slowly walked out of the kitchen.

"Good night, Dad," I called over my shoulder, really wanting to say, "I love you, Dad," but I didn't, and he didn't answer.

I loved my father with all my heart but somehow never felt that he really knew it. I felt so sad for him. To me he was an unhappy man, disappointed that his life didn't turn out the way it was supposed to. He was hit hard when he realized that his father had left him a failed business. Lots of things changed when his father died. He used to play golf on Saturdays with his buddies and his brother, Murray. He'd come home with that killer smile on his face, laughing and joking with Mother. As the business failed those fun days went with it.

"THERE HE IS again!" Gary interjected, stabbing his finger at the windshield. Watching the motorcycle man disappear in the distance, I wondered if my father ever did *anything* he really liked.

"Well!" Miss Havisham harumphed, "he loved being in those shows with you at Webster College. We know that for a fact." She bobbed her head for emphasis.

"Oh yes, my dear Miss Havisham, you are absolutely correct," warbled Good Witch Glinda. "Your father loved being in those shows at Webster. Absolutely." Yes, Ladies, he sure did. He was wonderful as Nathan Detroit in *Guys and Dolls*. He was a good singer too. He loved performing and singing. Because he had a good time doing those shows, perhaps he felt he could come home and talk at the kitchen table, just the two of us after rehearsal.

"And he was no slouch as Philly in *Playboy of the Western World!*" G.A. volunteered. At least I had the part of Pegeen Mike in *that* show. In *Guys and Dolls* I was in the chorus!

"Maybe losing his business beat him down so much he couldn't come back," volunteered my Inner Child, Anna. Maybe, but my dad was disappointed in life, starting at home when he was a kid like you. Those early years can form your character for the rest of your life, especially if you believed your parents didn't like you.

"Gary, do you think your father liked you as a kid?" I ask, shifting out of my private world.

"No, not really."

"How could you tell?"

"The way he treated me and the things he said. That was a long time ago though."

"What about the homosexuality?"

"When we talk now, he always says, 'give my love to Gary,' but I'm not sure he means it because he doesn't want Dontzig to inherit any of his money." This made Gary laugh loud and hard.

"He also said he has to lie to his buddies because they wouldn't understand."

"Hmmmm."

I guess things are different depending on what message your parents send you. My parents suffered as a result of their parents' behavior, and I suffered from the mixed messages my parents gave me.

Even though my dad worked hard, giving up his dreams for the love of his father, he never felt his father loved him, nor his mother, and consequently he suffered from a lack of self-esteem. I also think he was damaged by the war. We know so much more now what men and women suffer in combat, but back then it was a different story. I suppose his life, as it happened to him, made him feel a failure and he didn't know how or didn't have the energy to change it. And maybe there is something to be said for being a black Irishman—too much feeling, too much drink. Was he born thinking himself a failure? Maybe. What makes one person pick himself up and change his life and another live a life of quiet desperation? Conditioning? Beliefs? Karma? Maybe all of it. But his sense of unhappiness and failure was

so profound that I think his parents must have contributed in a major
way to his lack of self-esteem. They never made him feel loved. It was
the lack of unconditional love and approval, that's what. All parents
have to express and demonstrate unconditional love to their children
if they want them to have a positive sense of themselves. I think unconditional love and self-esteem go hand in hand.

"How do you know?" little Anna interjects.

Well, first of all, my mother told me that Nina, Dad's mother, was
also cold to my father. She openly preferred Uncle Murray and it hurt
Dad's feelings. I remember how differently she related to Uncle Murray. Another reason is, I know how he treated me, how both Mother
and Dad treated me. Their love for me, as they expressed it when I
was a child, seemed conditional. There was the threat of it being taken
away if I didn't behave the way they wanted. If they were mad at me
they withheld their love, saying, "How can I love you when you act
like that?" and "I can't love you because you're bad." Plus, my father's
punishments were much too severe for a child, any child. The impression I got was that he loved me, but I couldn't understand how because he hit me too hard too many times, just for doing things that
didn't hurt anyone, things that were minor.

Alcohol also has a lot to do with it. It changes some people's personalities. In my final year of college I couldn't take the craziness of
their behavior when they drank. On Christmas, they behaved so unbelievably that friends didn't want to leave me. I ran away from home
the next day, sending them a telegram from Harrisburg, Pennsylvania,
on my way to New York City, saying that I had to get away for a few
days, that I was safe and fine and I'd call them as soon as I arrived at
my destination. I spoke with them when I arrived at my friend
Leslie's apartment. Her name was Leslie Lowenstein, and she and her
parents lived on Park Avenue. They were terrific people. Mrs. Lowenstein was concerned for me *and* my parents. She convinced me to call
them, saying they would be relieved and glad to hear from me. She
said she was a mother, and that's the way she would feel.

"Yeah, but you're forgetting how much difficulty Leslie had with them!" That's true, Rebel Girl. Leslie shared her frustrations with me. I guess that's why it's so important to try to understand where the other person is coming from, but for me Mrs. Lowenstein was an angel that day. Anyway, I told her I didn't think my parents would be relieved and happy to hear from me. I hoped they would, but I thought they'd just be angry and punishing; and when I got home, they were. My father picked me up but said nothing until we were in the car, "Well, aren't you at least going to cry?" So I did. He didn't speak to me again the whole ride home.

"How could you do this to us?" my mother asked at the front door. "When the lead horse leaves the train, what happens to the rest of us?" They demanded I apologize to them, and to the nuns at school, for worrying them. Mind you, I was twenty-one at the time. Later that day, I overheard my sister talking to my mother in the kitchen. They didn't know I was standing behind them when my sister said, "I feel as cold as ice toward her, like a brick."

At least Sister Marita, the head of the drama department, put her arms around me and held me close. Several of the nuns did. Feeling their bodies through the wool habit felt like being given a bath after crossing the desert. Their natural scent of skin and wool gabardine is still with me today. That and the feeling of their breasts next to mine under the habit. You could feel the softness of their breasts. I realized in that moment, I had no idea what my mother's breasts felt like because back then she always leaned forward when kissing, not letting her body come in contact with mine.

The nuns expressed their concern for me and the pain I put my family through in a way that made me feel loved and cared for, even though they didn't really approve of what I had done. Sister Marita arranged for me to talk to a male lay teacher with counseling experience. It was fortunate because he helped me. He gave me my first therapy lesson about feelings being expressed appropriately. School helped me too. The drama department was a safe haven.

AFTER I MOVED to New York, Gary helped me begin to understand some of the dynamics of my family. I was able to look at their
behavior and mine and ask myself questions. I started with my behavior. I thought about how afraid I was of my father, and how my parents' behavior was sometimes so unpredictable and bizarre.

They came to visit once in New York shortly after Gary and I were
married, and they stayed with us on East Eleventh Street. My mother
irritated me; I felt on edge around her and I was barely civil. We exchanged angry words one night as we were leaving Sardi's Restaurant
and the tension continued when we got home. My father said nothing. Gary finally asked if we could all sit down together and talk. My
mother was dismissive, saying that he was behaving like a neurotic
priest! We had no idea what she meant. And then she announced that
they were leaving. "Come James," she said haughtily, "we're leaving." I
begged them to stay, but she marched out the door demanding my father go with her. I got the impression he didn't want to, but he said
nothing as he left the apartment. Instead he just patted the back of my
head as he walked out.

Dad sounded angry when he called the next morning and asked us
to meet them at a restaurant, The Sign of the Dove, before they were
to fly home. They were restrained, making small talk as if nothing had
happened, all of which made me feel crazy inside. As they were leaving for the airport my mother leaned forward and kissed my cheek.
Gary and I walked for a while. He was taken aback and asked me if
that was the way they behaved generally.

"Now you understand what I mean when I say I haven't the foggiest idea of what's going on with them. It's moments like that. . . . I
sometimes felt crazy when I was a kid."

During the summer of my freshman year in college, however, I
had learned a very important lesson when I realized how much, in
fact, I was like them. This shocking revelation came the first summer
I worked at Camp Pinecliffe, a girls' camp in Harrison, Maine.
I was in charge of nine- and ten-year-old girls. A principal rule of the
camp was that no child was to be hit or reprimanded physically. Be-

cause of my own childhood I was thrilled with this rule. Then one day during rest period my patience with the girls in my cabin ran out. I found myself spontaneously starting to shake one of my kids. I was stunned at how quickly I had resorted to a physical reaction for discipline. *Me* of all people! I had hated the way my father hurt me, and yet here I was, acting as my parents had. Growing up, I had sworn to myself over and over that I would never, ever, punish a child the way my parents punished me, yet I had, automatically.

"Why did you?" Anna asked softly. Because at that time that's all I knew, Anna. I hated that kind of behavior, but when I was caught off guard I acted out what I had learned and experienced at home. That's all I knew. That moment was a singular lesson in human behavior for me. That's when big questions about myself really began to surface.

"Questions?" Anna asked simply. "Yes, like, Why did I behave that way? I abhor physical violence, especially when an adult takes advantage of the power they have over children. Hitting a kid is easy. It's unfair and reprehensible. Yet I spontaneously grabbed that child's arm to shake her and I scared her as well. I felt horrible that I had done that. Another big question was, Why do I feel my parents didn't approve of me when I was growing up? Although my mother would probably be shocked to hear me say that.

What I've learned is that we often pass on what we've learned and experienced from the past. Both positive and negative lessons are learned or passed on from parent to child, church to child, school to child. If we want to change those negative responses and beliefs, we first have to want to change them, and then we have to get help in order to understand where they came from and why and then begin to learn how to behave differently and form new responses, beliefs, and patterns of behavior. That's why an unexamined life can be dangerous and very painful.

I wanted to break that chain of behavior that my parents couldn't. Some people withhold love and approval as a way to raise children and control them, but it's not a good way because the child grows up thinking and believing she isn't worthy of love and approval. Or she grows up thinking it's okay to hit children and abuse them the way she was hit and abused.

But breaking the chain can be hard; it takes courage and commitment. One Mother's Day weekend when I was married to Neil— we'd been together for four or five years—I went home to see my mother: have it out with her, so to speak. I took her shopping one afternoon, and she admired a beige suede coat, but when I went to buy it for her, she refused even to try it on. After we returned home and were seated at the kitchen table, I asked her why it was so hard for her to accept a gift from me. She said she didn't know what I was talking about and said something like, "Oh, you're crazy." I became adamant and asked again. She became anxious and angry and tried to leave the room. Suddenly, I jumped up, blocking her way out of the kitchen, and I said that we had to talk about this, that it was very important to me. She tried to push me away! I stood my ground. Suddenly, she backed up, her hands covering her ears to block sound, her eyes squeezed shut, and at the top of her heartbreaking voice she cried, "I just want to be loved! I just want to be loved! I just want to be loved!"

I'd come home to find out why my mother didn't want love from me, and here she was screaming for love herself. The voice I heard was the voice of her inner child, expressing her pain, the unspoken pain of a lifetime. Instantly I was aware of how major this moment was for both of us. A voice inside me said, "This is it, Marsha. This is what you have been waiting for. Show her what you've missed and wanted all of your life."

I walked to her and put my arms around her and held her so close that my entire body was touching hers. "I love you, Mom. I love you very much."

We stood there plastered together, breast to breast, crying and holding each other. Then I looked at her face and said, "Hi, Gorgeous. Now can I take you shopping tomorrow?" She cried and laughed and broke away, getting a tissue. We sat back down at the kitchen table and talked about Momsie and Grandpa. I told her I wanted to find a way to love and to understand her better, that her refusal to let me spend money on her left me feeling rejected and her rejection was painful.

We did go shopping the next day and I bought her the suede coat she had admired so much.

"MARSHA? WHAT'S THE matter?" Gary's worried and concerned voice brought me back to the present.

"I was thinking about my parents and I just couldn't help it—crying, I mean. They had such a rough time, especially with no information or skills to change anything. This trip is turning into a bloodbath!" I said and started to laugh at myself. Gary squeezed my hand and raised it to his lips.

"Now, *you're* making me cry!" I blubbered.

"Good!" he gleefully answered.

Mom and Dad came from a condition I think of as "love poverty," believing they had to maintain what little they had because that's all they thought they were worth. I call it "maintaining the status quo at all costs." Other ways to see it would be "living in a total state of fear," or "being a victim of circumstances."

Dad felt he was a victim of circumstances and I did too as I grew up; but, fortunately, I didn't want to live my life the way he lived his. He was too afraid to venture beyond the confines of the life that had been laid out for him. I didn't want to be a victim of my circumstances so I decided that I had to face my fears, whatever they are—whatever I'm most frightened of is the thing I must do—it's imperative if I want to grow, fulfill my potential, and know who and what I am.

It was considered a blemish on a man's character if he couldn't fulfill the role of the provider. And maybe my father's fragile identity was further bludgeoned by the fact that he couldn't provide for his family alone, and that my mother had to work so they could make ends meet.

But what was born out of necessity turned out to be a terrific thing for my mother. She hated being trapped in the house all day. "I had the house cleaned by 9 A.M., then what was I supposed to do? You and Lin were in high school; you had plans and activities. I stayed at home going crazy, just twiddling my thumbs. But your father never really understood."

She didn't like socializing with other women and she never was interested in any kind of sport. She sewed beautifully, making our special outfits since my sister and I were babies. She had perfect penmanship and could draw just as well. She'd attended two years of Fontbonne College before she quit to marry my father. Going to work after all those years of being a housewife thrilled her. She felt productive; she liked getting out of the house and doing something. "Using the old noggin," she'd say, rapping the side of her head.

She worked in a savings and loan bank and while flipping through some book Mom accidentally found out that our house on Elmont Lane was listed as a foreclosure. It was "on the block," as she stated it. She was shocked and devastated because she knew nothing about it. My father never had told her just how bad things were.

It was snowing hard when she came home that day. My father was bent over the shovel, pushing it as if he were Sisyphus, wearing just an overcoat and his battered brown felt hat. As I watched him work, his body reminded me of a question mark—a dark question mark against a drab, gray-white background. I felt so sad for him as my mother and I stood looking out the picture window, watching Dad shovel snow. She, though, was hurt, angry, and frustrated. When he came inside, my mother confronted him with what she learned at the bank. He said only, "I'm sorry, Jackie." In an effort to make him explain and to answer her questions, she beat her fists on his chest. He didn't say a word, but just walked into their bedroom and closed the door.

There was only one other time I remember my mother being so angry or frustrated that she hit my father and that time she slapped him across the face. My sister and I heard that cracking, stinging sound through the thin wall that separated our bedrooms. They were arguing about something that Lin and I couldn't understand because their voices would rise and then lower again. We did hear Mother say, "Keep your voice down!" Suddenly, we heard the slap. To me it rang out like a loud boxing ring bell, reverberating for what seemed a long time. My first thought was that he was going to hit her back because I knew what he was like. He didn't do it. Instead we heard silence and then my mother crying, sounding sad and frustrated.

How could he possibly hold all those frightening feelings of failure, bitter disappointment, and lack of self-worth for so long, never talking to anyone, never seeking help or advice and understanding? Perhaps that's why he could be vicious at times. "Jekyll and Hyde," Lin and I used to say. Of course therapy was out of the question. "That's for crazy people!" he said. When I was grown and divorced from Gary I tried to explain how it might help him, that it helped me and was a good thing. He just got up and said, "Not for me. I'm not crazy," and left the room. So much for heart-to-heart conversations. No wonder he gave up and died at such a young age, fifty-four years old.

The last time I saw my father he was dying and under the influence of morphine. It was in the hospital shortly before he passed on. I'd flown in from New York to say good-bye to him, knowing that the next time I came to St. Louis would be for his funeral. I was working at the time, costarring with Kevin McCarthy in Kurt Vonnegut's first play, *Happy Birthday, Wanda June*. We opened to good reviews Off-Broadway and played a successful run at Lucille Lortel's theater on Christopher Street in the Village. We did so well that the producers decided to move the show uptown to a slightly bigger theater. My parents were supposed to come to New York to see me in the show, but Dad suddenly collapsed a week or so before they were to come. He was rushed to the hospital where the doctors diagnosed him with lung cancer. They were optimistic and told him that many people survive lung cancer and live long and happy lives, and that he would be fine with one and a half lungs. It was very encouraging to all of us.

When the doctors operated on him for lung cancer, however, they found that he was riddled with the disease, so much so that they just closed him up. It was too late. He wasn't a good patient and didn't follow the doctors' orders after the operation while on chemotherapy and radiation. He knew he wasn't going to make it. That was before Thanksgiving. After the chemotherapy and radiation, however, he began to feel better and planned a trip with Mom to the Cayman Islands.

Thanksgiving Day 1970, he and Mother were getting in the car to drive to Aunt Mickey and Uncle Murray's for dinner. Dad suddenly collapsed in the driveway, his legs crumbling under him. A neighbor drove them to the hospital while I called ahead. The doctors made him comfortable, giving him drugs to ease the pain and stabilize him. I went back to New York to perform in the show, but with my mother and sister's promise that they'd call me in enough time for me to get back if it looked like Dad was going to go. The show's producers and the other actors were wonderful about it all. My understudy was put on notice.

Before opening uptown we had a break in the performances, rehearsing new blocking while the theater was being readied for the show. There was a pay phone on a wall in the space where we were rehearsing. My focus was split between the show and the phone. Every time it rang, I jumped. I had a talk with myself and tried to settle down and lose myself in the rehearsals. "So far, so good," I'd say. One day though the phone rang and my name was called out.

I think my Uncle Murray and Aunt Mickey picked me up at the airport although I really don't remember. At the hospital, Lindy and Mother briefed me before I went into his room. They told me he wasn't really himself because of the morphine, and that he looked bad because of weight loss. I opened the door to his room prepared for the worst and went in to see him. Slowly he turned his head in my direction and smiled. He didn't look so terrible, I thought. His smile was still the biggest thing on his gaunt, pale face. His teeth seemed abnormally large because he was transcendentally thin. Still, I didn't think he looked all that bad, just very thin and fragile. Looking at him I remembered that killer smile of his from the photo taken when he was in uniform. Lying in that bed, in some ways he looked more like his young self than his older self.

My thoughts went back to another time, and I realized I had been carrying the memory of what he looked like when I came to St. Louis while performing in the national company of *Cactus Flower* sometime in 1967 or 1968. His face was gray then, and he smoked constantly. We were in his car and the ashtray was filled to overflowing with cigarette butts and ashes. I had to roll the window down to get some fresh air. The lines around his mouth were deep gray slashes and his brow was etched and furrowed. I don't remember him smiling at all that week. He coughed though, a deep, wrenching cough, with heavy phlegm, the kind that makes you suddenly nauseated. He never went to doctors. He didn't believe in having checkups. He was probably sick then; we just didn't know it, although maybe he knew.

Now I was back again, in early December 1970, and Dad was dying. He lay in the hospital bed, looking childlike, with translucent skin and a big smile across his face. He didn't say much to me, just "How's it goin'?" and then turned to my mother and told her that there'd been large insects in his room all night. He said he couldn't get any sleep. Mother gently told him, "No, there weren't any bugs; it was the medication." He insisted there were bugs; they were on the wall, "right over there," he said. Mom came to his side and pushed his hair off his forehead. "No, Jimbo," she said, "the medication does that, makes you see things that aren't there." He looked at her intently for some time, like a small child looking up at his mother, and then suddenly chuckled and let it go. Mom giggled right along with him, and then Lin and I joined in. My mother was truly amazing during that visit. Upbeat but sensitive to his every movement, every word, laughing and taking care of his needs. I saw all the love she had for my father in her every gesture and look.

"Marsha's here, Jim. She just flew in this morning." My father answered, "That's nice. Where is she?" Mom and Lin laughed and looked at me. I was so impressed with the way they were relating to him, making everything light and easy.

"I'm right here, Daddy. Over here on the other side of the bed." I leaned down and kissed his cheek. He smelled sweet. I told him everything that was happening in New York with the play, mentioning the title *Happy Birthday, Wanda June* in case there was some chance he might remember. He surprised me and asked about Kevin McCarthy, what he was like to work with, and added, "He's a good actor." He was happy the show was doing well and sorry that he couldn't make it to New York. I told him about the move uptown and how terrific Kurt Vonnegut was and that the whole cast sent him lots of love. "You'll do fine; I'm not worried about you," he said. We all made small talk for a while and it almost felt like everything was fine, that he wasn't really in pain, that he wasn't going to die. Suddenly, a strange, thin, crying sound came out of his mouth. His neck arched backward, straining with his head to the side, his body contorting and shaking under the sheet, and his mouth opened wide as if in the throes of a primal scream. I remember thinking how vividly he looked like the mask of tragedy. Mother was right at his side, comforting him, gently stroking his forehead, asking him if he wanted the doctor. I looked at Lindy wide-eyed and she mouthed the words, "He's in pain." Her face contorted and the folded arms hugging her body jerked backward like a straitjacket. She turned away, her fingers wrapped tightly at her sides, white at the knuckles and tips. I knew she wasn't breathing, trying to hold all her feelings inside. Why wasn't I crying? I wondered. Why wasn't I upset like she was at this moment?

His convulsive pain finally passed. In a battle-weary whisper, he told my mother he didn't want the doctor. "What was he going to do?" he asked. "Give me more drugs so I could see more bugs in the room?" His comment made us all laugh. Mom helped him get comfortable, but rather quickly he started to fade and space out. As I stood at the side of his bed, studying him, memorizing the moment, I realized he wasn't even in the room anymore. I wanted to know where he'd gone. What was he thinking about? Was he seeing anything? He looked like a little boy staring at nothing, lost in his own

imagination. Then suddenly I realized he was back in the room, looking up at his wife.

"Brush my teeth for me, will you, Goombah?" he asked in a weary
voice, a voice that was getting weaker.

"Of course, Jimbo, of course." Mother explained to me that he
liked his teeth brushed because it made him feel better. I was struck
by the intimacy in their voices, the intimacy of the gesture. I thought,
this must have been what it was like when they were sweethearts just
married. As I watched Mom put a little toothpaste on his brush, it
occurred to me that neither one of them had known any other sexual
partner, not that I knew of anyway. I hadn't heard them use those affectionate names for each other since I was a kid living in North St.
Louis.

My father died December 17, 1970. At his wake tons of people
showed up, people Mom had never met. They were all the people he
did business with when he worked for the city of Crestwood. He really did have the right stuff to be a salesman.

"WHY ARE YOU crying? Were you dreaming?" Gary asked.

"I'm just tired, that's all. Trying to enjoy some quiet. My emotions
are all over the place, I'm sorry."

"Don't apologize Sweet Pea. I'm sorry I . . ."

"Not to worry," I said with a sigh, "want anything?"

"Would you reach in the back and get me some water? I was
thinking I'd call Gary before we get too far away. He'll be at work . . ."

"I'll dial it for you. I can tell him I miss him already." The three of
us have been family to each other for almost thirty years.

"You never really know how your life is gonna turn out, do you?"
I sighed, handing him the phone. "No matter what your dreams and
plans are growing up." Gary looked at me about to say something but
abruptly started chatting with his better half. I watched his face as he
talked on the phone, taking it in, memorizing it.

Gary Dale Campbell was born in New Mexico on November 22, 1939. He came from a wealthy family, thanks to his Granddad Arville—affectionately called G.A.—who brought Coca-Cola to the Southwest along with the Campbell Dairy. Gary grew up in Clovis, New Mexico, and spent summers on a big ranch outside of Santa Fe, the Diamond Tail Ranch. He used to come to Santa Fe when he was a kid, tagging along with his parents and his sister.

Gary left home when he was sixteen and headed for Hollywood, determined to become a movie star. He stayed there for a few years, long enough to study at the Pasadena Playhouse and then with Kim Stanley's teacher, Jacobina Caro. He appeared in a few B movies; *Too Soon to Love* and *Teenage Challenge* come to mind. He screen-tested for *The Sound of Music,* but it didn't work out. He decided that he wanted to be a serious actor, so he left Hollywood for New York. His best friend, Jennifer West, had already gone there and she kept telling him the city was fabulous. He arrived in New York City about a month before I landed there myself.

When I first arrived, in early September, I lived on East Thirty-first Street. It was lined with big trees, dipping and lifting their branches with lacy green leaves in a dance choreographed by the warm, late summer breeze. Directly across the street from my building was another brownstone, but it was dressed up with gay, striped, canvas awnings over the front windows just like I'd seen in the movie *Breakfast at Tiffany's.*

I'd driven from St. Louis to New York City in a beat-up jalopy, along with two friends, both recent college grads. Katie was tall and pretty with dark brown hair. She was from Kansas City, Missouri, and a fellow graduate of Webster College. The other girl was Katie's friend from Kansas City, who I hadn't met until the trip. She had the car, was headed our way, and needed to share the cost of gas and such. In return, she needed a place to sleep for a couple of days until her friends showed up and she could get settled. This was providence because Katie and I were on a very tight budget. Katie was given money by her parents, along with a time limit. I came to New York with five hundred dollars and a whole lifetime, proud of myself because I earned every bit of the money I had, and I'd put myself through school as well. I was twenty-two; I had a college diploma in speech and drama, was footloose and fancy free, and was ecstatic as can be.

Katie and I were determined to succeed in the theater. She was a singer with a beautiful voice and wanted to be in musicals. Her friend, whose name I can't remember, was a kind of Goldilocks fairy queen beauty, with long, silky blond hair, flawless skin, and sparkling blue eyes. She spoke with a slight accent of some kind, very melodious. Goldilocks fascinated me. She could stay in a bath forever and she was constantly taking one. She'd come out of the bathroom squeaky clean, wrapped in the perfect white robe that showed off her flawless skin, gracefully cleaning her ears with a cotton swab dipped in baby oil. Even the inside of her ears were clean and shiny.

I'd rented the top apartment in this brownstone, found for me by a boyfriend from St. Louis, Bob Burnett. It was on the shady side of East Thirty-first Street between Lexington and Third Avenue. Bob was ten or eleven years older than I and a fabulous date, interesting to talk to, sympathetic to my wishes and dreams. He explained everything to my parents, assured them that it was a good building in a good neighborhood, close to everything I'd need. Best of all, the rent was what Katie and I could afford. Besides all the amenities Bob enumerated to my parents, it was furnished—admittedly sparsely—but furnished still.

When I first saw the brownstone's entrance I burst into tears. It was perfect. There was a small frosted window on the left that bathed the tiny foyer in a golden light. The floor was covered in white and black squares, clean and polished. It smelled wonderfully musty, firing my imagination about the lives that had been spent behind those walls. It was immediately cooler inside and cozy too. I was about to ascend the heights to my apartment, when suddenly the door next to the narrow carpeted staircase opened and there he was—so handsome!—looking like James Dean with a great smile and a friendly hand extended.

"Hi, my name's Gary, Gary Campbell. I live here. Just moving in?

Need any help?" What a looker, I thought and so *nice!* I shook his hand; it felt strong but sensitive. I introduced myself, and without stopping, informed him that I was indeed moving in, that I was with two girlfriends, had just graduated college, and worked all summer so I could come here because I was an actress and was going to find fame and fortune in the theater. I think I may have said it all in one breath. He said it was nice meeting me and should we need anything, don't hesitate to just knock on the door or slip a note under it. As I started schlepping my bag up four flights of stairs, I thought about my handsome and kind neighbor and would have burst into song if it hadn't taken all my breath to reach our garret apartment in the sky.

After dragging my suitcase up the last flight of stairs, I plopped it down in front of my new apartment. I held what was left of my breath as I fit the key in the door and it swung open. My body didn't move except for my mouth, which dropped open involuntarily. I slowly walked in, hoping to find another room behind the door. Nope, this was it. One room, basically, facing front. Well, that's positive, I thought. The kitchen was in the closet to my right. If the oven door opened all the way I'd be surprised. I wasn't surprised. The bathroom was small as well, but at least you could get in and out of the bath without needing to become a pretzel; and the toilet was clean and approachable.

What was truly fascinating though was the bedroom, which was in a closet as well. There was even a shelf and a bar to hang clothes from, running the length of the twin bed. There was barely enough room to walk in without chafing your thighs. I leaned over to straighten a corner under the shelf and my tush hit the partition wall, throwing me forward. My head banged against the plaster wall, causing me to lose my balance and crack my shin on the metal mattress frame, which I didn't know was there because of the fitted, forest green corduroy cover that went to the floor. Well, I like the color, I thought as I managed to sit on the bed and check my leg for damages. The corduroy matched the corduroy sofa bed in the living room. The fifties formica table and the two ice-cream parlor chairs were a bit strange, but at least the apartment was furnished. This was my first lesson in New York City living.

Katie was the next one to hit the landing and I got to see what I must have looked like when I first opened the door. Her mouth dropped involuntarily and her eyes were bigger than I'd ever seen them. She brought some originality to the scene because she began to sputter. I got hysterical.

After seeing the space for the first time, we all decided that whoever came home first at night got the bed in the closet. The sofa bed was too small for two people unless you were in love. We decided that whoever came home last got the floor. If we were all home, we would take turns getting the pathetic bedroom.

Unpacking our bags and noticing that there were some mighty dusty corners, we quickly decided we needed to clean the place.

"Well, at least it won't take us long," I enthused. "Let's hit the old D'Agostino's around the corner. Shopping was no easy feat for three young women who'd never lived together. Exasperated with each other, we finally decided what we could afford, bought a small pad and a pen, and marked down the price of every item, then looked for a cheaper one.

Back at the apartment, after a lot of cleaning was done with rubber gloves and disinfectant, there was still the matter of dust and stuff on the wooden floor and under the furniture. The broom just wasn't doing the job.

"Well, that fellow I met downstairs told me to knock on his door if I needed anything," I announced.

"What fellow?" Katie asked. "You mean a super or manager?"

"Well, maybe. Although he's a very good-looking super and very nice, very friendly."

"Really?" Miss Goldilocks said, coming to life. Dripping honey, she whispered, "I'm next to the door; I'll just run down and see if he's there."

"*I'll* go," I commanded, tossing my head. "He knows me."

"GARY, DO YOU remember the first day we met?" I asked him.

"Yeah, you knocked on my door and asked to borrow my uncle's vacuum cleaner. You told me that you had just come to town from St. Louis, that you were an actress, that you were going to be playing Off-Broadway by such and such a time and then you were gonna be starring *on* Broadway by such and such a time. You had a whole list of things that you had planned for your future. I remember thinking at the time, 'Boy has she got a lot to learn!' But you know, you did do it, and pretty much within the time frame you mentioned. You did it all."

"I guess that says something about me, doesn't it? I've lost that clarity, enthusiasm, that . . . passion I had back then."

"You got sidetracked, darlin'. Anyway, we were children then."

And really we *were* children then. Experientially, Gary was much older than I; chronologically, he's just four and a half years older. Hell, everybody I knew then was older than me. Talk about rose-colored glasses. I was Miss Naive Pollyanna, a child let loose in a porno store. I hadn't a clue what was going on around me. Thank God for Gary. We became instant friends.

After Miss Goldilocks moved on in her search for fame and fortune, it was Katie and me against the world for about three months. Then it was just Gary and me against the world. He gave advice, told me all about getting pictures taken and about reading *Backstage,* a newspaper that listed all the auditions and job openings for the new kids in town. He took me to Forty-second Street, the old Great White Way, where then we could see second-run movies for practically nothing. I ate Cuban food for the first time, and Chinese food—real Chinese food. We walked and talked our hearts out.

Looking over at his profile on this day as he sits at the wheel of my car and grumbles obscenities at some poor driver ahead of him makes me smile because I am reminded of the time he taught me to say "Fuck." Growing up I wasn't allowed to say curse words, not any, ever.

No "damns," no "hells," definitely no "shits." It was considered extremely unladylike. There also were no "My Gods" or "Jesus Christs." That last one was considered blasphemous. My parents, of course, used all of them, Dad being partial to "Jesus Christ" in times of intense frustration or impatience with my sister and me. It was okay for them to use these words because they were adults. But it wasn't okay for me, because I was their daughter, they were my parents, and I had to obey because they "told me to." Being parents allowed them to do a lot of things that never made sense to me.

The first time I heard Gary say the F word I gasped.

"Don't *say* that!" I admonished.

"Say what? You mean 'fuck'? Why not? It's a great word. You can really express yourself. Nothin' like it. Go on! Say it. It'll do *you* good."

"I can't say *that*. It's a terrible word. . . . I . . ."

"Just try it once, okay? Just try it. Once!" I was embarrassed and started to giggle. However, feeling so "free at last," I decided, why not, I'm an adult now! I barely murmured the forbidden word for the first time in my life.

"Not like *that*. With gusto, conviction, enjoyment! You want to be an actress don't you? Well, what are you gonna do when you have to say that word onstage? Or in an audition!" That did it. I went for it, but in a reasonably ladylike way.

"No! You sound like some silly lady. Come on, get into it. Put some feeling into it. Put your upper teeth on your lower lip like you were gonna bite it hard and then stick your chin out like you had a chip on it."

"A chip on my *chin?!*" He just looked at me. So I stuck my chin out like I had a chip on it, bit down on my lower lip real hard, and let it rip.

"FFFFFFAAAAAAHHHKKKKKK!" It felt fabulous. Excited, I started to jump up and down, repeating the new word: "Faaaah-hhkkkk."

"Terrific! You did it. Congratulations, you now live in New York!

Just work on the attitude. Put more 'uh' in it . . . like you're on the toilet and you gotta push it out.

"Ggaaaaarrrriiiieee!"

Pretty soon the word "fuck" peppered every conversation I had. Then came "cunt." I liked saying that word, and between "fuck this" and "cunt that," I was expressing everything and describing everything with those words, plus a few others!

It got so bad that my agent, Peter Cereghetti, had to sit me down and tell me, "You've got the mouth of a sailor."

"So? What's wrong with that?" I asked. "Everybody on the street uses those words."

"Yes," he replied, "but mostly men and you use them the way other people use 'damn' or 'hell.' You're giving the wrong impression."

"Oh," I said, "I'm not acting like a lady; I'm acting like a woman. Is that it?" He looked at me weirdly and decided to drop the subject. I went home and told Gary what Peter had said.

"What's the difference between 'lady' and 'woman'?" he asked.

"Well, my father always demanded I act like a lady. A woman is a terrible person, he said, because she's round-heeled."

"What does *that* mean—round-heeled?"

"I know, I had to ask my father what that meant too. He explained that a woman is someone who falls back easily; she lies down on her back. She's easy . . . you know, for men." Gary thought about that for a minute and then asked me if I ever considered going into therapy. Shortly after that I did.

GARY INTRODUCED ME to marriage, therapy, and orgasm—in that order. We were married on February 21, 1965, by a nondenominational minister I found in the yellow pages. He had a small office in a large building on West Forty-second Street, sparely decorated with a potted palm and a podium but cluttered with lots of wooden chairs. There was a saying that was pasted in gold letters to the front of the wooden podium that read something like LOVE IS ALL. *Very* nonde-nominational.

On the day of the wedding, the minister was wearing an orange and brown tweed suit that must have been made for him in the early 1900s. He was a kindly man with white hair and a mustache to match. His wife assisted him and looked just like you'd expect his wife to look. She had gray permed hair, a soft pink face with a beatific smile, and a warm and friendly demeanor. After the proper words were said, the minister turned to Gary and informed him, in a smiling but serious tone, that if he didn't take good care of me, he'd come after him with a baseball bat! I was totally charmed by his concern.

"Gary, do you remember our wedding?"

"Yes, the minister did something unusual besides marry people."

"What do you mean 'unusual'?"

"He was an umpire or referee or something. I remember him telling me that if I didn't take good care of you he'd come after me with a baseball bat."

"Hmmmm."

"And I remember your dress!" he said, casting a pointed look my way. "It was a brocade Peter Pan thing, off-white, a suit that looked like it belonged to a grandmother."

"Why is it you *and* Neil both felt you had to dress me?"

"Well, Neil dressed you the way *he* wanted you to look! He definitely didn't want you to look sexy. I picked clothes that look good on your body. Remember that white satin dress with the short skirt? You looked great in that dress. Remember our first apartment?"

"Yes, I remember it well. I remember your father's nocturnal visit to our bedroom."

"I remember that disastrous visit with *your* parents."

"I remember how I suffered incredible migraine headaches coming home from work, tired from boring clerical filing at the New York Central Railroad, in such pain I couldn't go to acting class."

"I remember your first gourmet meal from scratch. Veal!!!!"

"You weren't a vegetarian then!" I laughed.

"I remember the night we decided to move!"

"Me too. That was truly weird." On a warm summer night we were watching television in the living room of our apartment on East Eleventh Street. Apartment 4A or B, I think. The two tall front windows and the door to the fire escape facing the street were open for some air. Upstairs, directly over our apartment, a neighbor was playing a guitar rather badly. The music suddenly stopped and there was a loud twanging crash, like the guitar had been smashed to bits.

"Well, at least we won't have to listen to that anymore," I said, turning to Gary. All was quiet for a moment and then came the sound of running feet on the floor above, coming from the back of the apartment straight to the front, directly over us. There was a strange "boing" sound that made us glance away from the TV set and look out the open windows. I remember that everything suddenly seemed to be in slow motion. I saw a fully clothed body, spread-eagle, sail past our windows on the way to the street. Just as suddenly everything was back to real time, and we leaped to the door and onto the fire escape, looking down to the street. There lay the body of our nineteen-year-old neighbor. His head was resting on the curb, his body still in a spread-eagle position on the street, his face looking up at us. There was no blood. It was as if he'd lain down to look up at the stars. He didn't see anything of course, because he was dead. He'd "flown" out of his apartment, we were told later, on an LSD trip. That was it. We decided it was time to move. A couple of months before we'd come home to a blood-spattered hallway and shortly before that another tenant was awakened by a robber coming in through the skylight over her bed!

We found the small ground-floor apartment on Jane Street in the West Village. We lived there together during my employment with David Merrick's company in *Cactus Flower*, appearing as Botticelli Springtime and understudying the ingenue lead, Toni. It was my first Broadway show and almost immediately I was given the opportunity to go on as Toni. Because I did a good job with no rehearsal, the Merrick office offered me the national road tour of *Cactus Flower,* playing Toni. I signed an eight-month contract, starting with rehearsals in Chicago. It was the beginning of the end of our marriage. Gary and I saw each other twice in those eight months. He'd been on the road too during the first year or so of our marriage, in a tour of *The Subject Was Roses.*

I'd been on the road for almost six months when Gary came to visit me in Boston at Christmastime. I suddenly felt claustrophobic, but didn't know that this was a fairly normal feeling for some people who are separated by circumstances. I was sure something was wrong with me because I felt more comfortable when I was alone. It was the first time in my life I was truly on my own. I'd lived at home all through college and lived with Katie and then Gary when first coming to the city. Experiencing a severe case of "shutdown" while he stayed with me left me feeling guilty and afraid—afraid of losing myself and my newfound sense of freedom, guilty and scared that if I became successful and he didn't, our lives would fall apart. And then what? Our unknown future together overwhelmed me. My father had warned me a career and marriage wouldn't work, and this experience was showing me that maybe he was right.

Going on the road was an incredibly overwhelming and thrilling experience. At night, after the show, and on days off, I had the freedom to do whatever I wanted, to explore all the different cities, observe human behavior, listen to what other people thought and felt and believed. I was gaining a perspective. I loved getting to know all the men and women who were responsible for the production. They became a family. We took care of each other, spent time together, creating bonds of friendship. It was a whole new world to me. I was learning how it feels to be free on the stage in front of an audience, finding my way through the complexities of comedic delivery. I learned why I lost a laugh, and how to get it back again through keeping my performance fresh and consistent. I was fully immersed in my passion for the work and didn't want anyone or anything to come between me and my newfound sense of freedom.

While I was on the road, I enjoyed being reviewed by critics every week or two in a different city—and reviewed well. I was enjoying it all and didn't think about what it would feel like when I got back home. I rarely thought of the consequences of my actions back then. Spontaneity was the order of the day—spontaneity in acting and spontaneity in life. I was mad with the fact that I could do whatever I felt like doing without having to answer to *anyone*. It all felt so delicious. Everything about my life in St. Louis had been controlled and programmed, defined by rules of church and family, restricted by what was considered "proper" behavior for a young lady. Judgment by others and proper appearance was everything. There was no chance for individuality unless I rebelled, ran away, got out, defied the expected.

All I knew back then was what the Catholic Church and my parents had taught me: love was controlling, conditional, and fragile and came with a very high price tag—the loss of one's individuality. If I didn't follow the rules, do as I was told, behave in a certain way, well then, the church and God and my parents would punish me by withholding their love. I was taught that even God's love was conditional. After all, if children weren't baptized they didn't get to see the face of God; their souls were left in Limbo. If I explored my individuality, did things that weren't proper or accepted, then I would inevitably be cast out, no longer accepted and approved of. I felt torn between the richness of freedom and the constraints of acceptable behavior for a young, married woman of good breeding, and I didn't have the experience of enough therapy to be able to work my way through all the guilt and conflict.

When I came home after the tour I was a wadded-up bundle of feelings and thoughts I just couldn't sort out. A friend of Gary's from high school days in New Mexico, Rell Lovejoy, had just moved from Los Angeles and was staying in our apartment on Jane Street. Rell was a hairdresser and had done very well, but like us, he wanted to be an actor. The fact that he was staying with us meant that I could put off any serious conversation with Gary, and I was glad. I wasn't sure what

I wanted to say. All I knew was that I wanted to be on my own, by myself, learning about life firsthand, not being told what I should and shouldn't do. I no longer trusted anyone to know what was best for me, let alone to understand me.

After a couple of weeks at home, I finally confessed to Gary everything I was feeling—how I envied him that he'd been on his own since he was fifteen, that I needed to be on my own as well—and that meant that I needed to leave. I didn't know what else to do. I told him, "I love you more now than when we met." I told him that he was a wonderful lover and protector, a far better person than me. As we sat in the living room talking, Gary's face was etched with pain and sorrow. He asked me to give him a chance; he said that if he was at fault in any way, he'd work hard to make our relationship work. I told him with total honesty that he was perfect. He'd done nothing wrong. It was me. There was something wrong with me, with my character. I didn't know how to love him and be with him and still feel free, maintaining an identity of my own. I told him I had to leave, that he deserved someone better, someone who knew how to be a wife, someone whose career was him. It was a devastating experience for both of us.

We decided not to do anything legal or binding, that we'd take it one day at a time because I was a mess of emotions without any clarity. All I knew was that I had a desperate need to be on my own and find out who I really was, with professional help.

I packed a bag with a few things, left, and went to the Dixie Hotel, of all places, in the West Forties, the theater district. Why the Dixie Hotel? It was cheap and in the middle of all the Broadway theaters. It certainly reflected my sense of guilt and low self-esteem. When I walked in, I thought to myself that it was a terrible place to stay, but what the hell—I deserved no better. It was a seedy place, catering to street trade, failure, some tourists on a tight budget, and the dark side of the city.

That first night I sat on the edge of the bed facing a closet mirror and sobbed at what I saw—a terrible person who had hurt the person she loved and didn't know why. The only good thing that came out of staying at the Dixie Hotel was the information, behavior, and impressions I gathered that a couple of years later would help me bring the character Maggie to life in the film *Cinderella Liberty*. Having gotten all the inspiration I needed, I quickly found an apartment on West Seventy-second Street.

Gary kept the apartment on Jane Street for a while, sharing it with Rell and Gary Dontzig. While I'd been on tour, Gary had met Gary Dontzig at the telephone survey company where Gary Dale was working. Dontzig was also a struggling actor who was involved with another struggling actress named Mimi. We all became friends and wound up in the same apartment building on West Seventy-second Street.

New York City Mayor Lindsay had declared a moratorium on new apartment rentals for some reason having to do with rent control, and the only available apartments we all could afford turned out to be in my building. Rell and the Garys moved in a couple of floors above me. I was often upstairs for dinner, just hanging out. Gary and I were still close, although I worried that he wouldn't find anyone to love, because he never seemed interested in any particular woman. Together with Dontzig and Mimi, his girlfriend, and Rell and his boyfriend, Ed, we played cards, made dinner, went to movies and the theater, and had deep conversations about relationships, giving each other advice about everything.

Dontzig started reading all kinds of books on Theosophy, magic, and the occult. Immediately intrigued, I began my education in religions of the world. When Rell, Dontzig, and Gary went on a six-month trip to Europe, I took care of their animals and watched over their stuff.

When they returned, Dontzig and Campbell decided to get a place of their own. Another apartment in the building soon became available and I asked the manager to please give it to my friends. He knew us all so there wasn't a hitch. Dinner, cards, parties, whatever, continued. I'd just call and say, what's for dinner and where, the Garys', Rell's, or mine? We became family.

The most beautiful woman in the world, my mother. This was her engagement photograph.

1.

2.

The most handsome fella, my father, James J. Mason, with his killer smile.

When Dad
was at war.

3.

4.

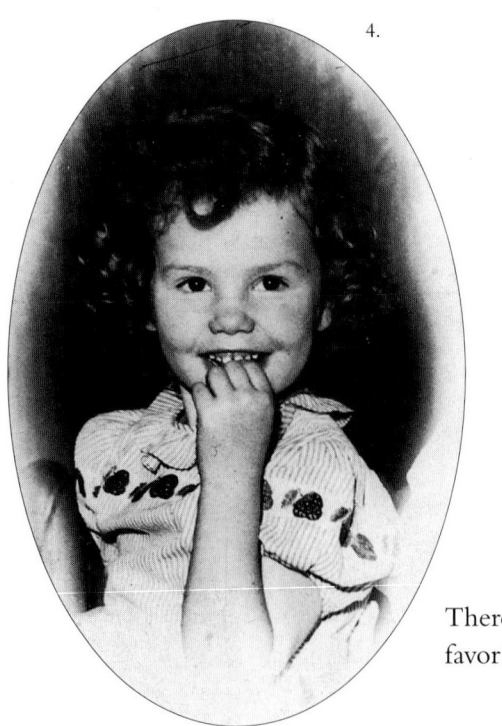

There it is, my
favorite dress.

5.

(left to right): My sister, Linda, and me on the back steps of Clarence Avenue. Love that hat!

6.

My grandfather Justyn and his well made chair.

7.

That's Little Gene, "Aunt" Flo, and "Uncle" Gene in the
background. They were Mom's cousins.

8.

(left to right) Santa,
Lin, and me. Mom
made the outfits.

Mr. Hilton on the chartered plane to the opening of the San Francisco Hilton.

9.

10.

The sale dress for Mr. Hilton's party.

12.

(*left to right*) Mike Nichols, me, and Neil. Wow! Look at the pointy collar!

11.

Me as Amanda in *Private Lives* with Paul Shenar as Elliot.

13.

Martha Swope took this photo of *The Seduction* from *The Good Doctor.*
Tony Walton designed the costumes.

14.

Jimmy Caan, me,
and Mark Rydell,
the director of
Cinderella Liberty.

15.

That's Kris Kristofferson and George Segal from *Blume in Love*

Gary and I decided we'd go to Mexico to get a divorce, but didn't get around to it in time. Eventually Mexican divorces were no longer legal in New York, so we had to get a New York divorce. Our lawyer told us that the simplest way to do it was on the grounds of desertion. Gary agreed to "desert" me, and Rell and Dontzig came to court and testified for me that Campbell had "deserted." After it was over we met up with the "deserter" and the four of us went to the neighborhood Cuban restaurant to celebrate.

I was aware that the two Garys had become close, but it didn't occur to me to think about homosexuality. I just thought of them as my brothers. I don't know when Gary and Gary became lovers, but I know I was the last one to "get it." Perhaps it was because I knew both of them when they were "straight," and because it just never occurred to me. I suppose you could call it denial, but by the time I was in Seattle shooting *Cinderella Liberty* some three years later, I was still worried that Gary hadn't found someone.

I called home the day I arrived in Seattle telling them all about the city and the hotel and all the exciting stuff about being part of a major movie. During our conversation I told Gary I was worried about him because he didn't have anyone. I didn't want him to be lonely, that it wasn't good for him.

"I'm not Sweet Pea. I have Dontzig."

"No," I said, "I mean someone to be involved with."

"I am involved."

"You are? What's her name?" Pause.

"Marsha, I'm involved with *Gary!*"

"You are?! Oh, thank heavens, I was so worried you were lonely." Later I asked him if I was the reason he became homosexual. He laughed and answered, "Never. I love Gary the same way I love you. To me there's no difference."

Rell eventually left New York with his lover and moved to Lynchburg, Tennessee. Several years later he became sick with AIDS and was dying. Gary and Gary flew to his home and helped Ed, his partner of many years, and his mother take care of him before he died. Rell and

I had a couple of great conversations by phone while they were there. Now, some twenty years later, it's the three of us. Over the years, Dontzig and I have formed as close a bond as I have always had with Gary.

SITTING IN THIS car today, looking over at Gary, my heart fills with love and admiration and gratitude. What I see is someone who . . . I suddenly realize I see someone who has a white-knuckled grip on the steering wheel, bent forward with his shoulders at his ears and a frown that is frozen in place. I don't think he's even breathing.

"Let's pull over," I order, "I'm gonna drive. Your shoulders are gonna be eye level any minute. Put the blinker on so Chris and Gary know what we're doing. And try breathing." The fact that he didn't argue told me he'd had enough. We pulled off at the next exit, making sure that the caravan was behind us.

"I hate driving on the freeways."

"Yeah, I noticed." Smiling, I climbed out and went back to Chris and Gary Da Silva, explaining we were changing seats. Buddy was exercising his lungs and vocal cords as if the car were on fire. Fortunately, the tiny tranquilizer made rag dolls out of Dulcie and Max who immediately flopped back to sleep. Unfortunately, the tiny pill seemed to have the opposite effect on Buddy the Bruiser.

CHAPTER FIVE

ON THE ROAD AGAIN

The solitary exercise of driving, being fully present in my car, paying attention to every detail—how the steering wheel feels in my hands at ten and four o'clock, what the engine is saying, what my eyes see straight ahead, and what my peripheral vision is picking up—is calming me now. What's the beat of the tires' music on the surface of the road? It's a mournful but comforting rhythm that reminds me of my breathing. Take deep breaths, Marsha. Get in sync. Yes, that's it. Deep and easy, that's what the road is saying. I like listening to the car while looking and driving. It's meditating. Driving can help a person to think or not think, to work some problem out in your head or just empty the mind. But you have to stay present (a form of meditation), or you will crash.

Racing is a form of meditation too. You have to stay present or you crash for sure. Most people don't pay attention while they're driving. They don't even take the time to sit properly in their car. They're not in tune. Right now I feel in tune and my body relaxes. My breath relaxes and the mantra comes easily to my mind. So-hum. When getting strapped into the seat of my race car or just driving to work, it's a little like finding the correct sitting posture for meditation. All the preparation to drive and race is a ritual, just like preparing for medita-

tion is a ritual. Ritual helps focus the mind: on the job ahead, the road
ahead, my new life ahead.

I follow a specific sequence preparing for a race and repeat that sequence exactly every time I get ready to race. Baba Muktananda
taught me the same thing in meditation practice. Meditate at the same
time every day if possible, wear special clothes when meditating because the Shakti stays in the cloth, have a regular cushion or mat that
you use each time when you sit, and concentrate on your breath.
When I race, I have special clothes that I wear, I have a special seat
that has been molded just for me, I follow a specific sequence preparing for the race, and I concentrate on my breath and the road ahead.
Same with driving, but most people don't know that.

The road stretches ahead with practically no traffic while my mind
stretches back: how little girls grow up . . . I liked playing with toy
cars, saying "vroom, vroom, vroom," so I have given my granddaugh-
ters little toy cars too. I wonder just how different my life would have
been if I'd been raised differently; if racing, meditating, and therapy
had been part of my growing up. Suddenly, the vision of me washing
the blue and white Plymouth Valiant that was my first car swims into
my mind, making me chuckle. I'd decided to "wash" the engine as
well so I took the hose and my soapy brush and went to town on the
engine. I was mystified why the darn thing wouldn't start the next
day, as was my father. He called a mechanic, who came to the house
later that afternoon, and he took one look at all the water in the car-
burator and asked me how the hell did all that water get in there. I
proudly told him I'd washed the engine. My first lesson in the myster-
ies of mechanics. At least my father didn't yell at me. I think I may
have begged the mechanic not to tell him what I had done.

God, I was always so afraid of getting into trouble, and of my father's anger. That Christmas night of my senior year in college was
the worst. He called me a slut in front of my friends as he stood at the
front door. He threatened the assistant manager of the store where I
was working during the holidays, a nice man who was standing next
to me while Edna, the sixty-something alterations lady, stayed in his

car. We all worked together at a Franklin Simon store in a mall near my house. They were very nice people who certainly shouldn't have been treated that way. The poor assistant manager tried valiantly to calm my father down but that only made him madder. I couldn't for the life of me figure out what was going on. I had no idea back then just how much alcohol can change a person's personality.

Later that night, in the dark of our room, I asked my sister what in the world was going on. I hadn't a clue why they were so mad at me. Lin told me it was because I hadn't called home to let them know where I was. I lay there in a state of shock.

"I did call home. I spoke to Mother, telling her exactly what I was doing and when I would be home." I couldn't say more because it hurt to be punished over an idiotic mistake. I went to sleep that night thinking about how much I wanted to get away and never come back. Unfortunately, I'd been conditioned from birth to be fearful of my father and never be angry or disrespectful to my parents, so I had nowhere to go with my feelings.

The following morning, my father forbade me to use the car to go to work. I told him I had to go because they were expecting me; December 26 was a busy day for the store. He didn't care, he said; that was their problem.

Feeling strangely calm, I replied in a quiet but firm voice, "Very well. I'll walk." The mall was about a mile away from the house. I don't remember how I got to the store. Perhaps he drove me; I'm not really sure. But I do remember that at some point that afternoon he called to remind me, "We'll be waiting for you." As he said those words, I knew I couldn't go home. I looked down at the black receiver as I placed it carefully in its cradle. Then a thought entered my mind and I called information, got the Greyhound bus depot number, and when the depot responded, I asked if they had any buses going to New York City that night.

"One at ten and another at midnight." The male voice sounded tired.

"How much is a one-way ticket?" He told me and I hung up. I

reached down under the cabinet for my purse and was surprised when I opened it. All my Christmas money was there. I had no recollection of putting it in my purse that morning. Counting it I calmly realized I had just enough money for the trip. I then calmly walked to the back of the store, stopping at the entrance to the alterations cubicle where Edna was working. She's so beautiful, I thought. White hair, gingham housedress, solid legs crossed at the ankles with sturdy beige lace-up shoes. She looked to me like a guardian angel with a halo glowing from the overhead work light. Quietly, I told her what I was going to do. She felt bad about the trouble from the night before and encouraged me to call my family. I said, "No." Something in the way I said it made her stop.

"Would you at least let me call them once you've gotten on the bus?" Again I told her no. I didn't want her to be involved; this was my decision—mine alone.

"Besides, I'm twenty-one years old," I said. "I'll be twenty-two in four months." I explained I was going to the home of my friend Leslie Lowenstein, who I'd known since my first summer spent counseling at Camp Pinecliffe. I assured her that they were very nice people and everything was going to be okay. My parents knew Leslie; she'd visited us one Thanksgiving.

"At least let me drive you to the bus station," Edna said.

"It's too far for you to go this late," I countered. "I just wanted to borrow the cab fare to the station. I'll pay you back, I promise."

She insisted on driving me, telling me it wasn't that far and she had nothing better to do.

"Okay," I replied. "I'll make you a bargain. If I have even a moment's hesitation or doubt that this is the right thing to do, I won't get on the bus. I promise." We drove downtown to the depot but had missed the ten o'clock bus.

"Come on," I said, heaving a deep sigh. "Let's have a cup of coffee. I promise, if I experience even a second's doubt, I won't go." We sipped coffee and she made me promise to get in touch with my parents once I was on the road and to call *her* as soon as I arrived in New

York to let her know I was all right. I, in turn, asked Edna to promise she wouldn't tell my parents where I was headed. This was most important to me. We drank our coffee in the empty Greyhound bus station that night after Christmas and it amazed me how calm I was. I didn't feel scared, although the jittery sensation I felt under my skin gave off a vibration of excitement. The surety of my daring decision made everything okay. When Edna tried to impress me with the thought of how worried my parents would be, her words made no impression whatsoever. I felt so sure—so completely sure—that what I was about to do was the right choice for me. My survival depended on it.

AS I DRIVE at the head of this caravan traveling toward my "new" life, in some ways I feel a little like that twenty-one-year-old girl who stepped up onto that bus thirty years ago, reaching for the handle of the door and pulling herself up. Thirty years ago, at that very moment, an image of a tall porcelain vase suddenly sprang into my mind's eye. I saw it clearly, right in front of me as I raised myself into the bus. At the base of the vase was a hairline crack that I knew was about to spread like a spider's web, breaking this beautiful vase into a zillion pieces. I took a deep breath and held it as I stepped up to the driver and into the vision of the vase, thinking it would shatter and me along with it. But it didn't crack apart. Instead, breathing came easily as I made my way down the aisle. I considered that vision a good omen. I was on the right track. As I sat down in a window seat I was fully present, alive, but with no idea of what the next hours would hold. When we stopped briefly to take on passengers I didn't even look to see who they were; it didn't matter.

Today, some thirty years later, this move feels, at times, like that vase right before it's going to crack into a zillion pieces, but this time I know that it's me that holds the vase together. I'm no longer a victim of circumstances; I'm the creator of my circumstances.

"Well, hallelujah!" Oh, be quiet G.A.

It is hot now, really hot. It feels good. For the past several days my bones had felt as if they were frozen. In a way, the desert through which we are driving seems like that darkened bus of thirty years ago. Both represent a passage through the dark tunnel, the unknown journey a person takes in order to grow and mature. In a way, this is my third rite of passage. Looking over at Gary, his head slumped as he sleeps, reminds me of the soldier who sat down next to me in the dark of that bus headed to New York. He too fell asleep almost immediately, his head nodding and swaying to the movement of the bus, and soon that bobbing head slid to my shoulder and came to rest. I didn't move away. I relaxed my body and looked out at the dark night comforted by the touch of another human being. As we drove east through the night I took solace in the fact that there is a bond between all living beings even if we are strangers. Sitting there, I felt connected to another person. Why I wasn't connected to my family was a question not answered that night. I slept some and came to as the sky was getting lighter. We stopped in Harrisburg, Pennsylvania, where I think the soldier got off and I sent my parents a telegram. It said: I'm all right. Don't worry. I needed to get away. I'll call when I get where I'm going. Or something like that. I don't remember what the scenery looked like outside that bus that morning. I just remember feeling safe.

Right now the scenery outside, the Mojave Desert, looks forbidding. It reminds me of Interstate 14, the route I took to Willow Springs Raceway, my home track for seven years. I'd pass signs pointing the way to the Mojave Desert, and now here I am, in the Mojave Desert with no gasoline or services available until Kingman, Arizona. Kingman is the main stop, if not the only stop, on the longest remaining stretch of the historic Route 66.

The blue Mazda has passed me and is cresting the top of the hill, instantly dropping below the empty horizon out of sight. I'm driving on a hot, shimmering tarmac of a road, in between my Mazda and my Porsche, with the air in here a rich effluvium of blood, heat, and doggy dank and I don't have to answer to anyone. "Except myself," I murmured quietly.

"Testy, testy," G.A. chided. The dogs are snoring, Gary in unison with them, and here I sit in a state of "in-between" in my life as well as my cars. Feeling "in-between" is a pretty constant state for an actor. In fact, it's a term actors use a lot. "What are you doing these days?" someone asks. "Oh, nothin' much, I'm in between engagements," or "I'm between jobs at the moment."

In-between is like plodding along. I plodded along those first years in New York. And I was often in between regular jobs like working in the suit and coat department of the Franklin Simon store on Thirty-fourth Street (don't look for it; it's no longer there). I left that and went to work for the New York Central Railroad, filing outdated hotel bills from the various hotels it owned. The old Biltmore ("under the clock") Hotel was a favorite. On Fridays I got to take the payroll sheets over to the main office. My treat for the week was getting a cup of coffee in the New York Central building. Talk about plodding. I nearly went nuts with so little to do. I had the filing done by noon and the afternoon hours dragged by unmercifully. I finally went to the filing room and totally reorganized it. Nobody saw or even cared, but it gave me something to do until a "real job" came along.

Hotrod Hullaballoo was a real job, my very first picture. A black-and-white teenage film for drive-ins. I played Sheila, the bad girl. The picture was shot on location in a redneck area of Maryland. We had the *promise* of sex, violence, and action. I provided the sexy part. I'm *almost* raped by the bad guy in our high school but fend him off with a rock to his head at the last minute. The big action comes at a demolition derby (my first ever) shot at night under big lights, forty or so cars all banging and smashing into each other until there's just one left that's still limping. What a trip.

I returned to New York from the wilds of Maryland with a cat and signed up for unemployment, once again in between engagements. I plodded and pursued my acting career, going to class and getting nowhere fast. I started working afternoons at a go-go club in the East Forties, hopefully to learn to be a waitress and earn good tips. They wanted to serve lunch with go-go dancing. I go-go danced for the suited clientele from the various advertising firms around the neigh-borhood, dressed in a black leotard, fishnet stockings, and high heels. I danced alone on the small dance floor to recorded music while the men ate their lunch and talked business. When not dancing I wait-ressed or sat on the swing over the bar and . . . swung.

One afternoon a man came in, sat at the bar, and ordered a drink. I was swinging to him alone; there wasn't another soul in the place. He said I had good-looking legs. I smiled and said, "Thank you." He took a sip or two and then volunteered he was a freelance photographer for *Playboy* magazine and could help me get a portfolio together. I smiled and declined. He persisted, saying he was sure I was a winner; just spread those pretty legs a bit and he could help me. I gracefully kept my gams together, thinking it's time to move on.

Next morning, I called the kindly fellow who ran the place. Sounding tired and sick, I explained I couldn't come in to work be-cause I had been diagnosed with mononucleosis, the catching kind. I picked mono just in case I ever needed to go back there for work. He was sorry I wasn't feeling well and said, "Well, you ain't the best dancer I seen, but you got class."

MIGRAINES, SALES, FILING and stupor, and go-go dancing motivated me to swear I would never, ever, work a dull nine-to-five job again. I didn't. It's true what they say about clarity of purpose. I had one great, overriding concern: how to pay the bills. The solution: TV commercials. I scoured the commercial agencies, handed out new pictures geared to that world, and tried my very best at every audi-tion. I felt guilty about this effort because I was a "serious" actor. Thankfully, divine intervention came in the form of my red-haired fellow from Procter & Gamble, my good friend Bob Burnett, pro-curer of apartments and first jobs. Because of him I got my first commercial, sitting on a car for Prell shampoo in a contest advertisement. Bob told me to give the job to a commercial agency for a commission. I did just that and they started sending me out on auditions. Pretty soon I clicked. I knew I'd "arrived" when the call went out for "a Marsha Mason type." When the money came, I bought my very first and only fur coat.

Because of that coat I was hired as an extra on a television series starring Peter Falk. I was told that doing extra work wasn't a good idea if you wanted to be considered a "serious" actor, but I loved Peter Falk's work and decided to do it anyway. I sat quietly and waited with the other extras until we were to be called, my gorgeous coat on my lap. Peter Falk walked by, noticing the coat and then noticing me. "Nice coat. What's your name?"

A little while later the crew started going into the old Filmways studio. While the other extras sat around and read or chatted, I meandered toward the door to listen. A kindly stagehand breezed by on his way in and I scooted right in with him, tapped him on the shoulder, and asked if I could please stand behind the scenery, far away, and just listen to the dialogue. I promised I wouldn't tell anyone and I wouldn't make a sound. He hesitated for a moment and then showed me a dark place behind some flats that were against a wall, telling me I'd better be quiet or he'd get into a pile of trouble. I snuck into place and waited.

Soon everything became quiet. A man's voice softly spoke the word "Action." Carefully peeking through the flats, I saw Peter Falk dressed in a raincoat, smoking a cigarette. He was speaking softly, looking down at the floor at someone off camera. The way he spoke made me want to see who it was so I inched out a bit to see who the other actor was. There was no one there. Peter was acting by himself . . . for the camera. I watched as he created a reality and a relationship in an empty space, just him and the camera. I was sure someone else was there. I promised myself that one day I'd be able to do that too.

Later that day we extras were "peopling" the escalators in what was then the Pan Am building at Grand Central Station. Shooting was to begin when suddenly Peter called out, "Wait a second."

"Come here," he said, motioning for me to stand in front of him. "Your folks will get to see you in the shot." Of course, I didn't know then that years later I would assist my husband Neil during the shooting of *Murder by Death* with Peter Falk and later play opposite him in *The Cheap Detective*. I left the Pan Am building that day three feet off the ground, and in my heart there was a renewed sense of conviction and passion for the work and my next audition.

Sometimes my auditions went well and I'd get a callback. Typically, if I was called back, I'd get called back two or three times as the list of candidates narrowed. This became a pattern. After a while I prayed for the day when someone would hire me from a single audition. That day finally came, but the job was not exactly what I had in mind.

I was hired as a spokesperson for Subaru at the Auto Show in the Columbus Circle coliseum. I had to rattle off a bunch of copy while standing on a revolving platform with a booming microphone in my hand. Eventually I got dizzy and lost my place in the pitch and went blank. I went "up" as they say in the theater. Trying to make up stuff about the car I was standing next to while going in circles led to some pretty silly stuff like, "And here we have the windows. Aren't they pretty! All the better to see out of while driving . . . this . . . car." Little did I know I'd play that scene again years later in *The Goodbye Girl*.

Sometimes auditions went well, but I still wouldn't get a callback. Sometimes auditions went appallingly and I'd get hired. Sometimes I'd audition forever, five to nine times, and never get the job. I learned to pick myself up, dust myself off, and start all over again, as the old song goes. Occasionally, when I did badly, I'd come home and crawl into bed, not get out of it for two or three days, and not answer the phone. One time I listened to the phone ring thirteen times and still didn't answer it. It was a weird victory of some kind. It was also safe to do because I could call my service and pick up the messages. This was in the prehistoric times of answering services, before answering machines. My emotional roller coaster was like a Six Flags demonic ride. The ups and downs were enormous, sometimes thrilling, sometimes chilling.

I finally got my first Off-Broadway job playing a small part and understudying a lead in Norman Mailer's first play, *The Deer Park*. Gary got hired too! Hugh Marlowe and Rip Torn and Will Lee were the stars. I had a small scene with Will Lee and a small scene with Rip Torn. I couldn't believe my good fortune. My scene with Will Lee was sweet or so I thought. When we got to staging it, "putting it on its feet," the director—whose name I have deliberately forgotten—wanted me to kneel down in front of Will as the lights went out. I didn't understand the staging at all but did as I was told. During one run-through I looked up at Will and asked him what on earth did this direction mean. He looked at me with his soulful eyes and smiled. "My dear, you're going down on me." My face felt as if it were on fire. Will looked at me and laughed. "The blush on your face is the color of a red, red rose and you smell as sweet. Don't ever lose that quality. You know one of the basic lessons of acting?"

"No," I answered.

"Ahhh, well it goes like this. If there's a pile of garbage, there always has to be a sweet-smelling rose perched on top. Otherwise you won't have a character, or a scene for that matter. Another favorite piece of advice: If the words are saying it, don't act it. It's the old salvo: When the messenger has to deliver the line, 'The king is dead,' don't act it, just deliver the statement as fact, and then see what happens."

The Deer Park was quite a physical experience for me. It was, first of all, my introduction to going down on someone, and second, my first experience of being pulled *by the ear* across the stage by the director. When the latter occurred I was so stunned I didn't know what to say. I was struck dumb, which was his obvious opinion of me. A third, rather bizarre physical moment took place in performance one afternoon. Rip Torn and I were seated next to each other with a telephone in my lap and his left arm resting behind me on the back of the banquette down center.

I'm supposed to be scared of him and truthfully I was. He's a wild and woolly guy. I'm to pick up the phone after it rings and say something he's told me to say. The phone rings, I pick it up, and with that Rip's left fist slugs me in the back! I was thrown forward and my breath was stuck in my throat. Gary, who was standing upstage with the other actors, let out a hissing sound. I didn't know what he was going to do, but I looked at Rip who just looked straight ahead. Somehow my breath finally came, I got out the lines, and we ended the scene.

"You anticipated!" he charged as he made his way to the men's dressing room. Instantly I felt guilty. Gary was instantly in Rip's face. He told him there was no justification for hitting any actor, let alone his wife, and if he ever did it again he'd have to answer for it big time. Rip was a bit taken aback and fumblingly responded, "Well, she *antici-pated* and . . ."

"I don't care if she does your part *ahead* of you! You are not to hit my wife again, ever!"

Years later I read an interview with Rip. He once studied with the modern dancer Martha Graham, and when he didn't do as she said, she hauled off and hit him. The image of Martha Graham slugging Rip Torn makes me chuckle. Now.

No one anticipated an understudy going on in previews but it happened. I was understudying Beverly Bentley, Norman's then current wife. Norman's then ex-wife, whose claim to fame was putting a knife in Norman's back, was understudying another part. It was a matinee, we were in previews, and there'd been no time to rehearse the understudies. Beverly, on her way to the theater, was in a minor car accident. She wasn't hurt, but she wasn't going to be able to make the curtain. I went on without rehearsal that afternoon, carrying the script in my hand. There was an announcement and then the play started. Beverly got to the theater by the second act and went on with the rest of the show. Being able to take advantage of surprises like that gave me confidence in my ability. For a while.

After *The Deer Park* closed I was again in between jobs. I filed for unemployment and the last week that I was eligible for it, I landed my next job, Israel Horovitz's two one-act plays *The Indian Wants the Bronx*. The first of the two plays was titled, *It's Called the Sugar Plum*. It was a two-character play in which I played opposite Johnny Pleshette. The second play had three characters, played by Al Pacino, Matthew Cowles, and John Cazale. Both plays were directed by Jimmy Hammerstein. We were opening a new Off-Broadway theater, the Astor Place, on Lafayette Street. I was thrilled to be working but I couldn't for the life of me figure out how to find my way into my character. Israel was patient and Jimmy was frustrated, although not as frustrated—and scared—as I was.

"What if I'm a flash in the pan? Don't have the stuff? Can't cut it? What if I'm mediocre?" These were my regular thoughts—not too positive.

I slogged my way through rehearsals, but everything felt heavy and unbelievable. By the end of the fourth week of rehearsals Jimmy was desperately giving me directions like, "Do it like Bette Davis!"

Valiantly I did my best imitation of Bette Davis. At least I had something to take on the stage that first night of previews. Doing Bette Davis quickly got old and I was left with "bubkes." On the last night of previews, we all went out for a quick Italian dinner down the street before the show. I ate my first meal in three days, fettuccine Alfredo. As we walked back on Astor Place I began to feel a bit more positive. I'm settling down, I thought. This is a whole new experience. My spirits began to lift as we walked inside the theater. Looking straight ahead at the stage, I passed out cold. Talk about not wanting to be someplace.

Opening night, the critics were kind to our play and loved *The Indian Wants the Bronx*. I remember them loving all the other actors. I gratefully remember a television critic who simply said my performance was "less than concise." What an understatement.

The play ran, but I left it to go into another play, my first Broadway show, *Cactus Flower*. After nine auditions over a two-year period, I'd finally been hired by the David Merrick office for the role of Botticelli Springtime, and I'd also understudy the ingenue lead, Toni. Just like

The Deer Park, I was hired to do a small part and had to go on in the big part with practically no rehearsal. Jimmy Burrows (of television fame) was an assistant to his father, Abe Burrows, who adapted and directed the play originally. Jimmy worked with me for a week and then Abe came in and gave me my first professional comedy lesson.

"You . . . Botticelli." His voice sounded like he was gargling pebbles. Very imposing. "Hey, you! Botticelli. You know how to deliver that line and get a laugh?"

"How, Mr. Burrows?" I squeaked.

"Count to four, turn front, and say the line."

I timidly tried it.

"Okay," he said, "just do it with confidence tonight." He then turned to Jimmy and said, "What's next?"

That night his direction worked and the laugh was big! My first *big* laugh. Thank you, Abe Burrows. Thank you for picking me up, throwing me into the air and catching me, and giving me a great big hug and a kiss. Comedy really is timing. Well, character and timing. Some say it can't be taught—timing, that is—but I've learned you can have a "feel" for it and can get good at it with practice. It too is a kind of meditation. It's being fully present in the moment, *feeling* the rhythm of the line, the air between you and the audience, and then landing it. Sorta like fly-fishing, I guess.

My second "go on with no rehearsal" situation suddenly developed in the first week or two of my engagement as Botticelli. The previous Botticelli's contract ended on a Saturday, as I recall. There was an error in somebody's contract that would have left the role of Toni uncovered for a performance or two starting on the following Monday. Sure enough, Toni got sick on a Saturday and wasn't able to perform. The previous understudy came and stepped in that Saturday as Toni. Then her contract was over. If the real Toni was still sick on Monday, that would have left the Monday night show without a Toni, and with an understudy—moi—who hadn't been rehearsed. The Merrick office tried to get the previous understudy to come in, but her agent asked for more money. He probably wanted to give Merrick a hard time because everyone knew that David Merrick was hellacious when it came to money and he had Mr. Merrick by the proverbial short hairs.

At rehearsal, May Muth, our stage manager, told us of the situation. She was waiting for the head honchos in the office upstairs to let her know what was what.

"I can do it," I squeaked. Everyone stopped what they were doing.

"I can do it," I repeated in a stronger, slightly more confident voice. "I've gone on before with *no* rehearsal *and* carrying the book. Besides, I can have it all memorized by Monday."

May Muth was a fabulous redhead with a man's voice, who was known up and down Broadway as "the Velvet Whip." She looked long and hard at me and then covered her eyes. "No way, José," she said. "That's crazy. You haven't even worked with Betsy and Lloyd." She was referring to Lloyd Bridges and Betsy Palmer, the stars of the show.

"Please give me the chance," I begged, "I won't let you down, I promise." I may have even crossed my heart.

May looked me in the eye. "Honey, you better not . . . my job's on the line! Are you *sure?*" she asked incredulously.

"Positive."

Sunday I crammed that role into my brain while Gary and Gary and Rell fed me and ran lines. I'd been meditating for a short while by then, using symbols that were given to me by a man in Italy, Oric Bovar. He turned out to be crazy, but the idea of concentration as meditation helped me learn those lines quickly.

On Monday, May crammed two weeks of rehearsal into four hours. That night the Merrick office was watching from the back of the theater. May was pacing the wings, destroying her nails, and mumbling to herself. I don't remember much about the performance. I do remember rushing backstage to change costumes, my script open on a chair, feverishly scanning the lines while someone dressed me and sent me back out again. When the cast applauded at the curtain call, I burst into tears. I knew the show was good because "the Velvet Whip" hugged me afterward and word came back from the office upstairs that *everyone* was very happy. Our Toni came back Tuesday night and I went back to counting four and saying my line. But not for long.

The Merrick office offered me the role of Toni for the second half of the national tour. It meant eight months on the road. I signed on and never looked back. Jimmy Burrows put me into that company and took us on the road. It would be almost thirty years later that he would direct me for the third time. The third time was a charm too—the television series *Frasier.*

"Thank God for *Frasier!*"

Yes! Oh yes, G.A. After my introduction to situation comedy with *Sibs,* I was left with a big nagging doubt about my ability to do television. After all, Jim Brooks is one of the best and so are all the people who worked for him over the years. He and I didn't hit it off though, and he thought me difficult. Okay. But also maybe I just couldn't "do it," "get it," whatever. It would be almost four years between *Sibs* and *Frasier.* This time the show was a winner with a great group of writers, producers, actors, and crew. And what a great character! I had the best time, a happy, healing time.

"Go back to livin' on the road, will ya?" pleads Ed.

I was on the road in a David Merrick production making seven hundred dollars a week. I was rich. I was making a living doing what I love. I never had to take "regular" jobs again. I was careful too because of all the in-between times; some of them can be quite long, like two or three years. After I came back and separated from Gary, I was back into the grind, looking for work again.

Soap operas paid good money; but the pace of the shows was scary to me, and I thought the acting was terrible. The characters didn't sound like real human beings back then. However, it seemed wrong to criticize them if I'd never even done one. Well, I did do *one* actually. It was a few years before. I played a vampire, for a day, on *Dark Shadows.* It was cool figuring out my reality as a vampire. However, it was not a career.

I did manage to continue working in commercials for a while, even though I still couldn't get hired on the soaps. I was very proud that my savings account was around fifty thousand dollars by the time I did a Manufacturers Hanover Bank commercial. The commercial played during the Knicks games in New York one season. I didn't make much money but the exposure was very interesting.

My future second husband would remember that commercial and the way I pronounced the word "insurance" when I went to work for him in *The Good Doctor,* and many years later Sly Stallone would tell me that he "knew that face was gonna go somewhere." From that commercial—and many, many years later—a handsome first baseman with the New York Mets, Keith Hernandez, would tell me he was turned on by that actress with the sexy voice.

Film auditions were harder to come by in that distant time when movies were on one coast and theater was on another. I did get an opportunity to be in a film of Norman Mailer's because of *The Deer Park* but I don't think I said very much, maybe just one line.

One lucky day I met the director Ed Sherin at an audition for a movie about young men coming back home from Vietnam. We'd never met before. I thought I might have a chance for the part but I didn't; and that was that. What I didn't know at the time, however, was "that" wasn't "that" at all.

After the disappointment of not getting Ed Sherin's film, I decided I *had* to get on a soap, if only to prove to myself that I could do it. I went on every audition for every soap that shot in New York. Not getting hired was starting to give me a complex, but that just made me more determined. Finally, Freida Rothstein, the producer of *Love of Life,* hired me. Hallelujah! I was hired to play a Brenda Starr, Girl Reporter, type with a guarantee of two shows a week. That meant I was paid for the shows whether they used me or not. Poverty was kept at bay.

I began work with the enthusiasm of a little beaver making a home before winter but I was in trouble immediately. They wanted a Brenda Starr who talked slower. I just couldn't understand why it took so long to say so little. Burt Brinkerhoff, one of the directors, told me they were short of pages whenever I worked.

I tried to adapt because I wanted to keep my job and I liked the idea of acting—almost live—on television. The show was taped but the atmosphere in the studio was as if we were performing live. One time, during a scene with two of the stars, a Styrofoam cup of coffee accidentally fell off the arm of a chair while the two men were talking. They just kept talking (slowly) and pretended it hadn't happened. Well, to me this was anathema. This was a golden opportunity to show what I could do, I thought, when it came to improvisation, and they wouldn't run out of pages! I gently nudged the actor who played my boss, interrupting him with some stunning ad-lib like, "Don't worry, I'll get that. Be right back," and I walked to the door and yelled for an imaginary copy boy to get me some paper towels, "pronto!" Someone off camera ran and got the roll, crawling back on the floor to give it to me out of the sightline of the camera. Turning to my fellow actors I announced, "Don't worry, I'll have it cleaned up in a jiffy. You were saying . . . ?"

After the scene was over the director informed me that the cup hadn't been in the sightline of the camera at all so none of my improvising had been necessary. But I think he smiled and rather liked what I did, although he admonished me, "You're *still* talking too fast."

During my time on *Love of Life* I was introduced to Darryl Hickman (the child film star). At the time, he was a vice president at CBS. I immediately engaged him in conversation by asking what it was like to be a child star working with great actors like Spencer Tracy. He then asked how it was going and I sheepishly told him I was feeling a little like a twelve-cylinder engine under the hood of a Pinto.

"I've been thinking about starting an acting class," he said. "I love actors and the process. I've got some ideas."

"I'm there. When do you begin?" It was great going to class again. There were twenty or so students that first year, all of us excited by Darryl's perspective. What made his work unique was the application of certain exercises for the process of creating and fulfilling a character in a scene. We learned to do the exercises before any scene work. Some actors wanted to do scene work but Darryl was unrelenting. I learned exercises of Boleslavsky, Bobby Lewis, Michael Chekov, Sandy Meisner, and teachers I'd never heard of. Going to class gave me renewed enthusiasm. We worked on those exercises until we could do them in our sleep. I even brought in some audition material and asked Darryl to show me how to apply the exercises to an audition. I was determined to "be prepared" for that lucky break whenever and wherever it came.

AND THEN, ONE cold, bright New York winter's day I went to meet with the director Paul Mazursky at the Sherry Netherland Hotel at Fifth Avenue and Fifty-ninth Street. He was casting a film, *Blume in Love,* and I was meeting him for a supporting role. Blume was to be played by George Segal. I was prepared to read if asked, having worked on the scenes in class.

The day was cold and clear and the buildings along Fifth Avenue glistened in the crisp air as I sat on a stone bench and stared up at the windows of the hotel across the street, collecting my anxious mind. "Well, here goes. Just be yourself, trust your instincts, and you'll be fine," I told myself. I crossed the street and went into the hotel.

Paul greeted me at the door of his hotel suite and motioned me to a chair that faced the couch with the window behind. I asked if he minded if I sat next to him on the couch in front of the window. I'm not sure why I did that, except perhaps to make the situation seem less like an interrogation. He asked me to read with him. It was just the two of us. After we read a couple of scenes, we talked and then he asked me to read again. When we finished I thanked him for meeting me and said good-bye. I felt good, very good; the scenes had gone well. By the time I got downstairs and back onto the street I felt cautiously optimistic. Then came the waiting.

I continued with classes, and with working and therapy. The therapy was difficult at times but necessary because I experienced weird anxiety attacks that took me completely by surprise. One particularly strong attack happened one Sunday afternoon. An acquaintance left

my apartment because he didn't want to wait for me while I meditated in the bathroom for fifteen minutes. When I came out of the
bathroom and realized he'd gone, my heart was pounding, I couldn't
get my breath to regulate, and I frantically searched for him on the
street. Needless to say, I added sessions to my regular schedule with
Blanche Saia, my first and longtime therapist.

Meanwhile, my agent, Jerry Kahn, hadn't heard "no" from Mr.
Mazursky, so "yes" seemed a definite possibility. As days turned into
weeks and the part still hadn't been cast, the agents stayed enthusiastic
and patient while I was going obsessively nuts. I had a week vacation
from *Love of Life* and decided it was a good time to get out of town. It
was a trip that Blanche and I discussed in light of my anxiety attacks
over abandonment issues. I was to travel alone. She thought a one-
week cruise was a good idea. I decided instead to go to London. I'd
never been to Europe and I thought London would be a good place
to start. I knew the language, and I could go to the theater every
night, even though in the past I had experienced a couple of attacks
of claustrophobia when trying to get out of a theater. And there was
plenty to see during the day since I'd never been to a foreign country
before. Lunch alone was fine; I could handle that. I often ate lunch
alone in New York, taking a book or play with me, pretending to read
while I studied all the people. So with no word from Hollywood and
a series of therapy sessions under my belt, I set off for London.

I was scared, mighty scared, the day I left. The anxiety of abandonment and terrifying fear of being alone ran my life. I ran into and out
of relationships with men because of it. Within forty-eight hours of
arriving in London, in the middle of the night in a strange bed at the
Hotel Europa, that familiar heavy blanket of anxious fear started to
envelop me, making breathing difficult and rational thinking nonexis-
tent. I called the Garys. They weren't home. I thought of calling
Blanche, my therapist, but I had just gotten there and if I called her I'd
feel like a wimp. So I called my good friend the actor Al Freeman, Jr.

I had met Al Freeman when I first came to New York through a
friend of Gary's, Jennifer West. We were introduced one night at the

favorite hangout for actors, Joe Allen's on West Forty-sixth Street. Al was a terrific young actor who had been acclaimed for his work on and Off-Broadway. His intensity and honesty onstage were remarkable and I was very impressed and a little intimidated to meet him. Sometime after Gary and I separated, Al and I ran into each other at a restaurant and became good friends and sometime lovers. Conversation with Al was always stimulating and challenging. We'd spend the night talking about all kinds of stuff, me asking a thousand questions about his life and what it meant to be black in our culture and he, kindly educating me. The places he took me were always fun. He introduced me to wonderful jazz clubs and restaurants with fabulous food. I was seriously smitten.

One night he challenged me by saying that I just liked him because he was black. His challenge made me feel uncomfortable. Was it true? Was my attraction about color, about what was forbidden? I couldn't allow myself to look at that possibility at the time because I'd feel guilty. Instead I argued the opposite. I said I cared about him because he was an interesting man. I said he had a mind that grasped the complex, he challenged me, he brooked no superficiality, he cared for me and about me. He was worldly and did interesting things. He loved music and literature and good writing. He was successful and talented and, yes, he was black.

We often disagreed, but he never put me down for my naive statements about common ground between "the white folk and black folk," as he put it. He once told me that I'd never know happiness because I was always so worried when I didn't have it and so fearful that I'd lose it when I did have it. When I wasn't happy, which was most of the time, he said I behaved like I'd never be happy again.

"Lighten up, girl," he'd admonish, putting his arm around me.

He was an honest man. He never promised what he couldn't deliver and he always told me the truth. It seemed impossible for me to tell the truth sometimes. I was too scared, I guess.

So when I called him that first night in London, he called back and patiently listened.

"This trip is a bloodbath!" I sobbed. "I'm not gonna make it." He stayed on the phone until he was sure I was okay and able to sleep. The softness in his voice, his concern that soothed my ear, the fact that he had arranged a way for me to call him if I needed to—all of it together enabled me to stick it out.

The next day was Sunday and it was gently misting as I walked in Hyde Park. I was feeling okay but a little lonely, not at all sure of what to do with the day since everything seemed to be closed. As I wandered aimlessly, I looked up from my soaked toes and saw, coming in my direction, a family of four. The man looked familiar. Just as I was about to see them clearly, they suddenly turned, walking out of the park and heading across the street. My heart quickened. Could it really be? I took off after them, running and then walking briskly to close up the distance. Yes! . . . Is it? . . . No . . . yes! I couldn't believe my eyes. What good fortune! Right ahead was George Segal and his family. This is a great omen, I told myself, getting so excited I didn't stop to think. I rushed right up to them and started babbling.

"Mr. Segal you don't know me but I'm an actress and I auditioned for your new movie *Blume in Love.* I'm still waiting to hear if I got the part, no news is good news I always say and seeing you here like this is such a great omen I'm so excited Marsha Mason's my name I hope you're not offended that I just came up to you like this I hope you and your family are all having a wonderful time and I don't want to bother you any longer hopefully I'll be seeing you soon."

He was gracious but wary. His wife and children just stared. It occurred to me that he might think me a lunatic, but I was so happy it didn't matter. I waved good-bye as they briskly crossed the road, and then I started singing and skipping down the cobbled street doing an extremely bad imitation of Gene Kelly in *Singin' in the Rain.* London suddenly never looked so beautiful and so perfectly quaint as it did that afternoon. The rest of the trip was a breeze. I even managed to meet some people my own age from Australia and went dancing in some clubs in SoHo. I flew home feeling like I could conquer anything. When I got back to New York I found out I didn't get the part.

Several days later, feeling decidedly discouraged, I called Jerry Kahn, my agent, and asked to see him and his partner, Barbara. Their agency was small, just three very nice people who cared about their clients. Their offices reminded me of a big living room in an Upper West Side apartment—cozy and lived in.

"I want to leave the soap and I don't want to leave it for another job," I announced. There was total silence except for some traffic sounds outside. They just stared at me. A phone rang and we all jumped. Barbara went to answer it but kept looking back at me, bumping her knee on a chair.

"What do you want to do, Marsha?" Jerry finally asked, speaking like a doctor talking to someone who is about to jump off a building.

"I don't know. . . . I just feel I . . . I don't know . . . but not stay here waiting for that lucky break. Oh, I don't know, maybe go to a repertory company somewhere for two hundred fifty dollars a week and find out if I can really act."

"I see." Jerry's tone was measured. "Well, what do you want us to do, exactly? You have a contract. You can't walk, the network will sue."

I don't remember what else was said. I just remember leaving there feeling somewhat better for having made a decision, but I hadn't the slightest idea of what to do about it. I didn't wait long.

A week or so after the meeting, Jerry called. The situation was this: an *offer* to appear in a summer package of Noël Coward's *Private Lives* for the American Conservatory Theater (A.C.T.) in San Francisco has been made. The leading lady of the company, Michael Learned, was offered a series in Los Angeles but couldn't accept unless a suitable replacement was found for the summer tour, preferably someone who had performed the play before because there were only two weeks of rehearsal. And they have to know immediately if I'm interested and *free* to leave for San Francisco in a week's time. Meanwhile they asked for a picture and resume.

"Send it! I'll worry about the English accent and the fact that I haven't done the play before after I get there!"

"What about your contract with the soap?" Jerry asked reasonably.

"I'll call Darryl Hickman and explain everything to him. He's a vice president of CBS and my acting teacher! Maybe he can help get me out."

I raced to Drama Book Shop and got the play, then raced to a dialect coach and explained that I had to learn an English accent immediately, that I had never done one before, and it had to be an upper-class Noël Coward English accent all in a week's time. I raced home, memorizing the play by rote, the way Darryl had taught us, stopping only to wonder who it was that recommended me for the part. I knew no one at A.C.T., but I knew it was a premier repertory company. So what if it was just a three-week run in Arizona and Central City, Colorado, during the hottest time of the year. I also belatedly wondered what it was paying.

"Two hundred and fifty dollars a week," Jerry answered, when I called. My chills were now ostrich bumps. They said be in San Francisco on Monday to start rehearsing on Tuesday. It was Friday.

"Darryl, I have an opportunity and I have to take it. I asked for it and it's here. I'm leaving for San Francisco on Monday morning. I'm supposed to work on the soap on Monday. I know I'm walking out on my job but I have to do this no matter what. It's too important; I have to go, even if they sue me." He was quiet.

"Let me see what I can do," he said with a sigh and hung up. I rushed to drag suitcases from the closet as the phone rang. Freida Rothstein was on vacation in Europe and not due back until the weekend. Darryl would try to reach her in Europe.

I memorized. I memorized and cleaned. I memorized and packed. I memorized and paced. The only break I took was brunch on Sunday with my friend Jonathan Reynolds. He insisted I come round and eat, telling me I needed to keep my strength up.

"We don't have to talk. You can eat and memorize," he said. "I'm making you eggs Florentine."

He thought I was crazy to leave the soap and run off for a low-paying, three-week gig in San Francisco, but made me the best eggs

Florentine I've ever eaten. He prompted me badly, correcting my words as I spouted lines between mouthfuls.

The morning I left, I had no idea what the producers and writers on the soap were doing. I imagined those actors that Monday having to speak very, *very* slowly. The last time I spoke with Darryl he told me Freida Rothstein's plane had been delayed somewhere due to some major storm and he still hadn't reached her. Jerry called several times, very worried. I told him to tell them that he had no idea where I was headed. "Tell them that I took off without speaking to you." I frantically finished packing and tried to deal with all the other last-minute stuff, including a final message for Darryl.

"I'm sorry to do this . . . but thank you again. I hope I haven't gotten you in any trouble. Tell them they can sue me, I mean that. I would if I was them; I understand their situation perfectly. I'm gonna take my chances." I didn't find out until years later, like the late 1980s, when meeting up with Freida Rothstein at Orso's, a restaurant in Los Angeles, that she told the network she had fired me so that I wouldn't be held responsible for walking out of the show and my contract. I believe in angels, living and imaginary, and Freida is definitely one of them. Her wingspan is mighty large when it comes to helping others. I shall always be beholden.

To top off this crazy, whirlwind decision, I almost didn't make the plane to San Francisco. My luggage definitely didn't. I tried to study the play on the plane but my brain had DOAd on the Long Island Expressway, so I dozed off looking at clouds and thinking to myself, I'll have to "wing" the tea party scene.

I awoke with the bump and screech of the plane's wheels hitting the San Francisco runway. Groggy, irritable, and panicked, I was met at the gate by a smiling, ebullient Italian, Gino Barconi. Everyone should have a Gino Barconi in her life. He's the perfect Italian grandparent who makes you feel wanted with a laugh and a "Now, now, don't you worry. We'll take care of everything." And there began the largest voyage in my creative life since leaving St. Louis some six years before.

CHAPTER SIX

BE CAREFUL WHAT
YOU ASK FOR

Where are we?" Gary groaned, barely awake. I envied his ability to sleep, but had enjoyed the sense of being alone. Immediately I was on edge, my solitary space suddenly shattered and my fragile sense of balance set askew.

"I'm in San Francisco and it's 1971."

"What do you mean?" Gary yawned, scratching his scalp and rubbing his face with both hands.

"Are you awake?" I replied testily, racing ahead to catch up with Chris while waving the Porsche to come with me.

"Well, there goes the peace and quiet," G.A. announces. "You're better off alone, old girl. Shouldn't try to communicate too much. Too edgy by far."

She's right, of course. Better that Gary drive and leave me to my internal ramblings. I realized I also couldn't answer Gary's question because I'd gotten lost in the past and hadn't a clue as to where we were when he woke up.

"I'll drive," he announced, stretching himself fully awake.

Stopping long enough to make the shift, I settled into the passenger's seat and reached for the map as Gary handed me the Evian bottle.

"Kingman," I announced. "We're near Kingman, Arizona. Must

have crossed the state line a while back. It says that there are no services available between Seligman up ahead and 93, which I think I
just passed. Are we okay for gas?"

"Yeaaahhh, I think so."

His yawning grated on my nerves. Slugging a big gulp of water, I
put the map down and gratefully closed my eyes, hoping for silence
and sleep.

"You didn't sleep that first night in San Francisco," Billie Burke
said, chiming in.

It always amazes me that the human brain can remember so vividly
certain images or scenes, certain rooms or certain moments in one's
life, pulling them up to consciousness level from some depth where
they have been unwittingly stored, like forgotten paintings that
haven't seen the light of day for years. The colors of that clean, slightly
funky hotel room in San Francisco are as clear to me now as they
were over twenty years ago.

"And yet you can't remember years of your life as a young girl."
Grace's tone was quizzical, not accusatory.

I didn't want to think about that now so I resettled myself in my
seat and tried to relax. Grace disappeared into the background as the
sunlight came forward through the sheer curtains that waved gently
in the window of that San Francisco hotel room. Funny, I can't remember the name of the hotel. I sighed as I watched the image of
those curtains, pushed by the soft bay breeze that fate-filled Monday
afternoon twenty-two years ago. I wonder if this trip, this ride to
Santa Fe, will be as chockablock a time as that trip turned out to be.

Sighing deeply and hearing the mantra, "Hamsa," I closed my eyes
and envisioned the blue pearl of meditation as my mind drifted back
in time.

Gino Barconi closed the door to that hotel room and suddenly
there was palpable silence for the first time in what seemed like forever. I stood there listening, watching the curtain flap and sway as the
soft breeze played with it. Slowly I began to hear sounds from the
street. I had made it. I was here. It had begun. I collapsed onto the bed,

feeling the welcoming breeze caress my tired body, allowing myself to sink into the mattress. Every muscle ached, but my mind was calm. I was floating on uncharted waters. I was beginning a new voyage, on my own terms. Much like now, I muse, returning to the present. I didn't know then what I know now, of course. Then I was in the flotsam of change, worrying about the impression I would make on a bunch of unknown people at my first day of rehearsal in this strange city. I desperately wanted a drink.

First, though, I reminded myself, I needed something to eat, and then a toothbrush and toothpaste. I'd have to be careful with my clothes. What I was wearing was all I had till the bags arrived. Better get up so they don't wrinkle, I told myself. My attention was drawn to the light outside; to my eye it was noticeably different from the light back east. I watched intently as it breached the sill of the open window and slid into the room, landing on the carpet and the bottom of the coverlet on which I was sitting. It kissed the edge of my left foot, a warm and friendly feeling on my bare skin. The light seemed translucent, and its effect was to make the pastel colors of the room appear friendly and benign.

After washing out my underwear, I turned on the television and skimmed the *TV Guide*. Vanessa Redgrave's film *Isadora* was the late movie that evening. What could be more perfect. Truly a great actress and the perfect role model for the part of Amanda in *Private Lives*. I can practice my accent, I thought. Accent! Oh my God, I forgot about my accent! They're going to know that I can't do an English accent! They're repertory actors; they do this kind of thing all the time! I'm going to be a laughingstock! My head suddenly ached so bad, I started to cry.

"Maybe *Isadora* will cheer me up," I said out loud.

After getting something to eat and buying a toothbrush and some toothpaste I slowly walked back to the hotel enjoying the evening air. "Time to do some work," I announced and pulled my script of *Private Lives* out of my bag and settled in for the night, waiting for the movie *Isadora* to begin.

Watching Vanessa Redgrave inspired me to renewed enthusiasm for my own work, and as I listened intently to her pronunciation throughout the film, I felt more confident about my own ability to do an English accent. However, sleep wouldn't come so I wound up channel surfing through the night and fell asleep around 5 A.M. After sleeping for only three hours, I awoke in an anxious mood, put on my tired clothes, and prayed that coffee would help. I remember very little of the first day of rehearsal. Isn't that odd? To remember the sunlight and the hotel room so vividly and not have a clue what that first day was like. I remember Paul Shenar breezing into the room, looking incredibly handsome, having just returned from vacation somewhere in Europe. Everyone was returning from vacations and I gathered they had to come back early because of me. Of course I would remember that.

Thanks to Gino, who was in charge of the rehearsals those first few days, things went along rather well. My bags did arrive at the hotel that morning and I managed to change clothes during the lunch break. The actors were nice and didn't seem to notice anything amiss with my accent or relative lack thereof. In fact, I was pretty much on a par with them as far as having my lines down; most of the time everyone was trying to remember the blocking, so I just followed along. Somewhere along about the third or fourth day, I confided to Gino that I didn't know the lines for the tea scene.

"Oh heavens!" he said with a chuckle. "Don't worry! They could barely manage to remember anything during that scene!" He then regaled me with a tasty story or two of riotous moments during the previous season's performances.

On the morning of the fourth day, Bill Ball, the artistic director, came to see a run-through with the original director of the show who had been in Los Angeles on business. The director's name was Francis Ford Coppola. Everyone told me what a terrific fellow he was, what it had been like to work with him, and that he had mortgaged his house in order to do the film that had just come out *The Godfather*.

After the run-through, Francis offered to take me for a ride in his new Mercedes sedan, which had just come off the boat from Germany. It seems that the powers that be at Paramount Studios, the studio releasing the film, had bet him that *The Godfather* wouldn't make $17 million domestically. He took their bet and obviously won. As payment, he asked for this special automobile, the last of a certain line to be made by Daimler Benz. It was with particular glee that he told me this story because he'd mortgaged his house to finish the film, even borrowing spending money from the cast while in rehearsal that past winter; and now here he was, all debts paid, being driven around in his just delivered luxurious winnings. He was having a great time.

Francis and his driver looked a bit like brothers. They had long scraggly hair, long scraggly beards, both were a little overweight, and both enjoyed themselves with a display of appreciation for the finer things in life.

"Now, about your performance," he began, and I immediately came crashing to earth. "She's the richest woman in the world. She's aristocracy, like this car. Smell this car, feel this leather. This is her world every day of her life."

I must have looked at him with dismay.

"Your work is fine, don't worry. Except in the fight scene. Your gestures are too American, too contemporary. You have to find something that constantly reminds you of who you are. What your world is like . . .

"Now, Marlon wore a pinky ring on his right hand that was two sizes too small, so his flesh would puff up around the ring. He picked it out very carefully. He wanted it to look like he had owned it a long time. And then there was the stroking of the cat on his lap while he was in his office doing business. That was his idea. He changed his face and voice by putting . . . Well, maybe that's not the right idea. Do you understand what I'm getting at?" he asked, looking at me intensely.

I blushed but forced myself not to look away. I quickly memorized his face. He reminded me of Allen Ginsberg.

"Get yourself some satin underwear, some very expensive underwear, to remind you that you are the richest woman in the world."

"Okay," I said. Of course, I couldn't tell him that I couldn't possibly afford such items let alone shop for them this late in the day. But I did say I would find something immediately. I thanked him and told him I would be much better tomorrow. I told him not to worry. I think I also thanked him several times. He dropped me off at my hotel and I waved good-bye. As I watched his gorgeous new car tool away, I sighed with yearning. If only I could enjoy life the way he did, be that much of a risk taker, know that much about so many things.

What on earth can I find at this hour? I wondered. Then I remembered that there was a small parfumerie around the corner at the St. Francis Hotel.

Jacqueline's Parfumerie appeared to be open; inside a petite, dark-haired woman was putting crystal bottles away in lighted glass and wooden cabinets. I tried the door, but it was locked. She looked up and smiled as I mimed begging, and she came toward me. In this tiny shop of glass, wood, and mirror, I saw the most complete and beautiful array of glittering bottles of parfum, poudre, and eau de toilette. Crystal flacons winked at me as she asked how she could help. I explained my plight as I peered about and studied all of her cases.

All the famous perfume houses of Paris were represented. Next to them lay silver and mother-of-pearl hand mirrors and all manner of vanity accoutrements. These items were part of my character's everyday world. Jacqueline was French, of course, and with a delightful accent she charmingly explained she was the proprietor and she had every French perfume available. I told her I needed the strongest scent made.

She selected various bottles for me to sniff; some were downright pungent and some just didn't "feel" right for the character. My eye caught a small mirrored tray of slender fluted bottles, holding a rainbow of various amber-colored fluids. I'd never seen perfume the color of tobacco before. I asked her the name.

"Intoxication," she answered. "This is the parfum for you. If I were the richest woman in the world, I would wear this."

"I'll take two," I declared. "And two bottles of eau de toilette and dusting powder if you have it." There went my entire salary. Thank God for American Express, I thought. I turned and looked out the window as Jacqueline carefully wrapped the boxes and placed them in a shiny white paper carrying bag. It was twilight outside and people were scurrying home from work. By contrast, the store was brighter inside as I signed the small fortune away and thanked her for staying open and helping me.

"*Bon chance!*" she replied as she escorted me to the door. "*Merci.*"

"*Au revoir,*" I replied in my best French accent. She smiled and said something else in French as she locked the door and pulled down the elegantly thin shade. The sidewalks were now dusted with shadows from street lamps and small stars had started to twinkle in the dusky blue-black sky. A fog horn sounded in the distance. What a strangely beautiful sound, I thought—my first fog horn. As the San Francisco twilight worked its magic, I drank in the cool evening air. Marlon Brando has nothing on me I thought as I sauntered toward my hotel.

At dress rehearsal the next day I took my prized possessions and doused and dusted my way through my wig and costumes, my hand-kerchiefs, my cigarette holder, my fan, my underwear—in fact, my entire body. We did the run-through, and afterward I sat there and shook while notes were given. I definitely was not Brando, but somehow the ploy had worked. Plus everyone thought I smelled divine, even Francis. In fact, after that experience, with every new project my favorite thing has been to find a signature scent for the character I am to play.

The tour was a success and the 114-degree weather in Phoenix helped saturate my costume, wig, skin, and acting with Intoxication. I loved every minute of it and didn't want it to end. I confessed to all that I hadn't done the part before and had memorized the entire play by rote the weekend before I arrived. There was surprise, laughter, and then some gentle corrections of my English accent.

"This is my life," I said out loud one night to the woman with the blond wig who stared back at me in the mirror. "This is what I was born to do. I can do this forever. Thank you, God. Thank you, thank you, thank you." That night after the show, I asked Paul Shenar, Elliot to my Amanda, if he thought I could apply for a position with the regular company that coming fall. He explained that usually you were invited to join and generally that meant you were promised one sizable role and the rest of the season you would be "as cast."

"There are always surprises with Bill Ball," he intoned. And when I asked him what kind of salary a new person got he answered, "Usually you earn about two hundred fifty dollars a week." Voilà!

We finished the tour in Central City, Colorado. Thankfully, it was cooler than Arizona. We were all flying back to San Francisco together, so I asked Paul and the other actors who were returning to the company that fall to put in a good word for me as we said our good-byes at the airport and I headed for Los Angeles.

I was nervous about the trip to L.A. because I would have to find my way into West Hollywood from the airport, and once there, find the hotel I booked on a good word from my agent while trying to follow directions on how to negotiate the freeways. The trip to Los Angeles came about when Jerry called to tell me that despite walking out on *Love of Life*, I was still in the business as far as he knew, and that although I didn't get the part in *Blume in Love*, I had done well in the audition and should go to L.A. and meet the head of casting at Warner Studios. He had suggested a hotel on Hollywood Boulevard that was inexpensive and had kitchenettes. Now, the idea of going to Los Angeles wasn't especially appealing to me. I had "tried out" L.A. once before, a few years back, by visiting some artist friends of Gary's. I lasted forty-eight hours. The streets in Beverly Hills looked cavernous and empty, and the freeways were daunting. Everything seemed too far away and exits on freeways whooshed by with no hope of ever being able to find them again. However, buoyed by feelings of success and confidence, I overcame my anxieties and decided to hope for the best. Just be calm, I kept saying to myself.

I was petrified as I pulled out of Rent-a-Wreck in my little blue Pinto, but it wasn't the old familiar, all-consuming blanket of terror. Fortunately, my virgin trip to London had helped. I drove into L.A., my nose practically glued to the windshield, my hands like a vise around the steering wheel, muttering to myself, "If you could get to London by yourself, you can do this, you can do this, you can do this."

Once, in college, some girlfriends and I drove into downtown Chicago early on a Saturday night. The trip, from the house where we were staying, took about twenty minutes. It was still light on the ride into town. At 10 P.M. I was driving us home and got lost leaving the city. By dawn, and some three hundred miles later, we got off the highway and stopped at a church in Indiana somewhere for Mass and directions. We had driven through parts of Illinois, Indiana, and, I think, Ohio. So much for my sense of direction. Thank God a race-track comes full circle.

The drive from LAX into West Hollywood went amazingly smoothly. I considered this a very good omen, but then reminded myself of the last time I thought something was a good omen. Oh well, at least I met George Segal. The directions had been carefully written out by the producer of *Happy Birthday, Wanda June,* who was in L.A. because Columbia Pictures was making the film of Kurt Vonnegut's play. I, of course, was not repeating my role on film; my part went to the blond British actress Susannah York. Harumph.

I found my way to the small residential hotel on Hollywood Boulevard at which I had booked a room. It had a palm tree in front and a Disney inspired sign. My room was clean and neat with plastic flowers, Formica tables, and Swedish teak furniture. As soon as I checked in and got situated, the phone rang.

"How would you like to be a member of the acting company at A.C.T.?" said the voice of William Ball.

"Oh my God, oh my God!" said the tremulous voice of the very grateful and happy actress. Then I burst into tears while laughing giddily. I could tell Bill was smiling his Cheshire cat smile. He explained that he was in the process of putting the season together and was prepared to offer me the leading role of Roxane in *Cyrano de Bergerac.* Rehearsals were to start on such and such a date. It wasn't soon enough for me, and I told him so. He wasn't sure what the rest of the season was going to be, so the contract would read "Roxane" with the rest "as cast," for $250 a week. I was thrilled, so was he, and so, he told me, was Gino Barconi. Suddenly everything was in a state of flux and I was in a tizzy. I had to think about what to do with everything I owned that was stashed in my place on West Seventy-second Street in New York City. I had to pull myself together for the 1971–72 season at A.C.T. Yes!

After squealing, laughing, and crying my way through all the details on the phone with Gary, I called my agents. "Can you believe it!? I have a job with a repertory company for two hundred fifty dollars a week! Just like I said that day in your office!" I was impressed by the synchronicity of events even if they weren't.

My agents were happy for me, but a little ambivalent about the eight-month contract. I, on the other hand, was so ecstatic about joining A.C.T. that I didn't want to go out to Warner Bros. and I told them so. They insisted, however, and gave me the time for my appointment with Nessa Hyams, head of casting, with instructions to call them after the meeting. (I didn't know then, of course, that Nessa and I would become great friends and write a screenplay together.)

I hadn't thought about how long I was going to stay in La La Land, and I still wasn't sure. I figured I'd take a week's time to see some friends, including Glenn Jordan, a director I had first met at the Eugene O'Neill Playwriting Conference several years before, who was in Los Angeles directing a TV remake of the old series *Doctor Kildare*. And of course I'd be meeting Nessa for the first time.

Warner Bros. Studio was somewhere over the hills and in the valley—another scary trip that caused me to sweat bullets. I figured I'd have to leave at least five hours before the appointment, just in case I got lost. I momentarily contemplated leaving the night before and staying in a hotel across the street from the studio (if there was one), but sanity came back and I figured I could find it in five hours.

I need to digress for a moment to say that I got to work with Glenn again in the *Kildare* series and again in *Only When I Laugh*. He is a wonderful director. He taught me a very valuable acting lesson:

"Don't *you* cry; make *them* cry!" He was an actor's dream of a director on *Only When I Laugh.*

Anyway, so there I was jumping up and down on the green shag carpet of my Hollywood Boulevard hotel room, so excited that I had to run to the ladies' room and pee. Next I called Glenn and told him the wonderful news.

"Now, I'm taking you out to celebrate your great news," he commanded. "Who's playing Cyrano, by the way?"

"Peter Donat," I responded.

"Good actor, very good actor. Come and be Nurse Lord on *Doctor Kildare* for me. You'll get paid some money, not much. Your outfits will be starch white with perky hats, nothing like the grand clothes you'll be wearing at A.C.T., but never fear, you'll get to wear glamorous white shoes that will be extremely comfortable because you'll be on your feet long hours waiting to say lines like, 'Yes, Doctor,' 'No, Doctor,' 'Right away, Doctor' while you hustle patients and visitors around the hospital halls and deliver scintillating variations such as, 'This way, Doctor.' And you'll do it brilliantly."

"The chance of a lifetime!" I whooped and thanked him profusely. Thank God. Money. Meanwhile I had to make my appointment with Nessa Hyams at Warner Bros. studio. Driving onto the Warner Bros. studio lot was like driving into a movie. I gave my name to a man in uniform at the gate and sat there watching the hubbub around me. It was just like scenes from a movie, with big lights being shuttled to huge beige soundstages, and people wandering around in costume and makeup. Glamorous, I thought, definitely glamorous.

"Here we go, put this on your dash. Straight ahead two blocks, you'll see the building on your left. Park where you can. They're expecting you. Good luck," he said and smiled. I loved him. I absolutely loved him.

The casting office waiting room was chocolate brown with brown furniture. Everywhere I looked there were bright yellow, construction-paper bound scripts with *Blume in Love* emblazoned in brown print on the cover. I felt a momentary glitch of disappointment.

Fuck 'em. I'm a working actress with A.C.T. .... and I'm on a series! I reminded myself as I marched up to the receptionist and stated
my name and business. I sat down and looked over at the scripts, but
decided not to pick one up. I figured it might scotch my good luck if
I even touched it.

"Miss Mason, you can go in now."

"Uh-huh . . . uh-huh . . . uh . . ." A woman with short, dark hair was
at a desk lighting a cigarette and speaking into a phone. "You'll never
guess who just walked into my office." The woman on the phone
motioned for me to sit on the couch, across from her desk, the top of
which was littered with all kinds of 8 x 10 glossy faces, a stack of
scripts, an overflowing ashtray, and a *huge* Rolodex. She hung up the
phone and swung around with her hand extended. She was pleasant
but definitely businesslike, and she had a great smile. I could tell she
was a New Yorker from the way she was dressed, and how she spoke
and handled herself. I liked her immediately and told her so. I think
that sort of threw her, but she kept right on talking.

"That was Paul Mazursky on the phone just now. The part that
you auditioned for in *Blume in Love* just became available. The actress
Dorothy Tristan wants to do another Warner picture *Scarecrow* with Al
Pacino that's shooting at the same time. Paul wants to see you. He's
right next door, up the stairs. Come see me after." I don't think she
even breathed until she took a drag off her cigarette. She pointed to a
building through her office window.

"He's in his office, second floor, second door on the right. Come
back here after you're finished. We can talk then." I didn't have time to
think or be nervous. I found myself bounding up the stairs and walking right into Paul Mazursky's office. His secretary was at her desk, on
the phone: the door to his office was open, and he was on the phone
too, only he was pacing.

He impatiently motioned me to come in as he sat in a chair, continuing to wave at me to sit down too. He continued on the phone
for a minute or two, and then hung up. "I've got a migraine from casting this damn thing. We start shooting immediately; I can't go back to

New York. You better be good. Let's read." He suddenly stopped himself and laughed. "What a terrible thing to say to an actor! I know
better. I've been acting a lot longer than you. Forgive me."

I don't remember the reading or what Nessa and I talked about afterward, I don't remember leaving the studio, and I don't remember
the ride home. But I do remember the next day while working with
Glenn, waiting to hear if I got the job. "Marsha, phone!" a grip yelled
between takes. I ran to the stage phone while Glenn was setting up
the next shot. "Yes?" I said breathlessly. "Starting when?" I asked, still
not breathing. My agent gave me the date and I scribbled and started
to shake. I looked down at the paper in my hand and counted the
days as I ran back to my hospital station and stood there in a state of
total numbness. It can't be, I told myself. I counted wrong. Stay calm.
Get this take over with and sit down quietly and figure it out.

While thinking these sane thoughts, another part of my brain was
verging on panic. This can't be happening. When it rains jobs it pours.
There's gotta be a way outta this. Maybe I can do both. Think positive.

"Cut! Marsha, darling, that's your cue. I realize you're a movie star
now, but let's not forget how you got there!"

After work I raced home to my Hollywood suitette and tried to
think. What I decided was that I had accepted Bill Ball's offer from
A.C.T. first, and it was that offer I must go with. I wanted it, I'd asked
for it, and I'd gotten it. Now I had to find a way to make it all work.

"Bill, I have to talk to you. I've been offered a supporting role in a
movie that shoots here in L.A. for Paul Mazursky, starring George Segal. It's a four-week contract and it might go over and into the rehearsal time for *Cyrano*. I want more than anything to come to San
Francisco and be a member of the company, and I said yes to you first.
I was just wondering if, maybe, well, I know this is . . . well, maybe
you could rehearse some scenes that I'm not in—fight scenes or
something—for a few days . . . ? But if not, I understand. I'll be there."

Silence. Great, Marsha, I thought, screw everything up why don't
you.

Naturally he was a little taken aback but I reiterated my promise that I would be there.

"Well," he finally drawled, "it's a very large production and you're in most of it! We have an enormous amount of work to do. . . . Let me think about it. I'll call you tomorrow." And he hung up the phone.

Bill called the next day and said that if I had the first two acts completely memorized by the time I came to San Francisco, he would work with the understudy for the first week of rehearsals but no longer. I promised that I would be there by a certain date. I think the fact that I had confessed to Bill about not having done the play *Private Lives* before, and I came to work for him having memorized most of it over a weekend had made all the difference.

"*You want what?!*" Paul Mazursky shrieked through the phone. "You want an out clause on your first picture?" I could imagine the redness in his face. "Nobody gets a finishing date on their first picture! Oh, my head is killing me. This picture is killing me. I'm serious. You think I'm joking. This is a living nightmare." I couldn't help but think that Paul was probably a good actor. I told him what Bill was willing to do and that I had to be finished and on my way to San Francisco by a certain date. I told him that I was sorry to have caused him all this trouble.

"This is a big production. We have locations, *Europe!* Well, not you, but there are hundreds of people involved. Do you understand what you're asking? I want to rehearse for at least two weeks before beginning shooting. You have a lot to do!" He sighed again. "I can't believe this."

I could imagine him shaking his head in disbelief.

Silence. "Let me think about it. I can't promise anything. I'll call you tomorrow," he said and hung up the phone.

I felt like a wrung-out dishcloth that had just washed a mountain of dishes. I couldn't move off my kitchenette bar stool. I sat there and stared at the Formica. "I need a drink!" I announced to no one but me and went to find one.

Paul called the next day to say that he had spoken with my agent and had agreed to an out clause. He was still in overwhelm, but actually was very nice on the phone. He was intrigued by Bill Ball's decision and asked me why Bill would let me come a week late to rehearsals. I explained how I had fibbed and gotten up in the role of Amanda in *Private Lives* so quickly.

"Really," he replied. "Well, I expect the same from you when we rehearse."

"Absolutely," I promised. As I lay in bed that night, I thought back over the past several weeks and tried to put the pieces together. It was amazing to me then and still is to this day how this part of my life unfolded. I didn't know at the beginning how Bill Ball had even heard of me, let alone hired me sight unseen. But when I finally asked, I was surprised by the circuitous route of destiny.

It turned out that the director Ed Sherin, who auditioned me in New York for a film he was shooting about two brothers home from Vietnam, got a call from his sister, a board member of A.C.T. She asked him if he knew any actresses who might replace Michael Learned, A.C.T.'s leading lady, who was being offered a lead in the series *The Waltons.* He told her that he had auditioned a young actress he thought might be good—me. And there you have it.

And there I was, lying in bed late at night, not able to sleep, having to get up at 5 A.M. to go to work being Nurse Lord, and at the same time I have to get ready to be in my first studio film, *Blume in Love,* then go immediately into my first production with A.C.T. in San Francisco as Roxane in *Cyrano.*

My next main concern was figuring out logistics and finances. How in the world was I going to keep my apartment in New York while living in L.A. for four weeks and then San Francisco for eight months? Change frightens me, just like it does most people. My suitette here on Hollywood Boulevard was inexpensive, but not cheap. I had to get back to New York before going to San Francisco. I was going to have to pay rent in San Francisco, probably rent a car, and pay for the car I was presently renting. I had my New York apartment rent to think about and all this on $250 a week. I couldn't touch the money I had in my savings account. As a struggling actor I knew I might not work again for a year and I'd promised myself I'd never go back to a regular, boring job again. Of course, the movie money was going to cover a chunk of it, but I was going to be gone for seven months and had to get all this taken care of by September. I also had to memorize my movie lines while working with Glenn, then shoot *Blume in Love* while memorizing my lines for *Cyrano de Bergerac*. How on earth was I going to manage it all? I asked myself as I lay in the dark listening to the cars whizz by in the night.

Glenn invited me to join him the next afternoon and meet his friends Louise Latham and Paul Picard. He affectionately referred to her as "Nonny," although Paul, her husband, called her "Nonya." Louise is an original, a talented actress, a wild and wonderful gal with an incredibly sharp mind and exquisite taste, a sensualist (in everything that's important, as she was wont to say) with a wicked sense of humor. She's worked with lots of directors, including Hitchcock, playing Marnie's mother in *Marnie,* and had done tons of television and lots of stagework. I was fascinated by her and her home and her incredible cooking and most of all her attitude toward life. She valued everything of quality, whether it was a gardenia, an excellent book, a bright mind, or a gifted actor. Surprise and elegance—those were the qualities she looked for and aspired to.

Louise took me by the arm and under her wing. "You're staying with me while you work on your movie." I'd have my own room and bath with a glorious grapefruit tree just outside the window that was in full perfumed bloom. I was to swim every morning, just like her, and have fresh orange juice squeezed from big, fat, organic oranges from one of her favorite trees. Then we'd drink freshly ground coffee, her favorite mix of exotic beans, by the gardenia bush that covered half the bay window of the kitchen. When Glenn made a droll remark about driving in the predawn dark to the studio, her bright, blue eyes twinkled.

"I absolutely love that time of day, don't you? Your coffee will be waiting for you."

"THE GIRL WHO scared the livin' daylights out of me!" exclaimed George Segal upon being introduced the first day of rehearsal. "Did she tell you what she did?" George asked and laughed as Paul Mazursky looked at me quizzically. After relating the tale of accosting George on a London street, we all got down to the first day of rehearsal. Susan Anspach was very serious and beautiful and very self-possessed. Kris Kristofferson was nervous and uncomfortable like me.

"I've never done this kinda gig before," Kris drawled quietly, sounding like he had gravel in his throat. I told him I hadn't either. He perked up and said, "Great! So you're a greenhorn too!"

Mostly my mind was preoccupied with nudity. I had never before taken off my clothes in front of strangers—well, almost never. Now I was going to have to be nude and act all at the same time. I came to rehearsal with my lines learned just like I said I would. Paul made every day fun and serious at the same time. When we rehearsed the nude scene, he promised that on the day I would be totally protected and made as comfortable as possible. Rehearsals were a breeze. There were lots of laughter and talking and questioning; I quickly realized this was the "Big Time" because everything was taken care of, including lunch.

"Clothes say *everything* about the character, honey, and you are going to look *fabulous.* You *are* fabulous! Your first movie, huh? Well! We have to make sure you look great for your first entrance. You'll look great in every scene. Are you in for a treat. There is *nothing* better than making movies, honey. I've done everything including dress windows and I love, love, *love* it!" Joel Schumacher was my first official costume designer in films and I love, love, love him.

"Now, the very first time we see you coming down the ramp at the airport is veeeerrrrrrry importanté. You have to look *smashing* and *sexy.* After all, it's your verrrrrrrry first entrance on film!" he said gleefully. "You have to have the right jewelry, everything will be perfect, you'll be fabulous. I'll be back with stuff for you to try and whatever doesn't feel right or look right, you just tell me and we'll change it!" It was then, I think, that he took his first breath.

All the interior sets that I was to use were up and ready to go. Props were at my fingertips for every rehearsal.

"If you want somethin' else, just ask, and we'll get it for you, anything at all," said the prop master. And whatever it might be, it was there a couple of hours later. When I mentioned that I had to find the right perfume for my character, the kindly prop man said, "You just let us know; we'll get it for ya, honey, doncha worry." And so it was: if you wanted something special to drink or eat or nosh on, it was there. I had never been treated so well in all my *life,* let alone my work.

The set was closed. I had never heard that phrase before, but found myself grateful for it.

During my actual "nude" scene, George got the frontal view of me, and the camera and millions of people (I assumed) were going to see my backside from tippy top to tippy toe lying on my side on a bed. I got to wear a tiny adhesive triangle and two tiny circles—I told Joel I thought this particular outfit was his best yet. Ultimately, the scene wound up on the cutting room floor. Whew.

Paul was the best director a naive Catholic girl from St. Louis could have for her first proper picture. I spent a lot of time in bed with George. I was, after all, the "diversion" for his character while he tried to get his wife back. Toward the end of our scripted affair, I had another scene in a bed. This time I got to use a sheet. George and I did the scene the way it had been rehearsed a couple of times, and we shot it. Paul then walked over to me and whispered in my ear.

"Now, you're five years old." I didn't say anything in response, but it didn't take any time to feel five years old. With just that shift in direction, we shot the scene again and that take was the one he used in the movie.

I've heard stories about Elia Kazan and other great directors using personal information and surprises to get a particular response or reaction from an actor. Movies are all about getting it on film once and then you never have to repeat it. Theater is just the opposite. You have to make it look like it's happening for the first time eight times a week, twice a day on matinee days. Movies can seem deceptively easy compared to the theater, but oddly it isn't all that easy because you *have* to be truthful for the camera. You have to reveal yourself in a way that you don't always need to on the stage. It's a weird business. I was incredibly fortunate or just damn lucky that for my first two films I worked with directors who were actors. Paul explained everything that was going to happen before it happened so I wouldn't get thrown, and we shot my scenes in sequence. Mark Rydell did the same thing on *Cinderella Liberty*. I don't think I've ever had that luxury again. With *Blume in Love* we rehearsed everything for two weeks, and then we shot everything the way we rehearsed it. Except once— it was my last scene in the movie, the one in which George is breaking off our affair.

"I didn't use you, you didn't use me, we used each other." That was his last line to me. As we rehearsed it, I turned away with tears in my eyes and walked out the door. When it came time to shoot, George said his line, I looked at him, and suddenly without warning I hooted at him and left. Paul said "cut" and I was mortified.

"Paul, I'm so sorry! It just came out; I know it's not what we rehearsed. I'm sorry."

"I loved it, it was great! That's a print."

"No, no, let me do it again the way we rehearsed, please."

We did the scene again, and when I got to that moment, the same thing happened again. "Huh!" just came out of my mouth. Paul yelled "Cut!", laughed, and the whole set applauded. I was so surprised and touched I couldn't speak.

A couple of days later Paul took me to lunch. "I think you could have a career in this business, if you want it," he said rather seriously as we picked at mounds of sprouts. "A lot of people are gonna tell you what you should do, what's good for your career; but just remember, do what *you* want to do, what you believe in, like this repertory thing, and you'll be fine."

I was reminded of Paul's sage advice some years later when Ray Stark, the film producer who guided Neil through some of his film productions, saw me in a production of *The Heiress* at the Westwood Playhouse and said to me, "You're not a movie star Marsha; you're a serious actress." *That* was why I went off to San Francisco after finishing *Blume in Love,* to find out if I was a serious actress.

IN THE ENSUING years there were a couple of times I *didn't* do what my inner voices told me because someone in power—well, truthfully, someone who intimidated me (in my case, always a man)— told me I should or shouldn't do it, that it was bad for my career, that it would destroy a marriage, ya-de-ya-de-ya. I was more hooked into being loved and approved of than I was loving and approving of myself. I betrayed myself in those experiences and they were neither rewarding nor did they do anything for my career. In fact they were awful!

"Now, surely you don't mean that, old girl. You have learned never, ever, to betray yourself again." Yes, okay, G.A., and hopefully I won't but I do wish I had been smarter and healthier back then!

"Oh come on, what's the big deal. It's life, isn't it? What can you do? You've learned the hard way, okay. But by God, girl, you have learned. The good that came from those times is the present. Sure, not doing *Norma Rae* . . ." Yes, G.A., I regret that decision. I made that decision out of fear. I gave up myself in order to keep Neil and the girls.

"This is the life you've chosen, old girl. Let's talk about what you have done," G.A. continues, "and who you are and who you are becoming! I'm mad about you, old girl, don't beat yourself up. You're just stressed to the max right now." My voice of reason.

Thoughts drifted as the car hummed along in the heat. Mantras came and went and emotions subsided. It felt good to go back in time. To go back to that phase, that synchronized time in my life. Was it astrological? Will it happen again? I hope so.

After saying good-bye to Paul I arrived back in San Francisco, bags and all, and went straight into rehearsal for *Cyrano,* determined to follow my bliss. Gino Barconi, my smiling Italian tanta, once again led the way. I stood outside the closed rehearsal room door and listened as I tied a rehearsal skirt at my waist. There was great commotion going on inside with enthusiastic voices raised in celebration. When I opened the door everything stopped. Hundreds of eyes came to rest on me as I walked into the room.

"Ahhhh, you're here! Just in time." And with a flourish Bill Ball got up from the table, cigarette in hand, and introduced me to Peter Donat, Marc Singer, and Deborah May, my understudy. "Our Roxane, ladies and gentlemen." Of course I tried to assess the vibration in the room, but sometimes I find it easier to *not* deal with the situation, although I knew mental questions were flying around the room. Who is she? How come *she* gets to come in late? She better be good. "This skirt will give you a better feel for your costume. It's a nightmare to get used to." Debbie May graciously handed me her rehearsal skirt with its big hoop. I thanked her very much for standing in for me, said my hellos to all the actors, and began where Debbie left off. To say that I felt the pressure of all those eyes on me is an understatement. Thank God I didn't step outside myself and fully grasp what the hell I was doing.

"Let's start at the top of the act, shall we, dears? Roxane, are you ready?" I took a deep breath, shook out my arms and legs and thought a prayer of thanks to the gods that I had learned these lines. Gathering my wits, I focused on, "I am Roxane and this is the man I love and these are the soldiers I've come to feed."

Everyone in the company stayed in that room and watched the rehearsal. I was terribly nervous, but just tried to stay focused and learn the blocking that Bill and the other actors had worked out. I figured that it was my job to get up to speed. By late afternoon we had run through the rough blocking that they had been rehearsing and Bill stood before the entire company.

"Good work today, everyone. Now, I want to tell you a story. . . ." Bill began to share with us his impression of me that first day he saw me in the run-through of *Private Lives*. He explained the necessity of technique, of learning how to use your instrument so that the emotion, the energy of creation, had a conduit for expression that could move easily from one feeling to another—rather like a personal Rolodex of feelings, he said. He geared his comments to the young students and journeymen who listened in rapt attention. I suddenly realized how valuable this moment was for all of us. We were there to serve a greater purpose than ourselves. We were there to serve the play and the audience who would see it. Bill was extraordinary—a man of vision. I was home.

MY SEASON AT A.C.T. was the next stage of my initiation into the secret world of alchemy. Acting is an act of service, a spiritual endeavor at its best and an ego buster at its worst. Total absorption into the creative world of art and theater was the order of the day at A.C.T. Classes upon classes of various disciplines were available to students and professionals alike. We even had the opportunity to learn meditation if we wished. Having been interested in spirituality since college, and continuing haphazard studies in that area when I went to New York, I was initiated into Transcendental Meditation at A.C.T., mostly because Bill was a major TMer and most of the company had been practicing it as well.

As I worked through the season, I found that my approach to the work became more "spiritually" motivated. I didn't abandon the basics of technique for something else; instead I added something intangible to my approach to the work. In performance, the "air" between me and the audience became palpable. I thought more and acted less. I surrendered the performance to a Higher Self by preparing in a more spiritual way.

The fruits of this discipline began to bud one evening during the balcony scene in *Cyrano*. I was up high, and Peter as Cyrano and Marc

Singer as Christian were down below in the shadows. I stood there and instead of trying to engage the audience by acting, I suddenly stopped and "felt" the air. Listening to the words of the play move in the air, I felt myself moving through the air. Suddenly each person in the audience was in my head and I in theirs. I put the audience in my heart. It was just us, and then not even me. I know I've related this experience badly because these "air moments" are beyond words for me; but the moments are as vivid now as they were the first time they happened, no matter how many years have passed. And life will sometimes show me that I wasn't just dreaming those moments. Sometimes I get corroboration that what I've experienced is felt by someone else and sometimes from the most unlikely sources.

Keith Hernandez, a great first baseman and a friend for life, told me one night that one of the most meaningful theatrical moments he ever experienced was watching a production of *Cyrano de Bergerac* on PBS. He said he'd been moved to tears while watching it, especially the balcony scene.

"How long ago was this?" I asked. He remembered it had been broadcast on PBS as part of the *Great Performances* series, in black and white. I couldn't believe my ears. I asked him who played Cyrano, and when he said Peter Donat I got chills.

For his birthday I obtained a copy of the show from the archives in Washington, D.C., and as we sat together on the bed, watching it and crying together, he charmingly told me I looked just the same. Ahhhh, what a guy.

For me the magical mystery of art, dance, and theater is the invisible line, or wave, of communication that exists between the actors themselves, and the audience. These invisible lines, or waves, connect us all whether we are aware of them or not. A person in the museum or audience, thinking he or she is just there watching, detached, suddenly, seemingly involuntarily, feels "something." That "something" might be his mind registering an emotion without knowing why, or his breath is inexplicably taken away; or he instantly remembers an image or emotion from the past or spontaneously finds himself guffawing, hooting, chuckling, and crying—all because an invisible connection exists in the air between the painting, or screen or stage, and him. Chemistry happens. I became an apprentice learning the embryonic beginnings of alchemy at A.C.T.

We opened the 1971–72 season with *Cyrano de Bergerac* to great success and immediately went into rehearsal for *The Merchant of Venice.* Because I worked hard and the gods and goddesses were with me, or maybe because destiny or the planets were well situated at the time, or maybe because Bill Ball was strapped and had to do it, I was lucky enough to be in the right place at the right time and given the opportunity to play in repertory Roxane in *Cyrano de Bergerac,* Jessica in *The Merchant of Venice,* Nora in *A Doll's House,* Alice in *You Can't Take It with You,* and Abigail in *The Crucible.* I had no time to do anything but work at my craft. I didn't even have time to shop for food. Mostly I would just run across the street to the deli. Everything was "right" and I was consumed with the work. There was a period of time, in the middle of the scheduled season, that we were performing two plays in tandem while rehearsing two other plays during the days we didn't do matinees. I just kept running across the street to the deli and ordering chicken soup to go, so I wouldn't get sick. I never even got a cold; I just got a little chubby.

IN THE MIDDLE of all this mayhem, the Garys came to see me. We threw mattresses on the floor and the three of us slept together like brothers and sister, with me in the middle. They came to a matinee of *A Doll's House* and, fortunately, one of those "air moments" happened. I was transported across the stage during one of the scenes. I couldn't feel my feet on the floor. I suddenly "found" myself as Nora on the other side of the stage. I said nothing to them about it afterward, but later Dontzig mentioned this particular moment. They said that the audience gasped. Had I heard them? No, I was fully in the moment of the play, in Nora's life at that moment, and yet the witness part of my brain was watching the moment too. I was Nora in that moment, wishing to fly out the window, and the witness to the moment at the same time. Those "moments" don't happen every day, and I was so grateful that the Garys had been there to see it.

When I was in Darryl Hickman's acting class, I was introduced to an exercise for getting in touch with an audience in a theater. Before the curtain rises, while I'm standing behind the curtain or some piece of scenery, I close my eyes and breathe in the audience, listening to the babble of their voices as they find their seats. This exercise often helped me overcome performance jitters. While standing there, taking in the energy generated by the audience, I repeated a prayer.

> Most generous Rewarder! Endow my body also with splendid clarity, with prompt agility, penetrating subtlety, and strong impassability.

I've yet to be able to achieve strong impassability when faced with a negative review, but I continue to pray and hope that some day total detachment will be a real experience.

Midway through the season with A.C.T., during the early performances of *A Doll's House,* I received a call from Hollywood.

"Hello," said the sexy voice, "Marsha? This is Mark Rydell. I'm a friend of Paul Mazursky's. I'd like to come up and see you in your show."

"Which one?" I replied. I loved being able to say that.

He chose *A Doll's House.* I arranged the tickets and afterward we met in my dressing room. I apologized to him because I didn't think I had done very well that night. I felt I was running to catch up with the play. He was complimentary, however, and asked if we could meet for coffee the next day. He wondered if I would read a script that he was doing. It was based on a book by Daryl Ponicsan titled *Cinderella Liberty.*

"Take a look at the role of Maggie," was all he said as he handed me a script.

I started reading the script when I got home that night and was amazed. The part was huge. I thumbed ahead and scanned the pages. Maggie appeared on practically every one. I was also amazed that he wanted me to read it. I didn't think I was physically right for the part. As I read, I realized I knew nothing about a character like Maggie, a prostitute with a tough black boy for a son. But there was something about her that I did understand, although I couldn't put it into words. I could see her in my mind's eye, standing on the corner of Forty-fourth Street and Eighth Avenue—we're talking pre-Disney here—trying to survive the best way she knew how. She was true and straightforward. I felt it was important her story be told.

I was surprised at my sense of ease during the audition the next day. I had confidence because I was employed, doing what I loved, so I didn't care about or even think of getting the part. I loved where I was in my career and what I was already doing, so reading for Mark Rydell didn't make me nervous. I have on occasion forgotten this most important lesson and invariably I don't do well when I want something too much. It is the gift of work—more work.

"So would you like to be in this movie?"

"Are you sure?" I gasped. "You mean, doing this part?"

"Why, do you know something I should know?" he said with a chuckle.

When I went down to Los Angeles to meet with Mark and the costume designer, I saw that Mark had pinned to a large bulletin board a photograph of the French actress Miou Miou. Seeing her finally gave me the confidence to do the role. She looked like an ordinary young woman you might see anywhere. I had pictured Maggie all gussied up with teased hair and too much makeup, hard looking like some of the women I used to see on Eighth Avenue in New York. The emotional life was no problem; how Maggie looked was my stumbling block. That experience taught me something about my own process as an actress. Sometimes it's the look of the character that is the key the actor needs to get into that character's psyche, and sometimes it's the emotional life. In *Only When I Laugh,* I found it was the character's emotional life that was my way in. In *Max Dugan Returns* and *The Cheap Detective* it was the character's physical appearance, including the details, such as color of hair and style, specific clothes and jewelry, and the character's economic level. One of the reasons I find the theater so much fun is that I am given the opportunity to change the way I look and experience what it's like to live in times remarkably different from mine, like Mary Stuart in Schiller's play of the same name.

We finished the season at A.C.T. with a trip to Hawaii, taking *A Doll's House* there for a couple of weeks. It wasn't as hot there as it had been in Phoenix, but the piña coladas certainly didn't help my waistline, especially in those corseted costumes. I said good-bye to everyone, thinking that I would be coming back for a second season after finishing the filming of *Cinderella Liberty.* Bill had asked me to open the next season as Kate in *The Taming of the Shrew,* which I was thrilled to do. Everything was great. I was off to Seattle to shoot a picture starring Jimmy Caan and I would be back in San Francisco in the fall. But that was not to be; fate or destiny was to give me another choice that took me in a whole other direction.

JIMMY CAAN HAD come to see me in *A Doll's House* while filming *Freebie and the Bean* with Alan Arkin in San Francisco. I was nervous about meeting him because he was handsome and a movie star and I assumed he had a say in who played Maggie. We met in a bar. It was my suggestion because that's how our characters meet. He was sitting at the bar as I came in, so I sat down next to him and flirted with him a little as we talked, not as heavily as I thought Maggie would, but enough to get a "feel" for the situation.

Jimmy had trained in New York at The Neighborhood Playhouse under Sandy Meisner, and he had loved it. His description of putting on his first pair of tights made me laugh so hard I was crying. What a great guy: really nice, very unassuming, sexy, and funny—an unbeatable combination and just like the character in the movie. Falling for him was going to be easy.

There was excitement in the air as I walked into Mark Rydell's office where production people were running in and out, travel plans where being made, dates and schedules checked and rechecked. I was introduced to Vilmos Zigmond, the cinematographer, and was told we were going to do makeup and camera tests. Mark told me to lose some weight—the piña coladas and chicken soup were showing. I was mortified and he laughed. We would be shooting the whole picture in Seattle, with the interiors being built from scratch in an old warehouse down on the waterfront. The ground floor of the building was being made into a seedy, sailor hangout bar. A movie production is a big affair, and the logistics of shooting outside of Los Angeles was all new to me. Shooting on location is like having to move a small city, all at once, to another place. Whole hotels are taken over. Transportation is organized. Electricity is brought in. Food, water, amenities, basics, you name it—everything is provided for. I was mesmerized by the organization of it all. And the "mayor" of this movable "town" is naturally the director. He has to sign off on everything—he and the producer and, in turn, the studio. It's an amazing feat.

We were all put up at a hotel in downtown Seattle with production offices there as well. Mark had taken a house so that his family could visit and the editors and assistants could have room to work. Jimmy and his brother, Ronnie, went out looking for a house as well after we arrived. I was given a big suite—my first—and a per diem. I don't remember exactly how much it was, but it was a lot to me. Jimmy quickly found a house to rent and we settled down to work. The first week we rehearsed at Mark's house. I remember sitting at a small glass table with Mark, poring over the script while the sun danced on the water surrounding his house. We would be moving over to the sets as soon as they were ready. At that time, the summer of 1972, the Seattle waterfront was a disreputable working waterfront with cargo ships, fish processing plants, sailors, and prostitutes.

Seeing the warehouse for the first time was a stunning experience.

It was an old building some three stories tall that had been unused for some time. On the street floor was the bar set. You stepped into a chiaroscuro world where the hard shafts of daylight caught the dusty mood of a seedy world. Actual sailors came to the door thinking it was a real place to get a beer and play some pool. It looked like it had always been there, totally real, right down to the dusty, broken knick-knacks by the cash register and that distinctive smell of cigarette smoke, booze, and beer.

I entered the place slowly, taking it all in, suddenly chilled and excited all at the same time. This was to be my world for the next eight weeks. Maggie's world. Looking all around at the artistry of the set designer and the decorators, I realized they made my job much easier. Their proven talent ignited the pilot light of my as yet unproven ability; I could feel my creative juices stirring. Upstairs, Maggie's rooms had been built and dressed, and they were perfect. I knew this was my home. It was all waiting for my approval: bottles and boxes of cheap cologne and powders that sailors had given me from the PX, scarves over the lamps, tiny figurines, and cheap girlie stuff—the trappings of prostitutes and poverty.

Sailors weren't the only ones who thought the bar was real. A couple of local gals came in as I walked back into the bar from upstairs. Their silhouettes against the hard glare of daylight looked like a black-and-white photo print. I'd never talked to a prostitute before, but here I was, making conversation, studying everything and every word they said. I invited them to stay and hang out, studying their mannerisms, the way they talked, what was important to them, what wasn't, where they came from, and where they thought they were going. All this real and imagined atmosphere helped me enormously. I began to feel "the skin" of Maggie.

I didn't think about how big the part was. I just kept thinking about "the life" and worked with Mark Rydell. He, like Paul Mazursky, is both a good actor and a good director. He knew what I needed to do the job well and he took every precaution to provide me with a safe and fun environment. We shot a lot of the movie in sequence, which helped me with continuity. The only real break came when the young boy who played my son was exposed to the measles. When one of his siblings came down with the disease, everyone scurried around to get all his scenes done within the twelve-day incubation period, throwing themselves into it with great enthusiasm.

The script supervisor became the most important person on the set since we shot whole scenes and bits and pieces of scenes, all out of continuity, with funny little shots like having to peek out a doorway and look left only. He was the one we all looked to when we needed to know what we were doing. "Now, where am I now?" and "Wait! What just happened?" were my two most asked questions. And sure enough, on the thirteenth day, the measles struck. Fortunately, Jimmy and I were immune. We'd dealt with those itchy critters when we were kids, but some of the crew, and especially their kids who were visiting because it was summer, had to get shots.

Jimmy Caan was wonderful to work with and wonderful to watch. He had eyes in his shoes, as Vilmos used to say, meaning he always hit his mark without having to look down for it. Also his energy level was amazing. He was always on the move, playing basketball, playing musical toy instruments, touch football, you name it. Oh! And pool too. Jimmy was good at everything it seemed, including rodeoing! I'd sit on the sidelines and watch in awe, trying to imagine what he was like as a little kid, totally hyper and full of it. He probably drove his mother crazy, but totally charmed her at the same time.

Even though everything was exciting and fun I felt a little lonely and a lot scared, so one day I called Gary and Gary and Rell; it was during this conversation that I learned that Gary and Gary had become lovers. There's something to be said for denial veiled in detachment.

The following day I went out to see Jimmy and his brother Ronnie at the house they had rented. I decided that I was gonna rent one too; after all, I was a movie star too. Jimmy gave me the name of his realtor and I made an appointment to look at two houses. The first one was pretty crummy, but the other was palatial. It was huge and modern and was surrounded by water. It was located on one of the islands off the mainland.

The rent for the place was my entire per diem money for the length of the picture plus a little more, but I decided to take it anyway. I wanted to be good to myself, and in retrospect, I think I wanted to isolate myself as well. Somehow the information about Gary's sexual shift, his love for Gary Dontzig, the question of my denial, and my enormous fear of being alone all came together that summer, and I decided that it was time to face that fear. Perhaps, in fact, it was time to face a lot of things.

One vivid memory of that house was of sitting one night in a black Mies van der Rohe chair located in the large living room. I turned off all the lights and sat in the dark, with just a candle on the table for company. I told myself to wait; wait for the fear to grab hold. I wanted no music, no TV, no distraction; I just sat there in the dark in a big, strange house, asking myself why I was so afraid to be alone. Was it because of a terrifying memory from childhood, when I was alone in a crib and no one came to save me? Was it because there was something seriously wrong with me when it came to choosing men? How come Gary's homosexuality never occurred to me? He'd been a wonderful lover, yet over time we became better friends than marriage partners. Would it be the end of the world if I didn't ever get married again? Would that be weird? Were my anxiety attacks all about what other people thought of me? I tried to come to terms with these questions.

Most of them got answered rather easily: I'd be okay by myself; I've great friends, so I'll never really be alone; I'm attractive and could certainly have sex if I really needed and wanted to—after all this is the seventies. And most important, I have my work. I'm not really lonely, except maybe when I look around at all the couples in the world. But hey, I see single people too. And I see how well I'm taking care of myself. Look at this beautiful house. And the owner had declined to rent it to John Wayne, but decided to rent it to me!

John Wayne was in town that summer too, shooting a picture. He had wanted to rent the house, but the nice lady rented it to me instead. She felt I would take care of her home. And so I shall, I said to myself as I blew out the candle and went up to bed. At least I had done something active about all my angst. And the sensations of fear that had plagued me for most of my life had not surfaced. All was calm, inside and out. I went to bed that night knowing that I had begun to change, that I had begun the process of taking care of myself, all by myself. I continued to feel like the outsider, but I also began to feel okay about it. Still, I was thankful we were working six days a week. Hopefully, Sundays will be enjoyable and not too strange. Surely there would be something going on.

Most Sundays, at the beginning, were filled with costume fittings, memorization, and work on the next week's scenes. But one Sunday, I went to the movies and saw *Blume in Love*. It was an odd sensation, going to see myself in a movie while I was in the midst of making another one. The movie was doing well in Seattle and everyone on *Cinderella Liberty* was really nice about it.

One Sunday shortly after I moved into the house, Jimmy Caan and his wild brother Ronnie came by boat to visit. They practically had heart failure. Jimmy immediately wanted my house, and I was very pleased with myself that I managed to score something he liked. On another Sunday, in the middle of the shooting schedule, when most of the wives and families came to visit, I invited everyone there for a big barbeque. It was my first huge party with lots of wives, children, and girlfriends. We ate fresh grilled Chinook salmon and I watched everyone enjoy himself, wishing I could feel somehow connected to someone like they all were. It was a familiarly uncomfortable feeling. I imagined everyone wondering to themselves why I wasn't connected to anyone, belonging to anyone, why there was no special "other person" in my life. The outsider was definitely the party giver that day.

I made my life pleasant in Seattle by working hard and, hopefully, doing good work. I made friends with the crew and their families and tried to enjoy it all. I'm proud of myself for facing some fearful questions, hoping to find some answers, all the while providing myself with a beautiful safe haven surrounded by water.

That summer was a major turning point and I was by water, just like when Neil and I went to Baja for the first time and he confessed he wasn't sure he wanted to be married anymore. "I've been married most of my adult life," he'd said. "Twenty years with Joan and now you." That was some conversation that day. And again, I was near water in Jupiter, Florida, a few years later when he called me about the divorce. And that certainly was another major shift.

"Good heavens, girl!" G.A. intoned. "It's a little late to be thinking about being near water right now; we're in a major shift all right, but we are driving through the desert to *live* in the *desert!*" Why aren't I going to the ocean, the *other* ocean, I wonder? Or the tropics for that matter? Okay, so the land in Abiquiu is beautiful, so what? There's no beautiful house on it—yet. I haven't a clue about what life is gonna be like there, and I don't know how to farm! So what am I doing going to live in New Mexico?

"You are so fucking impulsive, you just leap! Leap before you look, that's *your* MO. Jesus Christ, I can't believe we are doing this! You haven't a *clue* about what life is gonna be like there. You don't *know* how to farm! You are leaving a career behind, in the dust! Are you *nuts?* I mean *really!* You have really fucked it this time." My inner Critic is on a rampage and she's not all wrong. I am impulsive, but that's how I got to A.C.T., and that's how I got into movies and that's how I got married.

"And probably divorced!" she interjects. Okay, maybe this journey is a mistake, a major mistake. "I'll say!" she interrupts again. Now listen, I'm scared about this move, and I don't have a clue as to what's ahead; but I've been there—the unknown—before and, so far, with some regrets, everything has been pretty darn great. So relax and stop beating me up! What's the worst that could happen? I fail? I lose the farm? I'm a fool?

I could have told the truth and not lied about doing English accents and English plays, and I could have stayed with the soap and *not* gone to A.C.T., I could have *not* asked Bill Ball for the opportunity to shoot Paul Mazursky's movie, and I could have *not* asked Paul for an out clause so I could get to A.C.T.! *And* I could have *not* married Neil Simon! The point is I *did* do all those things and, yes, I did do them impulsively, just like now! I took a deep breath and calmed down.

"The desert," an inner voice mumbles, "we're gonna *farm* in the fucking *desert.*"

CHAPTER SEVEN

BEGINNINGS AND
ENDINGS

As the scenery becomes more and more unfamiliar, I can't help but wonder if what my inner Critic says is true. Maybe I have made the biggest blunder of my life. What if I am a complete failure, losing everything? Just because the past worked out well—for the most part—that doesn't mean the future will. My confidence in myself is fragile, to say the least. I'm feeling deeply scared and wishing I could shake off this feeling of fear about what lies ahead. Hell, I don't even know what lies ahead. I can't turn back . . . well, I could, but not really. Not now anyway. The trucks are on the road; the deal is done. I no longer live in L.A. Now I just have to find a john. Great! In the middle of nowhere and I have to pee!

There's something to be said about not thinking, as Miss Havisham, one side of my Eccentric self, is often telling me. I suddenly hear Miss Havisham join in, "Thinking—*all* thought—is your nemesis! Thought brings terror. Just pant and you'll be fine, dear." The thought of panting my way to New Mexico makes me chuckle.

"Please, dear." What have I got to lose? During times of stress I tend not to breathe at all! So following her instructions, I stopped thinking and quietly panted, placing the mantra "Guru Om" on my quick breaths.

As I panted and internally chanted, "Guru Om, Guru Om, Guru Om," bit by bit my breath deepened and my stomach eased (although my need to pee did not). As we drive on through the inhospitable desert I try not to think. Again came the inner Critic, "You're a fool! You're stupid. You don't know what the hell you're doing. You're a loser." Then another faceless voice whispers, "Oh Marsha, you're crazy." Okay. I'm crazy, okay! I put my attention on my breath instead of my mind and continued to mentally repeat the mantra, "Guru Om, Guru Om, Guru Om." Again my mind eased and my breath slowed.

I know that I'm protected. My guru gave me that, and I have faith and believe that with God's help, with my guru's grace, I'll make this work. Somehow everything will be all right as long as I live my life following the simple dictum, "Do unto others as you would want others to do unto you." It feels better when I come from that place. God knows, it's not easy sometimes, especially when I have my heart set on something. I'm not known for patience, but I know that if I honestly try to do what is best for all, whether it's loved ones, or asking the land what it wants to grow, I like myself better. And with that thought my mind quiets again, until I look over at the gas gauge.

"Gas!" I blurt out loud, searching the dry, lifeless, shimmering landscape.

"You or the car?" Gary queried innocently.

"We've got to get gas and I do need to get to a bathroom. Quick." Sweat began to trickle down my back and under my arms and I suddenly felt hot and cold at the same time. This was not good, not good at all.

"I see it, I see it." Gary says as an exit sign comes into view. Throwing on the direction signal to alert Chris and Gary who are behind us, he begins to turn off the highway.

"You have *got* to slow down, Marsha May," Gary cautions. "You're just gonna cause yourself *more* pain—and a serious accident."

"I'm already a serious accident!" I retort as I open the door and start to get out before the car even comes to a complete stop.

My face is slapped with a gust of hot dusty wind. My hair whips at my eyes, stinging them, as I feel cracks instantly forming inside my nose. All I can do is gasp, taking in the intolerable wind, grit, and heat. The gas station looks forlorn and seedy, and no one seems to be about.

"Is it open?" Gary yells as I charge here and there, looking for a bathroom. My throat is shut tight. Water. I need water. Rushing back to the car, I reach inside and grab for the Evian bottle on my seat. Buddy starts to lurch forward so I slam the door. Even his bark sounds drunken to me.

"A john, a john!" I slobber and choke as I guzzle the hot water. "My failed kingdom for a john!"

"Such a good idea Marsha, drinking water when you have to pee," G.A. says wryly.

"Saved!" I mutter as I spy a dirty white door marked LADIES in badly printed black letters. Bracing myself for the possibility of an ugly scene, I opened the squeaky door and tentatively sniffed for fetid air. Somewhat relieved, I entered. It was a little dank inside but could have been a lot worse. At least it *looked* clean.

Through the swirling babble of questions and exclamations raging in my head, Grace's soothing voice comes to the fore. "Now now, it's not the end of the world. You're not stuck forever in a mistake, Marsha. You bought land, two hundred fifty acres of it. You've rented a house closer to town that can take your furniture *and* it has a swimming pool and tennis court. You can always admit you made a mistake about the land and sell it." But what about Campbell and Dontzig, Grace? They want to build there too.

"You're going to be okay. You don't have to do anything you don't want to do." Grace's thoughts and her soothing tone begin to take hold. I took a deep breath and feel the viselike grip around my chest and neck begin to ease. The weird waves of nausea begin to withdraw, and breathing comes easier. The mantra "Hamsa" drifts into consciousness. Is it "hum" on the in breath and "sah" on the out breath, I wondered? Or is it the other way round, "so" or "sah" and then "hum?"

"Who cares!" booms Chuck Moses, my Pusher, "just *breathe!*" So I do.

BABA MUKTANANDA GAVE me a spiritual name: Sumati. He told me it meant "Having a good mind." He also told me he gave it to me in hopes that I'd get one! (So far, not so good.) He was fond of telling stories, and once told one about a king who traveled far and wide in search of spiritual enlightenment. One day the king came to a wide river. He wished to go across so he called to an old peasant man who stood with his raft at the edge of the river. The king instructed him to take them across. The peasant graciously poled them across the river, all the while quietly chanting, repeating his mantra. The king listened and then corrected the old man for not saying the Lord's name correctly. "Thank you, oh great king, for helping me to chant the Lord's name properly," replied the old peasant, graciously accepting the correction.

They continued on their way and the old man continued to chant his mantra. The king again noticed that the peasant still wasn't saying the Lord's name correctly. "Oh yes, yes, of course. I do apologize. Thank you, my great king, for teaching me." The old man repeated his mantra carefully, mindful of the king's correction, but as he poled and chanted, he soon fell back into his old pronunciation. The king became irritated. After all, the man was saying the mantra all wrong!

By the time they reached the other side of the river the king was practically apoplectic with rage. He stormed off the raft and up the bank muttering to himself about the stupidity and ignorance of his peasants. The peasant turned around and began poling himself back to the other side of the river. The king was so upset that this stupid man couldn't even say the name of the Lord correctly that he turned around at the top of the embankment and angrily shouted to the old man who stopped his poling in the middle of the river to listen. The king yelled the correct pronunciation to the peasant, but the peasant didn't seem to understand what the king was saying. He cupped his hand to his ear and leaned toward the direction of the king. Again the king shouted the mantra, correctly, admonishing the old man. The peasant shook his head. He still couldn't seem to hear the king so he laid down his pole, stepped off the raft, and walked across the water toward the king. Seeing the peasant walk upon the water toward him, the king was stunned. "Please forgive me, my great king," apologized the old man reaching the shore. "Please teach me."

The king rushed down the embankment and fell to his knees, kissing the old man's bare feet. "No, no, no!" cried the king. "It is I who am ashamed. It is I who needs to be taught. You chanted from the purity of your heart. It is you who has true devotion, not me. Please, won't you teach me?" The king stayed with the old man and became his disciple.

Baba's stories always touch me deeply. Sometimes they are so wonderfully humorous, and sometimes I cry because the simplicity and compassion of his teachings reach right into my heart. God, I miss him so much. I wish that I could see him again in his physical form. But he spoke the truth when he said that he would be with us even more strongly when he was gone, and he gave the greatest gift when he gave us Gurumayi. If Baba was missing at all in my life these past nine years or so, it was because I *chose* not to see him or to think of him. Yet when I've turned to him, he is always there. And now, so is Swami Chidvilasananda, his successor, known as Gurumayi. She is Baba and what a beautiful and resplendent representation she is of the Divine Self in human form.

Yogi Bhajan, head of the 3HO organization, once said that if you are truly loved you don't have questions. I think I now understand that statement. Dearest, most beloved teacher, my guru, my Baba Muktananda, you gave me understanding and consequently compassion and patience. You showed me my Inner Self. Now, if only I'd remember to look inside and see it, I'd have more compassion and patience for myself as well as others in these trying times! My prayer, as I stand in this cramped, dank toilet in the middle of the great Southwestern desert, makes me smile. Yes, I gained a sense of humor through you and Neil. I just wish the two of you could have been friends. But that was then and this is now, yes?

"You wanted to know and understand who or what God is," Grace reminds me. "You wanted to experience the rites of passage that Joseph Campbell wrote and spoke about. You entered the dark tunnel some years ago and thought you were entering it alone, but that wasn't really true, was it?"

No, Grace, I wasn't alone. For a long time I thought I was. It felt that way as a child because I thought God was somewhere I wasn't. I thought I had to earn that great love from someone or something distant and judging. I thought God would take his love away if I was bad and didn't do as I was told. I thought the same thing of my parents—abandonment and conditional love. Thankfully, I became suspect of those priests and teachers who preach conditional love and ugly punishment, and I've learned to view both the Catholic Church and my parents with love and compassion.

"At least you try, honey." Thank you, G.A.

Paul Zweig, a most beautiful spiritual devotee and a great man, told a story about an incident he witnessed. Baba was giving darshan one evening—welcoming people and talking to them as they pay their respects—and a distraught man suddenly got up and began yelling at Baba. Baba watched the man calmly as he threatened Baba, saying, "What if I pulled a gun right now?!" Baba looked at him and said simply, "Then I shall die loving you." Through Baba's example, through the teachings of the great sages and saints, I have been given true understanding. And because of Baba, I realize now, I've never ever really been alone.

The thought of Baba's face crinkling up, his shoulders jiggling in amusement, makes me giggle. His shoulders used to shake and jump when he tried to contain his joy. What a great guy he was, a living embodiment of the Divine Self in the body of a human being. He was a full-tilt-boogie example of matter and spirit. His humanity made him accessible and his divinity made him a realized example of what is truly possible as a human being. And what an organizer! He was a sensational CEO, in his orange silk *lungi* (Indian-style pants), flowing shirts, shawls, his tinted glasses, and jaunty knit cap, moving sometimes more than 2,500 people through programs, delicious meals, and great talks. A deep and satisfying sigh comes out as I think of him, and I stretch my body. Life sure is a great experience. I had no idea when I was a child that my life would be what it is today.

No matter how difficult or painful the past has been, I am grateful that I have chosen to examine my life, face whatever frightens me, seek a spiritual path and live it everyday, and consequently undergo a transformation. And I am eternally grateful and thankful for all the good teachers and mentors and coaches who have helped me to grow and understand myself. I feel so sad for my father and others who think investigation of one's mind and emotions is for "crazy people." I wish with all my heart that those who are fearful and scared could take the chance and move toward the fearful rather than run the other way. But I do understand the running away too: "Been there, done that" myself.

Baba took *mahasamadi* (leaving his physical form) in October of 1982. Then came the separation from Neil in April of 1983 and the finalized divorce in 1984. At the time, I thought I was okay. Looking back, I now realize that I was spinning out of control, spinning in and out of frustrating, unsatisfying relationships, hoping to repeat the past. But it didn't work; it didn't work at all. And to top off everything else, my creative work stopped as well. Not working for three years can scare the hell out of you, especially since my identity was totally de-pendent on working.

My dreams held furious, destructive images and during the day I was a couch potato, never getting out of my robe, not able to do any-thing other than wander around the house. I reminded myself of a fal-low field, and I became scared that nothing more would grow.

In later dreams, I looked up at a great phoenix midst the clutter and rubble of my life with nothing else in sight, a blue haze all around. In still another dream I was treading in a sea of pearlescent blue water with no land in sight. The dream scared me—they all scared me—but slowly, with help, I began to accept my fate, and eventually took the dreams as a good omen. What else was I to do? Everything had crashed around me. Everything that had brought me happiness in the past was now gone, taken away. I fought against change by trying to re-create the past, but it didn't work. I just wound up a lump of flesh with no enthusiasm for anything. My mind and emotions had no energy for life, for anything really.

Slowly, over the year, my dreams showed me that change was taking place, deep inside. In my dreams and through meditation I found myself in new, unfinished buildings, new construction sights waiting to be finished, unfamiliar houses with long corridors that led to all kinds of interesting rooms. I dreamed that a beautiful white cobra with green eyes was seated in front of me and suddenly lunged at my face intending to eat me, and I wasn't at all afraid! In fact, in subsequent dreams I called upon the white cobra as a friend and protector. I became attractive again in my dreams, and I had confidence and curiosity as I searched the various rooms. The color blue was often present, and Baba Muktananda's voice would be in my ear, or I'd be wearing a string of blue pearls—a sign of the Self.

Baba didn't hold much weight with Western psychology. His human experience was that the Self was enough. Negative thoughts and feelings needed to be replaced with positive thoughts and feelings. "Remember," he would say, "God exists within you, *as* you." Baba and his teachings, coupled with the work I undertook in psychological therapy, gave me strength, became the vehicle through which I made the dark and fearsome rite of passage, a transformation that is still happening today. I wouldn't have been able to go through the challenges I have encountered without Baba's teachings and without the living example of a practical spirituality, coupled with the sound advice, support, and loving help from Blanche, Marilyn, Roger, and Hal, my four "head doctors," and the love and understanding of Nancy, Ellen, and my family of friends. I am only as strong as my understanding, my choices, my beliefs, my experiences, and my faith. Everything I have experienced in this life, and even past ones, has led me to this moment and has enabled me to make choices. Ah yes, choices! And decisions too. It took so long to understand that choices and decisions can be either freedom or slavery, depending on how you deal with them. I wish they taught decision making in school.

RIGHT NOW, STILL in this dank, cramped toilet somewhere in the desert, the decision to calm and focus my stressed-out emotions was uppermost in my mind, that and washing my hands of the grit that feels embedded in my skin. I don't want to look in the clouded mirror that is glued to the crumbling wall, so I keep my eyes averted. I don't want to lose the soft feeling that has come over me while thinking about Baba. As I look around for something with which to dry my hands, it occurs to me that this cloudy, distorted mirror might actually make me appear normal!

"What the hell," boomed Chuck Moses, "grab a glimpse."

My reflection startled me. Expecting disaster, I didn't look half bad! With no paper towel to be found, I dried my hands on my frazzled hair, staring at my image in the warped, foggy mirror.

My first experience of verbalizing thoughts and feelings while looking into a mirror came one summer evening when I was a young girl. I was in pain, deep psychological and psychic pain. I conversed— actually, vented is more accurate—with my image in the mirror of the medicine cabinet in the small bathroom of our house on Elmont Lane, in Crestwood, Missouri. I exploded, releasing all the pent-up feelings stored inside, saying all the things I wanted to say to my fam- ily and God but couldn't. I surprised myself at how articulate my anger was, and how intense. After running out of steam, my face was all red and blotchy and swollen with spent emotion, but I felt better, lighter. Releasing all the hurt, all the venom and anger had helped. After that, home alone, venting to my image in the mirror became my safety valve.

I'd even wait for my family to leave so I could be alone. Then I'd go to the bathroom and look into the mirror and wait. It usually didn't take long before the emotions came up, thoughts and feelings that I couldn't or wouldn't say to whoever was the source of my pent-up hurt, anger, frustration, and rage. Then, venting away, I'd watch my face as it contorted in peculiar ways, changing colors. I'd hear the searing, sometimes harrowing, tone of my words and feel satisfaction from saying them. It was during one of these mirror sessions that I realized I wanted to kill. I knew I wouldn't, but I was taken aback by how deeply I felt the need. I felt the hate *and* the hurt, and I wanted someone else to hurt too, just like me.

I was raised in a house where one of the rules was "Children are to be seen and not heard." And if you weren't good and didn't obey, then came, "Wait till your father gets home!" which meant some kind of physical punishment. Being able to talk back to an adult was forbidden. In fact, any expression of anger or frustration was discouraged. It was accepted that my parents could get angry but my sister and I were not allowed. Perhaps that's why we got so angry at each other, with what I now know is called "displaced" anger.

Not being able to express anger or upset created a lot of stress, and as a result, I didn't learn how to argue or express my feelings appropriately. Besides, it was drilled into us that it wasn't "ladylike" to behave that way, and that it was disrespectful. I was raised to believe that behaving like a lady was one of life's most important rules. As a result, shutting down these forbidden emotions became the order of the day.

It occurred to me that my unique brand of therapeutic Krazy Glue really did hold me together, that and becoming an actress. Becoming an actress had saved my life, had led me to psychology and to an appreciation and understanding of the mystery of human behavior.

The "why" of things has always been important to me, perhaps because adults never answered me as a child, and when they did, I knew it often wasn't the truth. So what if other people thought I was looney tunes, talking out loud to myself, meditating, venting my feelings, immersing myself in the philosophies and religions of the world, or mimicking the various voices in my head while staring into mirrors. At least I got the anger out. I even learned to kneel at my bedside and pound my mattress. Talking things through, learning to express feelings appropriately, and getting truthful answers to questions all go a long way toward emotional stability.

"Let's get out of here," Moses, the Pusher, commanded.

"You got it, Chuck," I said, taking one last look in the mirror before flinging open the dirty, white-painted door. Stepping out into the harsh glare of the Arizona sun, I found everyone else waiting for me. The Mazda suddenly roared out with Chris in the lead as the Porsche gingerly followed, heading for the highway. The plumes of dust, grit, and heat smacked my face.

"How do you feel?" Gary asked as he rounded the driver's side.

"Better," I answered, reaching for the car door handle. Suddenly, without warning, I leaned against the hot metal of the car and started bawling. Gary stood at the door of the driver's side and peered at me, waiting. Buddy drunkenly lurched toward me from the back seat of the car, hoping, I suppose, to give me some doggie comfort or perhaps to just get out of the car. He probably was thinking he had to get out; everything was so crazy and unfamiliar.

"Get back," I blubbered as I pushed hard against his weight. He didn't budge. "Gary, help me!" I cried. "Buddy's gonna get out of the car!"

Gary rushed over and pushed against the poor dog's chest, barely managing to restrain him. "Grab for the leash," he ordered. "I'll take him for a quick walk." Dulcie and Max didn't even look up from their supine positions as Gary grabbed Buddy's leash.

I slumped into the car seat and allowed myself to cry some more, convinced I'd done irreparable damage to the animals. By the time Gary got Buddy back in the car, my nose was so stuffed I could neither blow nor breathe.

"You have hyperseemia," he announced breathlessly as he climbed in and started the car, heading toward the highway.

"I haff *wad?*" I growled stuffily, reaching for more tissues.

"Eat something. Get a piece of fruit or something out of the cooler. We'll be in Flagstaff in a couple of hours."

"Hyperseemia?" I asked archly, staring at the ceiling of the car. "You mean, that *hypoglycemic* thing?"

"Yeah, that . . . thing. You and Dontzig get it like clockwork."

"Mind if I play some music?"

"Of course not," he replied smoothly.

I slipped Aretha Franklin's *What You See Is What You Sweat* cassette into the tape deck, leaned back, and began chomping down on potato chips and peeling an orange. My eyes suddenly felt leaden (hallelujah) and I let them close against the burning light and harsh landscape as Aretha wailed a Bacharach–Sager–Roberts song:

This is my life . . . and it's my right to live the way I want to live each day. . . . And this is my song. . . . And for too long I sang some-one else's melody. . . . Somehow I took myself for granted in some-one else's eyes . . .

Listening to the lyrics I realize how true it was of me, and of my relationship with Neil. I was Neil's actress. In order for us to be to-gether, he wrote for me, and he wrote brilliantly. He knew that being an actress was important to me, but he was in conflict about my working and being away from home. It was a maddening, complex problem for both of us because we respected each other's talent and loved being together. Privately we had a great time too: fun, great sex, deep conversation, enjoyment of the girls. Yes, he required all my at-tention, time, and energy when he wanted it. And yes, there was little room left over for my friends, my interests, my private time.

. . . I saw reflections of the girl I was. . . . Caught me by surprise . . . seein' a woman who's defined by you . . .

Is that what I saw in the mirror the morning of my thirty-ninth birthday? I remember that moment so vividly, stopped dead by my own image in the mirror. Where had I gone, the me that used to be recognizable to me, that pleased me and made me feel good about myself? Where was the familiar Marsha, I wondered? I couldn't relate to my image at all that morning. Then began a terrible, terrible year, the start of an odyssey through the dark tunnel. I felt I had no sexual appeal; I felt down, depressed, sorry for myself, angry, upset, panicked, scared, even terrified—you name it—if it was negative, I felt it. Little did I know I had started menopause, and what's worse, I didn't know a thing about it. My mother had never mentioned it and neither had any doctor. My periods were normal and painless. Who knew!

"REMEMBER THE DOOR incident?" G.A. asks with a chuckle. "That was one of my favorites."

Mine too! I don't remember what Neil and I were arguing about, but he started to walk out of the bedroom; I was so angry I slammed the door behind him and had no intention of letting him come back in the room. There was silence for just a beat. Then through the door I hear his muffled, somewhat pleading voice, "Marsha, open the door?" Instantly, I opened the door and said, "Okay," as if he'd just asked if I wanted to see a movie. The moment broke us up. That was a milestone for me, instant gratification for someone who typically couldn't even get in touch with her anger until two or three days after some incident. I was so excited and pleased with myself. I had gotten angry, said my piece, slammed the door, and violà! immediately opened the door with a big smile on my face. Anger all taken care of, thank you! I could tell I was getting healthier as indicated by the shorter and shorter time it took for me to get in touch with my anger.

"You had a terrible fight one night, though." Anna's voice sounds so painfully sweet.

She's right. I'd come home from the studio and the house was quiet. "Where's everybody?" I asked Reddie, our cook and housekeeper. She seemed a bit anxious and told me Neil had left a letter for me on the breakfast table.

It was written on a yellow legal pad. He basically had decided he wanted a divorce, the reason being that I hadn't returned his phone call that day at work. He also wrote that perhaps I should be married to someone younger, someone who didn't feel bothered by having his wife work. I tried to eat some dinner, but my hands shook so badly I poked my lower lip with my fork. So much for eating.

I decided to write a letter back and placed it on his desk, informing him that I had no idea that he'd called that day, that if he didn't want to be married, fine, but *I* was not packing a bag and leaving as he suggested. *He* could pack a bag and leave since it was he who didn't want to be married anymore. I was staying. I was staying because that's the commitment I made and why on earth would he think I wouldn't return his phone call!

We made up and the whole incident was forgotten, but problems lingered, like his insecurity about age and his feelings for Joan, which he hadn't really sorted out because he remarried so quickly, even picking the same wedding ring for me that he had given her. Her death had left him with a deep sense of abandonment that no amount of love, assurance, surrender, and commitment could erase, and it took its toll on both of us.

Neil is incredibly verbal and facile with words and his mind works in a completely different way than mine. Therefore arguing with him wasn't at all easy. I found it easy to be flexible, whereas he had difficulty with that. He handled being successful and adored with ease, it seemed to me, because he had been successful for so long. I felt incredibly uncomfortable and undeserving of success and adoration. He spent a lot of hours working by himself, which was not my modus operandi. When he came out of his office having worked hard on a play or screenplay, he wanted me there waiting so we could spend time together. And when I wanted to have an office outside our home, like he had, he became upset.

I'd found a little stone cabin in Topanga that looked like a doll's house. I wanted it as a place to meditate, draw, paint, write, commune with the wild nature of the canyon, and be in a different world from Bel-Air with servants and gardeners and opulent wealth. I wanted some kind of safe haven that I could go to during the day—not every day—someplace that was private and mine. He didn't understand why I needed to have a space that was all my own away from the house and suggested I make an office for myself in what had been Ellen's bedroom and was now a guest room. But through all the differences we learned from each other and loved each other and had wonderful times together as well.

Why was I so scared of him, fearful of his disapproval? Because the bonding pattern we had created was one of patriarchal controller and dutiful needy daughter.

"Yes. Because in your mind," Grace concurs, "he was the grown-up and you were the child."

It was the kind of relationship I'd known before, but at the same time, didn't know at all. Gary was quite different in how he dealt with me, although he picked out my clothes, just like Neil. But Gary was a contemporary, a peer, a pal, an understanding friend, a rebel, a misunderstood self who didn't make demands that were counter to my desires and my needs. Gary represented something quite different; I looked up to him as well because of all he had been through with his family. Of course, I looked up to Neil too. He was from another generation. He was successful and powerful and a protector, and everyone thought him a genius, a great man, a loving father, which he was. Everyone felt that way, including me. He was the father I wished for but never had; he was a wonderful and sexy husband as well. I was the inexperienced girl scared of success, the naive but determined head-over-heels-in-love student, just like in *Pygmalion*. And I reminded him of Joan.

My life with Neil was full—full of parenting two beautiful girls into womanhood, full of his work and our work, and full of the running of the house. None of which I had done before! It was *all* wonderful, and all difficult, and we spent the majority of our years together very happily.

But then Nancy grew up and went off to college, and Neil turned to me one day and said, "We have to find new reasons to be together." Ultimately, after some nine years together, I wasn't what he really needed or wanted. When we first met in October of 1973, he had just buried his first wife of twenty years that previous July, but hadn't really grieved her death. At the time, I didn't realize how powerful a presence she was for him, nor did I realize how necessary it was for him to be married and continue the life that he had with Joan. I only saw this extraordinary man of wit and sensitivity who was totally charming and sad and very caring. It was instant chemistry between us, at least *I* thought it was; he was smitten with me and I with him. I can't really explain *why* the chemistry was so strong; it just was. I suppose you could say it was destiny; it certainly felt that way to me.

After all, I jumped Neil Simon from behind in an alley in broad daylight the first day I went to work for him. He brought out the kid in me that day. I felt about fifteen years old at the time, although chronologically I was twice that. I didn't even think about it, jumping him, I mean—I just did it. It was a totally spontaneous impulse that just seemed the right thing to do at the time.

We'd taken a break during the first day's rehearsal of his new play *The Good Doctor* and Neil had gone somewhere outside. When I noticed he wasn't in the theater, I felt compelled to find him so I went outside too, hoping I might "accidentally" run into him. I ran across West 46th Street to one of those corner stores in New York City that sell just about everything from newspapers to condoms to children's candy. While I waited to pay for my gum, I searched the streets through the window of the shop, hoping to catch a glimpse of him, but I didn't see him anywhere. Drat. Otherwise it was a beautiful Indian-summer day in October and the world looked mighty fine to me.

I took a deep breath and let out an audible sigh as I left the shop and started to cross the street just as a cab came careening around the corner and almost took me out. I'd just begun to breathe normally again as I rounded into the alley that led to the stage door, and there he was, just ahead, ambling toward the back of the theater. His head was bent, his left hand was in his chino pants pocket, and his right hand was patting down the funny little curl his dark hair made at the back of his neck. His shoulders were hunched forward, and although his walk was definitely sexy, the back of his body sent a message: tired and sad. He was tired and sad for good reason. Joan, his wife of some twenty years, had just died in July. She had been ill with bone cancer for well over two years. He had two daughters, Ellen and Nancy, to look after. When we said hello that first day, I'd noticed his eyes were very sad; it was easy to see his pain even though I didn't know him.

As I watched him walk ahead of me, I suddenly felt like a kid who wanted to make someone happy, so I took a skip and ran up and jumped him from behind there in the alley, scaring him half to death. I didn't intend to scare him; I intended to playfully surprise him, but I scared the bejesus out of him, practically giving him a heart attack. His immediate response was unadulterated fear. The spontaneous sound he let out stunned me. "Of course!" I thought. "He thinks I'm a mugger!" As he brought his arms down from over his head and straightened up from his crouched position, I blurted out, "I'm so sorry! I didn't mean to scare you." He recovered a bit and a charming, lopsided, shy smile played at the corner of his mouth.

"I thought you were a mugger," he replied breathlessly as his hand again went to his hair, patting it down.

"Want some gum?" I sheepishly asked as color started to return to his face while mine was crimson. I guess you could say I bowled him over. And I'm glad I did it, even though he was a complete stranger.

"Well, not a *complete* stranger, if you know what I mean."

True, G.A. We definitely had some kind of deep mysterious connection. Otherwise why did the touch of his hand on my shoulder that first day of rehearsal affect me so deeply?

I didn't know any of the other actors seated around the table that first day, and I didn't know Neil. But as A. J. Antoon, our director, called us all back to the table to resume the second reading of the play that day, Neil uncrossed his long legs and got up from his chair. He then cleared his throat and walked around the long side of the table, stopping directly behind me. As he thanked us, saying that he loved us and what he was hearing, he put his hands lightly on my shoulders. Without hesitation, I reached across my chest with my left hand and gently patted his fingers, in a rhythm that was both ancient and familiar. As I did this, I felt a sharp, clear, recognizable feeling. I had made this gesture, this exact gesture, before.

Immediately dropping my hand, I lowered my head because my face was blushed with heat. My heart was pounding, and as I looked around the table at the other actors to see if anyone else had caught the intimacy of the moment, no one else's eyes met mine. As Neil finished speaking and conferred with A.J., I touched my cheeks with both hands. My face felt so hot I excused myself from the table and hurriedly went to the ladies' room.

"My God," I whispered out loud as I moved away from the table. What was that? What just happened? Reaching up and patting his hand like that—way too intimate—I thought; I don't even know the man. But it had happened spontaneously; it felt so familiar, so old, as if I had done it a thousand times before.

I took stock of myself in the mirror of the ladies' room and fluffed my hair, murmuring to myself, "*Twilight Zone* time" and told myself "get a grip." Purposefully, I went back to my seat at the table, determined to be diligent, focused, and concentrated on the second act. What I didn't realize at that moment was that I couldn't "get a grip" at all: I was gone—long gone—head-over-heels in love.

PERHAPS NEIL FELL in love with me and wanted to marry because he understood his need for continuum, his need to replace Joan so he wouldn't feel abandoned. Perhaps he didn't really feel as romantic about me as I felt about him; perhaps he wanted more than anything to continue his life the way it was before Joan died. And perhaps too he wouldn't have gotten married so quickly if it hadn't been for

Ellen and Nancy wanting us to. However, I didn't really see any of that back then because I was madly in love with someone I wanted to share the rest of my life with.

Whatever the reasons, the most important thing about it all is that I grew up in my marriage to Neil Simon a much better person than when I went into it. In retrospect, with the clarity of the psychotherapy work I've done, I now know that I was drawn to, and drew to myself, someone who personified everything I thought I wasn't. And I can be honest with myself and say I was scared of the film world I had just entered when I met Neil and I wanted protection. Neil was a great protector. He can be a terrifically affectionate, warm, and sexy guy who loves women and loves being taken care of by them. And I loved knowing I could make that kind of commitment and I did it very well for a period of time. Besides, I loved Ellen and Nancy instantly as well, and they wanted me in their lives and have continued to want me in their lives, thank God.

When we were a family, I identified with the girls when we went out in public. I held back to walk with them, took their hands, protected them from the shoving and pushing, feeling the shoves and pushes from the crowds myself. I certainly didn't identify with Neil; I didn't know how because he was so powerful and important, and I didn't feel that way about myself at all. Neil was scared and insecure just like me, but I didn't see him that way when we first met. However, I think that during most of the years we spent together, we were in the same place: in deep romance about life and in love with each other.

I thought it would last forever. It was supposed to. We were crazy about each other. I lived for him and I did it willingly. I don't know when it was exactly that I slipped away from myself.

"Yes, you do. When you turned down *Norma Rae*." Maybe, G.A., but maybe I didn't take myself for granted, like in the song; maybe I didn't *have* myself in the first place. I was scared of all the attention over *Blume in Love* and *Cinderella Liberty*. And yes, then there was *Norma Rae*. I wanted to do that film so badly but I didn't want to risk the marriage. It would mean eight weeks on location and no visit from Neil.

And there were Ellen and Nancy to think about. Ellen was away at college, and Nancy was home, but in school. I just didn't take care of myself when I was taking care of everyone else. I did this willingly though. I made those choices and decisions myself. That earnest little self of me was determined to do right by my family. So if becoming Neil's acolyte—a good wife, a good mother, a good student—if sacrificing and surrendering some of my own needs and wishes was necessary for the family's happiness at that time, so be it. Besides, from the moment I saw him no other man interested me the way he did.

"Well, what about . . . ?" Be quiet, G.A. Shadow Man was different and at a different time. Completely different and you know it.

"You thought Ben Bradlee was interesting, and don't say you didn't."

I danced with Ben Bradlee *once* the night I met him at a very large party. That was it. We had an interesting conversation and I found his candor stimulating.

"But you couldn't tell Neil that, could you." No. Whenever any past relationship came up in conversation, or any talk about attractive men, he didn't like it. It took him a long time to accept that Gary was my family and a true friend. Neil came from another generation. People his age weren't friends with their exes.

Neil hated it when I told him the truth about Al Freeman; but I told him because he asked and I didn't know he would react so strongly. He couldn't grasp the idea that I had a life before I met him. Fortunately, Gary and Gary stuck it out with me, although Gary Campbell was hurt that I withdrew into the relationship for a while. Neil eventually became friends with them and always included them on his opening night guest list. When we divorced he told Gary that he wanted to have the kind of relationship with me that Gary and I have, but I don't think it was possible for him. Ultimately he couldn't accept Baba in my life either.

Grace is correct though, when she says I didn't see Neil clearly back then. I didn't see his insecurity; I saw only his power, his demands, and his need to control. I saw my father in those moments and that's what triggered my feelings of claustrophobia and anger. Those moments are good examples of the bonding patterns in relationships that Hal taught me about.

"Didn't you see him clearly the first moment you looked into his face?"

Gosh, G.A., that very first moment, seeing Neil? . . . Yes, I did see him clearly. I saw the sadness and fragility and . . . the charm too.

It must have been August, late August 1973. I'd come back to New York City after shooting *Cinderella Liberty,* thinking I was going to San Francisco for a second season with A.C.T.

My new agents, Phyliss Wender and Jean Guest, called and said that Neil Simon's new play *The Good Doctor* might interest me. What was odd about this comment was that Eli Wallach had said exactly the same thing to me in Seattle during shooting the film some weeks before.

"But I want to go back to A.C.T. I love repertory," I told Jean and Phyliss.

"And you probably will go back," they replied. "But it's important to audition for Neil Simon and his producer Manny Azenberg; they don't know who you are. And the play is a series of vignettes so you'd get to play more than one part, a mini version of repertory. Besides, the casting people think you're a California actress."

A California actress?! Here I'd been struggling and working my tush off for years in New York, hoping to be taken seriously, and just because I got lucky and shot two pictures in the same year they think I'm a "California actress"!

I went to the audition having studied the "side" I'd been given. It was for a segment of the play called "The Seduction." I hadn't read the whole script, but didn't really worry about it because it was a series of vignettes and, truthfully, I figured I had a job already in San Francisco at A.C.T.; so I'd go and read for Neil Simon, Manny Azenberg, and the director A. J. Antoon, and then I'd be headed back West.

There's nothing like already having a job to raise one's confidence level.

I blew into the theater via the stage door and plopped down on a rickety chair. Suddenly the "powers that be" walked right past me without so much as a hello. I looked up at them, or rather the backs of their heads, hoping to recognize Neil Simon since I wasn't at all sure what he looked like. The last person filing through the door suddenly turned back.

"Aren't you the girl from *Love in Blume?*"

I was momentarily jolted by his reversal of the title of the movie (*Blume in Love*). "Ummmm, hmmmm," I answered, nodding my head. He ducked out of sight and shortly I was called to the stage. I stood in the glare of some overhead lights and looked out into the dark of the theater. I couldn't see a thing. God, I hate auditions. I read the scene they had provided partnered with the stage manager. After I finished, a voice from the dark asked, "Would you read the next scene please?"

"What next scene?" I replied. "I was only given this one." There was some mumbling and murmuring.

"If you like," I suddenly offered, feeling no fear, "I'll read it for you cold. I don't mind. I just won't know what I'm reading." More murmuring.

The stage manager gave me another side; this one was called "The Governess." A young man with an open, sweet face and a full head of thick curly black hair came to the lip of the stage and introduced himself. "Hi, I'm A. J. Antoon, the director." He gave me a quick rundown on what the scene was about. I quickly looked it over.

"Would you like more time to study it?" came another faceless voice as A.J. receded into the dark.

"Nah," I answered, scanning the dialogue, "I'll just go for broke."

"Whenever you're ready," said the stage manager, looking at me rather oddly.

The freedom I felt was exhilarating. It was so rare! I really didn't care about the outcome—that was the secret. I was confident of my own talent and it didn't matter so much to me whether these strangers approved of me or not. Looking the stage manager in the eye, I read "The Governess" scene without a care in the world.

A man stepped out of the dark and into the spill of light from the stage. It was Neil Simon.

"So you're from California?" he asked.

"Noooooo," I answered, "I'm from New York. I've lived and worked here for quite some time now." Neil told me later he turned to Manny and A.J. and said, "Hire that girl; I'm going to marry her." I was to start rehearsals on October 3, 1973. What I didn't know then was that I'd be married to Neil Simon on October 25.

The table for the first day's reading of *The Good Doctor* was placed on the stage of the Eugene O'Neill Theatre, which Neil happened to own. It was a rather drab theater with the interior painted all shades of one color, beige. I didn't know that first morning as I looked up and around at his theater that my first foray into interior decorating would be the redecoration of the Eugene O'Neill Theatre.

All I knew on October 3 was that I had auditioned for the ensemble cast, with Christopher Plummer in the lead, and was the last actor hired for Neil Simon's new play *The Good Doctor.* I knew the cast was stellar. Christopher, Frances Sternhagen, Rene Auberjonois, and Barnard Hughes. In addition to not knowing that day that I'd be married and a stepmother in three weeks, and soon would learn how to redecorate a theater by just doing it, I also didn't know that day that Neil would write a scene for me called "The Audition" in which a young actress auditions for the playwright Chekhov by doing all the sisters in his play *The Three Sisters.* Such is life in the theater.

I can honestly say I love all actors. I also love the process by which a play comes together, and I love old theaters and old soundstages too. I especially love standing on the stage of an old theater with just the work light as my companion. I like to look all around me and out into the audience, the dark void, feeling the subtle presence of those who have been there before. And that was the way "The Audition" was staged: just me on the stage alone, dressed by Tony Walton and surrounded by his set and Tharon Musser's magic lighting design, looking out into the darkened theater, with the voice of Chekhov, as played by Chris, asking, "What are you going to do for the audition?" I answered, "*Three Sisters.*" "Which sister?" Chekhov asks. "All of them," I replied, and then proceeded to do the last scene of the play.

Theaters are not unlike churches or cathedrals. You step inside or on the stage and immediately feel a shift in the air. There is all about you that sumptuous smell of history, desire, and the emotional vibrations of hundreds of individuals who have "lived" there before. The word "hallowed" comes to mind.

There's this tangible emotional chord that exists between me and the experience of fulfilling a character, bringing her to life. This chord, this lifeline between myself and the process, the character and the space, becomes whole when the audience comes in. The celebration is most exciting when it is moved to respond with laughter and/or tears, and it's especially thrilling when the silence is palpable. The audience's responses become part of the dance of creation, expelling painful and/or joyful recognition of what it takes to be a human being. It's like magic when an audience or fellow actor responds in a way you least expect. And if there is to be magic, it sometimes happens on the very first day.

"There was magic all right!" I'll say, G.A. There was magic reading the play and there was romance magic as well. For me, each first day of rehearsal for a new play is like experiencing sex for the first time with a new partner. Feelings of vulnerability, insecurity, nerves, excitement, and giddiness race through my body, along with everything else that is humanly possible to feel. I worry that I wore "the right thing," that I might say "the wrong thing," and, most important, I always hope and pray that I will pass the test, that they will like me, that I will affect them, that I'll get a laugh. And when I go through those, I worry about whatever else usually makes me feel insecure. During work on an episode of *Frasier,* Jane Leeves asked me if I still get nervous. "Always," I answered. "It never goes away."

"Then how come your heart and hands weren't jumping all over the place when you got that phone call from the lawyer?" Gloria, the Collapser, whines.

Fear comes out of us in very different ways. If it's a really major fear, or major scare, sometimes we act differently. I tend to get very quiet and calm. *That* phone call, the one from Alan Alexander, our lawyer, came without warning. I guess I was in denial, whatever. I didn't see the signs.

"What a bizarre transition," quips G.A. "From the beginning of your relationship to the beginning of the end!" Yes, of course. You're right, G.A.—funny how the mind works.

I began to feel the strain of it all when I went to direct my first play in Jupiter, Florida. Neil thought it a good idea that I branch out; he said I wasn't going to be a movie star forever.

"I wish you'd understood that better, old girl." Me too, G.A. Another case of my impulsive personality blithely bopping around without a clue as to what's actually going on around me. I thought actors worked all the time if they're good, like the English actors do. I can be so dense sometimes.

There I was in Florida at the Burt Reynolds Theater, having agreed to direct a two-character, single-set play titled *Mass Appeal,* but because of the schedules of the play's two stars, John Travolta and Charles Durning, they needed to do the show during Christmastime. Well, that wouldn't work for me and the family, so I wound up directing the eight-character play, in four acts with four different sets, titled *Here Comes Mr. Jordan,* starring Robert Hayes and Jack Gilford.

"Jeez, that sounds hard. 'Specially for a first time." Thank you, Ed. Neil thought I was up to it though, so off I went to Jupiter, Florida, and off he went to Hartford, Connecticut, to try out a new play *Actors and Actresses.* He was snowbound and I was set bound, and actor bound: Jack Gilford and another character actor in the play didn't get along and tensions were building. Bob Hayes, the leading man, was trying to work through it all and I was trying to act professionally and be a referee at the same time.

By the second week or so, Neil was calling every night, upset that we were apart, and that he was having trouble with his play. We were both so wrapped up in our own problems and wanted the other to be supportive and helpful. Being apart only created greater tension. My friend Dixie Marquis came to Jupiter for a visit for a couple of days, and at one point we took a walk on the beach. When I got back to the room the telephone was ringing. Neil went ballistic that I hadn't been in my room, that I preferred Dixie's company to his.

"I think we'd better have a serious talk about our relationship when you get home," he said. The gauntlet of divorce had been thrown down again. I took a beat and found myself answering his challenge.

"Yes, I think you're right, Neil. I think we do have to sit down and have a serious talk." After saying it, I felt kind of okay because I'd stuck up for myself instead of feeling panicky and threatened and guilty that I'd done something wrong. Before I'd always been the one trying to make nice. This challenge of "divorce" came at a time when I had no more endurance or patience left in me. I was at my wits' end trying to get big, lumbering sets on and off the stage and, truthfully, I liked taking walks on the beach at night after a long day of problems and was tired of feeling guilty about it. I'd never challenged Neil's behavior when he went off in a mood. I'd never asked him not to work or not do something he wanted.

"Well, that's not totally true, old girl. You did ask him to stop off in New York before going on to England and Wimbledon."

That was because of his back, G.A. He had a bad back and that trip was important for us. I was to meet him in Italy. We were going there to spend time together, just the two of us, getting in touch with each other, finding new reasons to be married. He didn't do what I asked; he flew from L.A. and went to England and straight to Wimbledon the next day. When the phone rang at three in the morning I knew the news wasn't good.

He was on the floor of his hotel room, staring into the dead eye of some fish that the waiter had to put on the floor so he could eat. No Italy for us. No sex. No stroll down European streets. No nothing. He needed care and he needed it badly. It was serious. I flew to London and stayed there until he could get on a plane to go back home. I went to the theater at night by myself and tried to put on a happy face. If I showed my deep disappointment, he'd get angry and feel terrible, so I'd go into the bathroom and cry into those big fluffy towels while running the shower or bath. It was awful.

Eventually I went on to Italy and took Nancy with me instead. We had a great time, but I was worn out—worn out from work and worn out by fear and unexpressed anger and hurt. It was not a good thing, not a good thing at all.

I didn't stop to think and try to understand, to "see" what was behind it all. I didn't catch on to the fact that he was scared and insecure about his play, our relationship, his health, everything. I was scared too, and sadly I heard only a demanding and willful voice.

On the opening night of my play—I think it was Valentine's Day—Neil was supposed to come to Florida. We'd gone back and forth about it. At first I didn't want him to come because it was going to be a disaster. Then when I said okay, he didn't want to come. We finally agreed he'd come. On that day, Hartford, Connecticut, and all of the New England area, including New York, was hit by a blizzard. Manny Azenberg once said Neil and I probably would still be together if that blizzard hadn't hit.

After saying good-bye to the cast opening night, I drove to a scruffy fishing lodge in Key West that was a couple of hours away from Jupiter. I was in trouble, big trouble. I didn't want to go home to L.A., I didn't want to face Neil, and I didn't know what I wanted to do. I arrived at the lodge around one in the morning and fell asleep to the sound of raindrops hitting the leaves of a rubber plant that was outside the screened porch. I awoke the following morning at dawn and heard on the television that Tennessee Williams had died that night, having accidentally swallowed the cap from some eyedrops or something. I cried for a long time. I cried all the tension and tiredness of the past four weeks and the past eight years. After a couple of days of staring out at the Gulf I knew I needed a break and some help. I needed Neil to give me the time and understanding that I'd given him the first year of our marriage. I needed him to trust that our love was strong enough to weather the storms of a relationship, whether it was his grieving for Joan and wishing that I was her, or my midlife crisis, my need to be by myself to grieve for me, the girl who got married eight years before. Divorce wasn't an option. So after returning to L.A., when Alan called that day and informed me that I had to get a divorce lawyer, that Neil was divorcing me, I was stunned. I had no emotional reaction like screaming or yelling or bursting into tears. I just started to shake a little and then I stopped breathing. I didn't feel myself not breathing; I didn't feel at all. When I asked if Neil had gotten a divorce lawyer, Alan paused and said, "Yes." I told him that I didn't know any divorce lawyers and asked if he could recommend one, a woman lawyer. I don't remember much after that and I don't remember calling Roger Gould, my therapist; but I must have because I went to see him that night. I'd been going to Roger for about a year, I think, maybe more. Neil's therapist at the time recommended him to me. I'd had women therapists before Roger, and when I hit that midlife crisis birthday and acknowledged my ambivalent feelings about my marriage, I thought that going to a man might make a difference. He had written a book called *Transformations* that was the forerunner to Gail Sheehy's book *Passages*. In fact, she had interviewed him or read some of his work while preparing hers. I must have told him it was very important that I see him because I saw him that night and had never been to his office at night before.

I chose to sit in the exact center of Roger's brown leather couch. The therapy session that night was different from any I'd ever had. It seemed important, for some reason, to physically move carefully and slowly, to make each step a conscious choice and each gesture and movement a careful, conscious decision. My life had split apart with a single phone call. I didn't know it at the time, but it would take years to put myself back together.

It was strange going to Roger's office that late in the day—twilight time, literally and figuratively. Never having been in his office in the evening, the familiar room wasn't familiar anymore. It felt strange, shadowed by oncoming evening and two lighted lamps. I'd never seen the lamps lit before. There was a standing lamp across the room lighting nothing but a blank gray wall and the soft gray pile carpet. Waiting for Roger to come in, I remember saying to myself, "The wall's a blank. Fitting."

There was a table lamp next to me, and its soft glow gently embraced part of me, placing me half in light and half in darkness, giving me a kind of pale protection from this particular night. I heard the swoosh and hum of the speeding cars outside on Ocean Avenue. I looked to the picture window across the room; but the office was on the second floor so I could see neither the Pacific Ocean across the street, nor the lights of those speeding cars. All I saw was my shadowed reflection, indistinct and undefined.

I remember thinking to myself, They're going home. They're going home to their families, to lovers, children. Going home to dinner. And then I just stopped thinking, willing myself just to sit back and wait for Roger. I heard my breathing as I stared ahead, which drew my eyes to my chest, as if to make sure it was *my* breathing I heard. I remember being surprised that my heart wasn't noticeably pounding, that there were no sudden heaves, no shudders, no cessation of breath.

The door across the room opened and light beyond streamed in as Roger and one of his associates exchanged evening farewells. He emerged through the shadows to sit in his usual chair. We sat there in silence, waiting. Swoosh. Hum. Woosh. Dhrum. Nothing came to mind. Slowly, as if afraid my skin would break, I placed my hands at my sides. Then, mentally, carefully, opening my body, I looked at Roger, hoping that being physically open would open my mouth. The light from the table lamp continued its vigil, encircling a part of both of us as we waited for me to say something. I looked at his graceful, long lean figure and his gentle gaze and finally began to speak.

"I know something important is going on because I don't feel anything," I said softly and then stopped. The room became quiet again except for the muffled sounds of life going on beyond the picture window.

"Where are you, Marsha?" Roger asked softly. His question hung in the air between us.

"*Chorus Line,*" I replied simply. "I was thinking about a particular song from that show titled, 'Nothing.' I saw the show for the first time when it was in previews down at the Public Theater. Neil had been going down there because he was helping Michael Bennett with the book but no one was supposed to know.

"Michael and I had first met when he came to New Haven to help with *The Good Doctor* before the opening in New York. I remember him saying to me that the theater was such a great place to work because everyone helped each other. It was natural then that he asked me to come one night and see *A Chorus Line* and give him my thoughts. I told him that Cassie had to make the chorus line. She was one of the leading characters. It wasn't fair to the audience if she was cut from the line. It wasn't fair to all the performers who've come to New York hoping to make it in the theater.

"Michael argued that the ending was truthful, that most dancers do get cut. I countered with the fact that we all know how tough it is, the ones who stay and try. I shared with him a similar conversation I'd had with Mark Rydell. I tried to get Mark to change the ending of *Cinderella Liberty.* Having lived the character Maggie, I knew she should have learned *something,* some small glimmer, something from being loved and cared for. I was confident she'd show some kind of change, something. But Mark felt that life wasn't like that. I argued that the audience roots for Maggie and her sailor savior to make it just like we all do when we first fall in love. I asked Mark if he thought Maggie wasn't capable of changing, of learning something valuable from being truly loved by someone who knew everything about her. Mark decided to lay some dialogue over the last shot of the movie that suggests that Jimmy Caan's character was going to New Orleans to go after her. But that wasn't what I was trying to explain. It wasn't about a guy *saving* her. It's about her taking a small step to begin to save herself, by *not* running away. The same was true for Cassie and her learning to be part of the chorus line. I told Michael that life was difficult enough—we know that in spades. What we all need to be reminded of is the possibility of change. We need hope.

"Michael Bennett was there at the beginning of my marriage to Neil. He saw me through a difficult time, our first production together. Oh, he wasn't at the ceremony. Nobody was. Just us four—the family—Ellen, Nancy, Neil, and me. We were married in the criminal court building in downtown Manhattan, somewhere near Wall Street. A judge married the four of us. Judge Gold. We married the day before we left New York for New Haven. Afterward, we all went back uptown to the theater for rehearsal. Manny, Neil's producer, arranged for champagne and a cake, or that's what I remember. The company was gathered onstage with some staff, and Manny gave the toast.

"May the show run longer than the engagement!" We had known each other, Neil and I, exactly twenty-one days when we got married, and we'd postponed it a week. Michael Bennett came up to New Haven, and then I also remember him standing at my dressing-room door the night we opened in New York. 'Don't worry about the audience,' he said. 'Yes, a lot of 'em are dying to see who this young, unknown actress is who's married the famous Neil Simon after a three-week courtship. Fuck 'em. You go out there and do your job. That's what you're paid to do. And don't worry, you're good. Real good.'

"And I did too; I went out there and faced all of Neil's friends and colleagues of twenty some years, and his mother, *and* Joan's mother.

"And now . . . it's almost ten years later and I'm sitting in this office, having been told that Neil wants a divorce, and I'm trying to get in touch with my feelings."

"What happened today, Marsha?"

"I received a call from our lawyer, Neil's and mine, Alan Alexander, and he told me Neil wants a divorce and I have to get a divorce lawyer. Alan felt bad, I could tell. I think I must have started going numb then, 'cause I can honestly say that since that moment I've felt nothing."

"What does 'nothing' feel like?"

"I don't know. My mind's a blank. And so is that place that holds my feelings. Where is that place, really? Is it my heart? I have literally felt my heart hurt in the past, but not tonight. I was so sure Neil and I would last forever. In the first moments of grappling with the announcement of this . . . death, this end of the most important relationship of my life . . . you told me that once, remember, Roger? You told me that Neil was probably the most important relationship that I'll ever have . . . because it was important for me to learn to stay, not run away: stand toe-to-toe with Neil, you said; don't run away. You said that if I did leave, then it had to be a decision, not a reaction, that I should *decide* to *walk* out the door, not run out of it. . . .

"Anyway, all I can truthfully say is that I feel like I can't move. I'm in a kind of heavy ooze. A dark, green, gelatinous, sticky ooze. If I could move off this couch my foot might make a thick, slurpy, popping kind of sound."

I don't remember leaving Roger's office. I don't remember the ride home. I don't remember where Neil was. He wasn't home; he was away. If only I'd been wiser, more psychologically aware, perhaps I could have soothed his fears and maybe even met his needs without thinking and feeling like I was dying inside.

But, of course, that was exactly what was happening. The familiar me was dying along with the death of our marriage. I just didn't feel it then.

But Nancy and Ellen felt it. They felt it big time. Ellen was supportive at first, but after some months she became conflicted and felt she needed to take sides. It was understandable, but that didn't make it hurt any less. I learned something very important during that time. I learned to love even though I felt wronged and panicked that I would lose both of them. I had learned to love unconditionally from Baba and I was able to live it with the girls. And we are together today, stronger for our experiences, and I think more understanding and compassionate.

During the separation and divorce, Nancy went through a very difficult and painful time as well. Our divorce triggered something she had buried deep inside, and it was then that she finally was able to get in touch with her feelings about her mother's death and the kind of relationship they had and a lot of things that had been impossible for her to look at until then. I, on the other hand, began to spin out of control.

Nancy came to visit me in San Diego while I was performing Viola in my friend Jack O'Brien's production of *Twelfth Night*. She needed support too. It was such a painful and difficult time; she was dealing with it on a conscious level and I wasn't. I'd thrown myself into the work and partying so that I would have to neither think nor feel. She on the other hand had come to visit so we could share feelings and be with each other. By example, she helped me to slow down and take stock. I'd given a party for the cast and tried to kid myself that she would enjoy it too. I realized my mistake when I saw the deep sadness in her eyes as she quietly excused herself and went into the bedroom. That night I climbed into bed with her and held her and stroked her hair. I hadn't realized until that moment how deeply tired and sad I was.

In the ensuing year, I ran. I went back to smoking and drinking and picking hopeless situations with men. I kept trying to replace my marriage with another relationship, but that didn't work because I hadn't given myself the time to grieve—to grieve the death of my marriage and a relationship with a man I loved and, although I didn't know it at first, the death of the girl who had lived in that marriage.

Funny, isn't it, that I created—opted for—*chose* a protective, controlling, seductive, supposedly safe marriage just like I'd hoped for as a child. But ultimately it became painful and unsatisfactory for both of us. After that initial phone call, and the reality of a separation set in, I realized that I desperately needed some time to be alone, to be by myself. I went to the Bel-Air Hotel and stayed there for a couple of weeks. Neil and I spoke by phone and I had lunch one day at the house that was no longer mine. I asked him that day if I could stay at the house while he went to New York. He said no, probably because I couldn't tell him how much time I needed.

"If I don't do this," I told him, meaning taking time for myself, "I feel like I'm gonna die."

"Well how long are you talking about?" he asked. "Six days, two weeks, what?" I wanted to tell the truth so I said, "I don't know. I don't want to lie to you. I honestly don't know."

"Well, if it's going to be six weeks or longer, then I can't continue this way." I died a little that night.

CHAPTER EIGHT

DESTINY RIDES AGAIN

E eeyyyyaaaahhhhhooooooooo!"

"What! What is it?!" Being awakened from a heavy sleep by
a screeching, victorious sound pronounced with a Western
twang can totally disorient a person. Jangled, I sat up and looked
around. I was still in the car, it was still moving, and Gary was still
driving.

"Flagstaff!" he said. "We're head'n' into Flagstaff."

I closed my eyes and moaned.

"You got some sleep; that's good."

"Yeah, now I probably won't sleep tonight," I grumbled as I rubbed
my face. My eyes felt weird, crusty. I couldn't open them all the way.
"My eyes are funny."

"Not much further now. We're almost there."

"Flagstaff?" I asked.

"No! Santa Fe!" He was so cheerful I wanted to slap him. Instead I
washed my eyes with water using a paper towel. Eight eyelashes
looked back at me from their position on the wet towel.

"Jesus, my eyes are balding!"

"It's your mean dissipation that's causin' it," he chortled. "Just kiddin', just kiddin', Marsha May." I shot him a look, or rather, tried to,

through my crusty balding eyes. I'd been stopped dead at "dissipation" as opposed to "disposition," wondering what would either have to do with losing eyelashes.

"That's good luck, your eyelashes. We're gonna be there soon!" His good humor made me feel irritable and guilty for not sharing his enthusiasm. I'd probably say something bitchy if I answered, although my "mean dissipation" made me smile. I guzzled water instead and tried to stretch the skin around my eyes by blinking hard.

"Let's stop, stretch, and feed the dogs. What time is it?"

"Little after four. Look at those mighty fine pines."

"Mighty? Mighty fine pines? Since when did you start talking like Gabby Hayes?" I asked.

"They're ponderosa pine." There was no talking to him in my state of mind.

We parked in the shade of some of those mighty fine ponderosa pines while I fed the dogs and even Max ate a little. Being out of the car, stretching and stooping, started the blood circulating again. The change in the environment made me feel better, more hopeful that this move was the right one.

"What *are* you doing, Marsha May?"

"What does it look like? I'm trying to get some blood to my tush." I proceeded to jump and jog and hop through the trees and around the rocks and the dogs, stretching my arms, sides, and back. I quickly wore myself out and started to wheeze.

"Gosh," I gasped, "it's hard to breathe."

"That's what happens at this altitude," Gary responded. "You'll git used to it."

"Git?"

"You looked funny jumpin' and dancin' around out there," Gary said. "Like a kid. That nap did you good. Any dreams?"

"Nah," I answered, not wanting to revisit the depressing feelings about Neil's and my divorce. Soon we were back on the road and once more seat-belted in place, staring at the sleek back end of my Porsche as Chris, having changed cars with her husband, set the pace, and I wondered if my general behavior seemed strange to other people. Of course, I've always worried that my behavior might seem strange to other people, especially when I am starting a new project. As the years have passed this worry has lessened, but in 1973 at the first day of rehearsal for *The Good Doctor* I was my usual worried self. The only thing that ameliorated my anxiety was the reading itself.

Someone in the theater once said that we actors spend three and a half weeks of rehearsal trying to get back to that first reading, that we spend the rehearsal time re-creating that original virginal experience so we can do it eight times a week. At the first reading I listen to a play with an intensity that rarely exists in my daily life, unless I'm in a life-threatening situation. The first reading is a kind of meditation. Well, actually, I think acting is a meditation. But what transpired at the break that first day of rehearsal for *The Good Doctor* in 1973 was a kind of realization or transformation or maybe just destiny coming into play.

INSIDE THE THEATER everyone was gathered round to read the words of Neil's new play. This first reading is a sacred ritual that happens only once and can never be exactly repeated. Every part of my mind, body, voice, and spirit is on red alert, ready to record, react, adjust, taking in everything that's going on around me. I listen intently as the others read aloud. The voices in my head speak as well, alerting me to anything and everything, helping me to remember and record these virginal impressions. They alert me to bits and pieces of information that might aid my initial understanding of the material and my character's place in the story. I jot down anything and everything that comes to mind, hoping for the unexpected, the opposite, the surprise.

"I wish I could say that about life," Gloria, the Collapser, volunteers. "I don't like it when someone responds to me in a way I don't expect. I get scared."

"I don't like it either," Anna says. Now, why is that? I ask myself. Why do I get scared in life while I don't get scared in acting? I sup-

pose it's because while acting I have some kind of control over the situation so I feel safe. As a child, I had no control over my situation and
I didn't feel very safe when my parents sometimes behaved erratically,
especially when they had too much to drink. They could become angry or irritated or emotionally carried away for no apparent reason. I
didn't know then that liquor can change a person's behavior and personality. I only knew they had changed suddenly and their unex-
plained behavior scared me. These impressions from childhood stayed
with me for a long time, into my adult years, so that would explain
why I become nervous when people behave erratically or have too
much to drink.

Once, I became shockingly belligerent and aggressive when I had
too much to drink and behaved in a way I couldn't imagine myself
behaving if I had been sober. I went to an after-hours bar in L.A. with
some friends and they were serving a blue, psychedelic-looking drink.
I didn't feel drunk but practically came to blows with a tall, dark
woman who I thought was flirting with my date! It wasn't until the
next day that I realized how erratic and inappropriate my behavior
was, and that lack of awareness scared and embarrassed me. I wonder
if Mom and Dad ever realized how much their behavior could
change when they drank. I don't think they did.

"You behave differently when you act," Anna says. Yes, but acting is
different. When I'm acting, I'm in control, I'm making it up. That's it!
That's what has frightened me in the past—loss of control or being at
the mercy of someone who has no control. That would be very scary
to a young child, wouldn't it, Anna? "Yes, it's very scary when people
drink and get angry."

Well, acting isn't the same at all; you have to be very *in* control
when you act. You have to know what you are doing and what everyone else is doing on the stage at all times, otherwise someone could
get hurt. I remember the first time I got hurt in acting class; my acting
partner wasn't in control. It was a scene from *Cat on a Hot Tin Roof,*
and the actor playing Brick threw his crutch at me and hit me in the
eye. He felt terrible but I was the one who was bleeding!

In stage acting, you have to be perfectly in control in order to be able to "fly": it's a paradox (I think). Each performance is really a new experience, even though the words and moves are the same. That's the magic of theater. Each performance is new for me, as well as the audience, because the "dance" or "play"—the interaction between me, the other actors, *and* the audience—is informed and defined by whatever has happened to us that day and all the days of our lives. Once in a great while I have been lucky enough to totally lose myself (but not lose control) in this dance, this communication, this communion of spirit. When that happens, I "fly" during a performance like when it happened during *A Doll's House* and during a performance of *Cyrano*. I don't know how else to explain these special moments except to say that when they happen, I am not me; I'm the character and the witness as well. Everything that's happening feels effortless; no "acting" is taking place, just being. At times, I've been fortunate enough to get lost in the play during the first reading—not often, but often enough that I get excited, thrilled as I sit for the first time with the other actors and read.

"Honey," G.A. made the word sound like a declaration. "You started to fly the moment you met Neil and you didn't come down for years!" True, G.A., true. At that first day's reading I couldn't take my eyes off this magnet slash playwright as he sat listening to the reading of his play, and I found myself watching him intently as he sat slouched in his chair. He was totally absorbed in the reading of the play, which is what I should have been. His eyes were cast down, his chin was pressed into the palm of his hand, and his long legs were crossed as well. Fortunately he didn't notice my stare.

"Get a grip, girl!" came the barking voice in my head. "Concentrate! What's the matter with you?!"

What was the matter with me, indeed? During that reading I watched him every chance I had. Talk about no control! It was disconcerting to say the least, my attention being pulled in two different directions. When we took a break after reading the first act, I casually strolled up to him, feeling like a flake of metal drawn to a magnet. I tried to appear nonchalant and relaxed, but inside everything felt like those huge reverberating speakers that loom over the stage at rock concerts. Outside, calm; inside, a million decibels of reverb.

I remember coming home after that fateful first day and the phone was ringing as I came into my apartment.

"Hi, I was calling to ask you if you'd like to have dinner . . . but not now, it's too late . . . I did call earlier . . . to ask you to dinner . . . it's Neil."

"Ah-huh."

"Ah-huh? Does that mean, you know who it is and that's good, you want to have dinner?"

"Ah-huh . . . I mean, yes! As a matter of fact, I would like to have dinner with you, but not tonight, I just ate."

"Ah-huh," he replied. I laughed. He laughed. I was a goner. Inside, I was a teenager in the first flush of her very first romance, the Sandra Dee of West Seventy-second Street, gone bonkers over the handsomest, most popular fellow in school. On the outside, I did retain some semblance of maturity, I think. When I'd hung up the phone that night, I was so proud of myself because I'd made him laugh, something I considered a major feat. He has the quickest, wittiest mind of anyone I've ever met, but his shyness and vulnerability were evident as well. For me, our conversation was a dance of electric chemistry.

When I came into the theater the next morning, wearing a fabulous outfit (I hoped), Neil was seated in the front row, so I sat down right next to him. I'd sit next to him whenever I could. And when I was away from him I couldn't think of anything else. We'd look for each other and slip off to stairwells to cuddle. Yes, cuddle. We got caught in our first kiss on the stairs backstage by his assistant Jane who was as embarrassed as we were. Her blush was just a shade lighter than mine.

Fairly quickly I began to think I looked like an old woman! Well, not really, but my life and emotions were revved so high that I started to show the effects of some of the stress and strain happiness and life-changing events can manifest while trying to rehearse for a new Broadway play. God, when I think back on that time I'm amazed at the energy I expended just trying to keep up with my life. Thanks to the stress, my upper lip blew up so badly I couldn't eat, let alone kiss. I think I can safely say that my lip looked like a gargantuan bee had stung me.

"Cupid's arrow, no doubt," G.A. wryly answers.

If it was a sign to slow down, I was looking the other way, driving 110 miles an hour.

"What about Ellen and Nancy?" Anna suddenly asks.

"Yeah, what about them?" Ed responds.

Well, it was Ellen who had suggested to her father that he ask me out for dinner that first day. I remember how shy and somber she seemed when I was introduced to her. Her long, shiny brown hair was pulled up in a bun, she was wearing glasses, and had no makeup on. Because of her demeanor and her appearance, she seemed much older than her fifteen years. Both she and Nancy were very nice and pleasant but when I looked into their faces it was apparent that they were in deep pain. A great sadness shrouded their eyes. I wondered, *What was it like to lose your mother at such a young age, Ellen, fifteen, and Nancy, almost ten?* Ellen spoke for both of them most of that first time I was with them, but it was Nancy who, one night after dinner, asked the startling question.

"Why can't Marsha come and live with us?"

I'd stayed over a couple of nights during those first two weeks of rehearsal. It felt odd sleeping in Joan and Neil's bedroom, in their bed. Neil and I just cuddled and slept together those first few nights, and the girls had separate rooms on the floor above. Ellen and Nancy seemed to like me almost immediately, and I found myself paying careful attention to the dynamics of their relationship with their father and each other. Also, the same chemistry that existed between me and Neil was present with Ellen and Nancy, although not in the same way of course. I tried to be sensitive to how they behaved, what they said, and especially the way they said it.

One night we were all seated together in Neil's office. He decided to tell them about us, that we were in love, and he wanted us to get to know one another. They sat facing us on the couch, Neil sat at his desk, and I sort of leaned on him. Nancy still had her school uniform on, I think, and both looked incredibly sweet and earnest. I don't know what I expected, but I definitely didn't expect what happened next. After Neil spoke Nancy piped up, "Well, why doesn't Marsha come and live with us?" And Ellen immediately countered with "We won't tell our friends you're not married."

Neil and I talked long into the night and decided we would get married before we left for New Haven, the only out-of-town tryout that was scheduled before the play's opening in New York. This all transpired by the middle of the second week of rehearsal!

"Perhaps, my dear, Neil was pushed into it by his children? Has that ever crossed your mind?" Well, yes and no, Miss Havisham. Looking back now? Maybe. I think I was so . . . what? I suppose I felt so incredibly needed and wanted by the three of them that I didn't think of anything else. It all seemed so sure and right to me. I don't know why exactly, but that's how it felt. What I didn't know of course was what was ahead for all of us. I thought only of those sweet and loving children asking me to be a part of their lives. I was incredibly touched, and grateful in a way. They made me feel worthwhile. Besides, for some reason, I could intuitively relate to them.

"But my dear," Glinda asks, her voice quivering, "why didn't you stop and think of what you were doing?" I just didn't, Glinda. Like I said, it simply felt so right. I wanted very much to be wanted. I wanted to matter to them. I don't know, fate, destiny, timing—they all conspired, bringing me to that moment.

I remember calling Blanche Saia, my first therapist, who was still practicing in the same place. I knew I'd need help taking on an instant family, and she'd had children as clients; so it seemed perfectly natural to seek her advice about Ellen and Nancy. I remember sitting in her office on the Upper West Side off Central Park West and announcing my plans to marry. I was sure it was the right thing to do. And it was.

I'm sure of that today as I drive along, headed for God knows what kind of life. The marriage didn't last forever, but my life with Ellen and Nancy continues to this day and is still the most important thing to me.

I REMEMBER THAT first winter we were married, 1973, when we still lived on East Sixty-second Street. Neil would sit in the darkness, in the little room by the front door that was a favorite of the girls, I think, because it was a favorite of their mother, Joan. The record player was in there, and Neil would listen to Frank Sinatra croon sad love songs and think of her.

"I think Joan liked it 'cause it was small and cozy with a fireplace and everything. Sort of like a miniature room." What an apt description, Anna. It was a tiny room that seemed somehow sweetly protective. Perhaps that's why Joan liked it. She also had a favorite place to sit in her bedroom upstairs, right by a large paned window that looked out onto the back garden below. Ellen told me that she would come home from school and often find her mother sitting there, waiting to hear all about what had happened at school. I have a feeling she spent a lot of time sitting there, just thinking about things.

Anyway, on a particularly bitter cold night I was washing Ponti, their dog, down in the basement. The girls were up on their floor of the townhouse doing homework. After getting the dog all fluffed and clean, I followed the sound of Sinatra singing some love song and was surprised that the doors to the little room were closed. I noticed as well that no light was seeping out into the foyer. I wasn't sure what to do. There was no answer to my knock, so I gingerly opened a door and was startled by the sight of Neil seated in the chair, his face covered by his hand. He didn't look up. He just sat there in a shaft of light coming from the foyer chandelier. I asked quietly if he was all right, if there was anything I could do for him, and I started to lean toward him.

He didn't look up when he answered, "Don't come in. I want to be left alone. . . . I miss her so much. . . . I miss Joan so much." I understood and quietly shut the door. Suddenly, I felt like an outsider, an unwanted outsider, so I took Ponti for a walk around the block and cried my own sad feelings away.

"When do the dead die? When they are forgotten." *Who* said that? The statement startled me into the present.

"I did." It was Grace who spoke. "It's a quote from a book that you've read." I'm always amazed at what the mind remembers and what it forgets.

DRIVING ALONG ON my way to a new home, looking back in time and knowing how I feel today, part of the sureness of that decision to marry Neil must have come from a deep unconscious connection and desire to be part of a family. Perhaps Neil was accurate about our life together when he said to me, "Now that the girls are gone we have to find new reasons to be together."

Whatever the reason he wanted to marry, the important thing is that I grew up better and wiser, and I gained two extraordinary daughters who allow me into their lives and secrets and help me to be a much better mother than I ever thought I could be. It was a difficult time for all of us at the beginning, but we all thought it was worth it. Of course, I admit we did show some wear and tear, especially in those first three weeks, and over the entire first two years.

On the morning we were to get our rushed blood tests, Neil crossed the street, walking toward me wearing a navy-type pea coat. His head was bent, his hands stuffed in the pockets of his jacket. He was pale and he wasn't smiling. He looked at me with such pain.

"I can't go through with this," he said.

"Okay," I answered, speaking slowly. "Are you all right?" Clearly, everything was happening too fast. We didn't know each other. Joan had been such a big part of his life. We talked as we walked arm in arm.

"Okay," I responded. Marriage wasn't that important to me, it was

Neil that mattered. I told him I loved him and whatever he wanted was what I wanted. So we postponed getting married.

"We might as well go ahead and get the blood tests since we made the appointment," he said.

"Okay," I answered. So that's how we came to get married in *three* weeks, having postponed it a week. We were married within three weeks of meeting, and then lived in marriage almost ten years, from October 25, 1973, to April 5, 1983. Divorced, March 1984.

BABA MUKTANANDA ONCE said that one's destiny was written in one's actions and choices today, and that one's life today was written by one's actions and choices in the past. So, was the marriage to Neil destiny? Somehow I think so. Maybe destiny is the power of one's fate. Perhaps it's predetermined, although I don't think so because we do have free will—we do have choices. Some people think we don't, but I now know we do. Were we destined to meet? Was our meeting fated? If you believe in past lives, then perhaps we were. Is fate a power or event that supposedly predetermines future events? Baba says that your karma (your past actions), and your destiny (your future), are altered by the guru's grace and your best efforts. And what about the old adage, "Character is fate"? If that's true, then by changing my character or revealing it to myself in order to change, I change my fate. I think getting the offer to go to A.C.T. and the act of actually going helped decide my destiny. I left for San Francisco so sure that it was what I had to do. I met and married Neil and I was sure I had to do that as well. And going and meeting Baba Muktananda and making a heartfelt commitment to my spiritual life changed my life for the better.

How I handled those experiences perhaps determined my fate, as did the divorce. And my character today is quite different from what it was before. Perhaps my character is revealed in my past choices and actions; but I'm not sure about that because I sometimes surprise myself by the way I behave. As I've gotten older and put into practice what I've learned, I am fully aware that my choices are very different from what I might have done in the past. My personality is perhaps pretty much the same, but it seems more expanded to me now. I know I've grown. I learned to be a good actress at A.C.T. I learned to be part of an ensemble. And I learned that acting is also technique, a skill. I learned to follow my deepest intuition, and that when I do, I'm much better off. I also learned that when I don't, I suffer. With Baba's help I learned patience and surrender those first two years with Neil. And through it all I learned to have a good time. I gained a sense of humor and liked it when I made Neil and the girls laugh. I learned to love unconditionally. I learned that not everyone can communicate clearly, but that communication is paramount in any relationship. I learned healthy ways to deal with my anger and hurt, as well as how to have an "appropriate" argument with someone I love. I learned to honor commitments and, at the same time, how to stick to my guns when I'm tested. Not bad for a naive, somewhat neurotic, midwestern Catholic girl.

"THERE IT IS! There it is!"

I look over at Gary Dale as he jabs his finger at the windshield, pointing the way. I've never in my life been so happy to see a Holiday Inn.

CHAPTER NINE

MEETING MR. HILTON

Having reached Flagstaff, Arizona, at the end of a long hot day of travel, with a little more than half of our journey behind us, Chris and Gary Da Silva parked their share of our caravan and set out in search of Flagstaff's biggest margaritas and some Mexican food. Gary and I and our three animal charges opted for some food from the cooler, a shower, and, hopefully, sleep on a nice clean bed with a mattress. Please God, may I never sleep on a hardwood floor in a sleeping bag again. I craved a drink, anything alcoholic, but figured if I had one I'd truly be wasted tomorrow when we hit Santa Fe. Besides, I decided, it's good to discipline myself and get through this trip without a glass of wine.

The room Gary and I found had two double beds and the usual motel-type furniture, but it was clean, it smelled fine, and we could open a window. Such small pleasures cheered me. I've been on the road a lot in my life, and I know what it's like not to be able to open a hotel or motel window for fresh air, to get the peculiar smell of the room's many previous occupants and cleaning solutions out of my nose.

Despite my exhaustion, sleep did not come. I had a small corner of the bed while Max and Dulcie took the rest. Gary was saddled, literally, with Buddy. Eventually a kind of resignation set in as I lay there thinking mantras and feeling like I was having an out-of-body experience due to sleep deprivation. Getting up early the next morning was no problem; getting the dogs up, however, was another thing altogether. Max didn't look good at all; we had a hell of a time getting him into the car.

It seemed eerily quiet as we drove, Gary at the wheel, me with the trip map in my hand. If all went smoothly, we'd be in Santa Fe in five or six hours, and suddenly I realized I couldn't even remember what the house I'd rented looked like. The sun was coming up on another day. The dogs were in the back, sleeping a drugged sleep, even without drugs. I looked at Max. His second operation didn't look—or smell—like a success to me. He still had the hard, baseball-size growth on the side of his head, in spite of the operation to remove it last week. It was apparent also that his spirits were low, way too low for comfort.

"I'm gonna have to find a vet when we get to Santa Fe, Gary. Max doesn't look right. I'm scared."

"We'll call Warren when we get there. He'll know somebody. Don't worry."

Warren Thompson was a big burly fellow with a kind face and warm manner. I'd been introduced to him by Shirley MacLaine, who had bought land out in Abiquiu too. He'd sold me the two hundred fifty acres there and was renting me his family's house to live in while I figured out what kind of house to build, something I still hadn't given much thought. Talk about living in the moment. And here we were, three cars, three dogs, and 33,000 pounds of stuff crammed in two trucks rumbling toward a new destination. I sighed heavily. No snazzy repartee came to mind. Even my inner voices were quiet.

The empty road stretched hot and arid ahead of us. Suddenly a sign went whizzing by. It said Socorro and the number of miles, which, of course, I didn't read. Socorro, New Mexico. Why, that was where Conrad Hilton came from, I realized.

"Gary Dale, is Socorro very far from here?"

"Yep," Gary drawled. "It's quite a ways away, down south."

"Is it far from Santa Fe?"

"Oh, yeah, some two hundred miles. Why?"

"That sign back there said Socorro. Mr. Hilton came from Socorro, New Mexico! Conrad Hilton. Do you remember Connie Hilton?" I asked.

"Uh-huh," Gary said, starting to yawn. "I met him with you, in New York. You'd go out with him, come back, and then we'd go out." He finished his yawn with a laugh. That had been in the winter of 1964. I met Conrad Hilton in St. Louis at Webster College, in the spring of that year.

Boy, he looked mighty tall that day as he strode up the college's main walk. His gait was strong and impressive and he had a definite spring in his walk, with his large, bony hands swinging at his sides, making the sleeves of his suit seem too short. As we were introduced he clasped my hand firmly, and with a courtly smile said, "How do you do?"

I was nervous, but looked right at him, surprised that his eyes were blue, bright, and mischievous. His teeth looked a bit too big for his lean face, but those sharp blue eyes caught and held my nervous gaze as the vice president and president of my school, Sisters Jacqueline and Francetta, respectively, continued their introductions. Mr. Hilton was seventy-two years of age that graduation spring. I was just twenty-one.

Back then, Webster was a small Catholic women's college. Now it's a huge secular university with campuses all over the world. I was able to go there because of a four-year, half-tuition scholarship the school awarded, plus the thousand dollars I had won as the first runner-up in the Junior Miss contest my senior year of high school. I felt very proud that spring morning in 1964 because I'd put myself through four years of school, working hard in the drama department, holding down part-time jobs, performing in all the productions, and producing that year's musical.

Webster was a haven for me. I loved being there, especially during final rehearsals, when I'd spend my nights on campus as well.

The Sisters of Loretto, who ran the school, and their board of advisers decided that the school should have a proper fine arts building with studios and classrooms and a first-rate theater. Enter Mr. Hilton. He had pledged $1.5 million to the school and came that spring as the guest of honor for the celebratory weekend, culminating with the Loretto-Hilton Theater and Fine Arts Building groundbreaking ceremony, and the annual Senior Father-Daughter Banquet.

At our first official meeting with Conrad Hilton I couldn't help but smile as I watched Sister Jacqueline and Sister Francetta flutter around him, making nice. Together they made an impressive team. Mr. Hilton dubbed them "the Crescent and the Star": Jacqueline, "the Crescent," had wooed him and Francetta, "the Star," had charmed him. He was totally smitten. The gossip in the halls was that he was partial to Francetta because she behaved like nuns were supposed to behave.

Jacqueline was another matter. She had come to Webster College a year before me from Nerinx Hall, my high school, where she taught Geometry and English. She was passionate about both teaching and her students. I remember my struggle with math and a conversation she and I had about my borderline grade. She asked if I was serious and passionate about my acting, and whether I was sure that acting was what I wanted to do. When I said "Absolutely," she responded, "All right, don't worry," and she passed me in geometry. She left Nerinx Hall to become Sister Francetta's vice president at Webster College. She and Francetta smartly realized that the college had to change drastically to survive and that their order, The Sisters of Loretto, would have to change with it if they were to continue to be an effective and vital force in education.

Jacqueline was deeply committed to teaching and had strong beliefs and opinions about education and the teaching profession, and because of those beliefs she became somewhat of a "personality."

She was appointed to President Kennedy's Education Task Force and was the only woman and the only nun on the board. While in Washington she met the fashion designer Oleg Cassini, who was a favorite of Jacqueline Kennedy's, and asked him to design the first "modified habit" for the sisters. She felt that the traditional black habit was intimidating to the lay person. I was very impressed by her relative worldliness and her adventuresome spirit, and by the fact that she had totally charmed Oleg Cassini into designing a very attractive, suitable outfit. We giggled together as she showed me his drawings and told me that the main concern expressed by some of the nuns was that they would have to wear a girdle!

She and Sister Francetta decided to accept male students into the drama department of this all women's Catholic college and began the process of turning Webster College into a secular university. I was also impressed with her vision and her energy. She enlivened many a late-night conversation as I toiled over my studies while sitting on the floor outside the small theater during technical run-throughs of the various plays I was in. Rumor had it that she had been called on the carpet by an apoplectic archbishop because of an article she had written for the Sunday *New York Times Magazine* titled, "If You Haven't Questioned the Existence of God by the Time You're 18, You're Either a Fool or a Liar." I marveled at her vocabulary and grit and vowed then and there that I too would distinguish myself and have the courage of my convictions no matter what others might say about me. What I didn't know then, of course, was that an awful lot of people would have an awful lot to say about me and my life and my work.

I also didn't know on that warm spring day as we welcomed Mr. Hilton to our school that I would soon be flying to the West Coast as Conrad Hilton's date for the opening of the San Francisco Hilton Hotel and the beginning of what I can rightly call my adult education. I also didn't know then that some ten years later Sister Jacqueline and I would lunch together at Maxwell's Plum, a restaurant in New York City, and compare notes on what it was like to be married to a nice Jewish widower with two children. She would be Mrs. Jacqueline Grennen Wexler and I would be Mrs. Neil Simon.

"And *she's* still married."

I had to smile because my inner Critic sounded distinctly like a Jewish mother.

Being asked to the opening of the San Francisco Hilton Hotel by Mr. Conrad Hilton was a very heady thing. He had extended two invitations, one to me, and another one to a fellow senior from the South. I assumed we were chosen because of our relative stature that year: She was the student body president and I was in the drama department and the producer of our major theatrical event of that year. She was invited to a grand Republican fund-raiser, or convention of some kind, and I was invited to the opening of the hotel.

"Forget the inner voices! I'm amazed no 'outer' voices raised any questions considering you were a very naive, midwestern Catholic girl going off for a weekend, unchaperoned, with a seventy-two-year-old multimillionaire who was once married to Zsa Zsa Gabor!"

I know, I know. It sounds crazy now, but you have to understand the innocence and naivete of the people involved. They assumed I was to be chaperoned by Ms. Wakeman and, in fact, I was. It didn't occur to them that Mr. Hilton might do something ungentlemanly because he behaved like a gentleman and was a gentleman. I was raised in a very unworldly way with little or no experience with the sophisticated world of wealth and big business. I shall always be grateful that I had that experience. Besides all of that, wealth of that sort can often blind the best of us, especially if your world doesn't go beyond Webster Groves, Missouri.

The nuns and my parents were all atwitter. They were very pleased and excited when Mr. Hilton properly asked if they would give their permission, and everyone said, "Of Course!" With those two words my life changed.

"And you've been changing ever since, old girl!" Be quiet, G.A. I hadn't the foggiest notion of what it was like to fly anywhere, let alone fly to Los Angeles, California; stay at a big hotel, the Beverly Hilton; and then fly on a chartered plane to San Francisco with Mr. Hilton, his executive assistant Olive Wakeman, and some of his other guests. I also hadn't the foggiest idea of what would be expected of me once I was there. This would be my first trip away from home with a male stranger.

"What to wear!" became the all-involving mantra for the next several weeks. It was decided that Mrs. Candido, my sister's boyfriend's mother, should make my dress for the formal dinner dance celebration, and my mother and I went shopping for material and a pattern. We settled on a black-and-white small print sheath, with a scoop neck, an empire waist, and a long straight skirt. We also bought a pair of imitation pearl drop earrings to go with it and decided that a long solid black coat of similar material would look perfect. Now, this expense was a burden for my parents. We didn't have money; both my parents worked to make ends meet. I had worked every summer since I was sixteen, as well as during holidays, for my spending money and college tuition, and I also put in extra hours working in the drama department for two dollars an hour. I was very proud of putting myself through college and maintaining a B+ average. My first experience of self-esteem.

My mother and I pored over the schedule that Mr. Hilton's executive assistant sent us. There were two days in Los Angeles, then the trip to San Francisco, then the Gala Opening Ball, a big luncheon (an unusual word to me) the following day with various dignitaries like the governor of California, Pat Brown; the head of Bank of America who had a funny name, Serge Semenenko; some of the Hearst family; a gentleman by the name of Colonel Crown from Peabody Crown Coal (I think), out of Chicago; and a very wealthy rancher who took care of his vast ranch property via helicopter.

By the time the airline tickets arrived, my mother and I put together what we thought was a very nice wardrobe for the various events that I would be attending with Mr. Hilton. As the day grew closer for me to leave, I felt confident that I would be fine as far as my wardrobe was concerned. I think my entire suitcase as packed for this major trip was worth about four hundred dollars and that included jewelry.

Fortunately, when I landed in the City of Angels, an angel was waiting for me, Miss Olive Wakeman. She stood about four feet five inches in high heels, with soft curled strawberry hair piled high on her head. She was Mr. Hilton's executive assistant and proved to be my fairy godmother. Her eyes were a sparkling blue, framed with just a hint of the palest of blue eye shadow, and she smiled as she took my hand.

"Please call me Olive," she said as she welcomed me to California. She also inquired about the flight; arranged for my luggage; filled me in on the social events of the next two days in L.A., including the trip to San Francisco; and immediately put me at ease as we negotiated our way through the terminal to the blinding light outside. We were accompanied by a nice-looking man who immediately attended to my luggage and alerted the driver of a private car, via a walkie-talkie, that we were on our way.

As she and her companion escorted me to my first limousine ever, I also met my first chauffeur. He was dressed in a uniform, complete with hat, standing by the open door of a beautiful, pearl gray machine. He seemed perfect, and so was his warm, friendly smile as he introduced himself. He offered me his strong brown hand and asked me if I wanted something to drink. *My goodness!* I thought to myself as I got in that car, *these are very happy and friendly people!* I settled into the back seat next to Olive and admired the crystal whiskey glasses, cloth napkins, and vase of flowers, all secured in the side bar. As I took in the elegance surrounding me, I felt that my life had suddenly become a movie!

Olive's companion worked with Mr. Hilton too. His name was Bill. They joked with each other and seemed to enjoy each other's company. Olive would later confide to me that he was in love with her and wanted to marry her; but it couldn't be because he was already married and she was Catholic. As I watched them I noticed how beautifully put together Olive looked. Her clothes were perfect. Her hair and makeup were perfect. Her nails were beautiful and sedately polished a color that matched her lipstick, and I knew that her toes were probably perfectly polished inside those lovely perfect shoes that matched her perfectly lovely bag.

As I gazed out of the big tinted window and saw my first palm trees and a Los Angeles freeway zipping by, I thought about what was in my suitcase and immediately stopped breathing. When terror and panic set in, I automatically stop breathing. It's my usual response to just about anything traumatic. I don't choke or explode or cry or laugh; I just get quiet and stay emotionally suspended while a small but quietly intense voice whispers inside my head, "It's okay, don't panic!" as I panic. Usually I consciously take a couple of breaths and try to get some control, but often my immediate response is to run away. I couldn't do that in this situation, of course, unless I wanted to die on the freeway in front of these very nice people who were taking such good care of me. Instead of running or breathing I just kept looking out the window, hoping I was giving them the successful impression of Audrey Hepburn as she might behave in this situation. But I quickly realized I was in a situation way over my head. I had no frame of reference for something like this. How am I going to get through this? I wailed internally. I can't disappoint my parents *and* the nuns! My solar plexus contracted and sent my stomach and heart to my throat.

"We're almost there," Olive said as I turned toward them.

"This is Beverly Hills," Bill said. "The hotel is right in the center of the world's best shopping." He glanced at Olive and winked.

Olive returned his smile and said, "We will get you situated at the hotel and then Bill and I have to go back to the office, but I'll leave my number. You'll be picked up and brought to Mr. Hilton's office before we have dinner at his home."

As we pulled into the circular drive of the hotel I found some air somewhere in my suspended state and quietly gulped.

"Olive, could you maybe come up to my room with me and take a look at what I've brought?"

"Of course," she graciously replied, gently squeezing my arm and giving me a cherubic smile. This was the moment where I first began to suspect she had angel wings.

After I was warmly welcomed by the staff of the Beverly Hilton and ushered upstairs to my two-room suite that was bigger than my parents' house, Olive took a quick look in my suitcase. She studied its contents carefully and thought for a moment. As usual, I held my breath. She looked up and smiled.

"Hmmm. Your dress is lovely. But you need a little extra something for a cocktail party the board of directors is giving for Mr. Hilton and his guests."

I gulped for air again and must have looked like the terrified fish out of water that I was.

"Now, don't you worry," she said, patting my shoulder. "There are shops downstairs that will have what you need. I'll call them right now and tell them you're coming. They will happily help you and you just sign for it. Mr. Hilton insists. And I have a beige fur stole that you can borrow that should go nicely with what you have."

"Won't you need it?" I asked.

"Oh, I have another one that I was intending to use. I'll show you both of them and you can choose."

Two fur stoles! I thought to myself as I smiled my relief. I've landed in Oz and she's my Billie Burke, my Glinda.

So off I went, down my yellow brick road, passing through the lobby where everyone smiled and nodded as I asked a handsome bellman how to get to the shops. He smiled, bowed, and pointed me in the right direction. I wanted to bow or curtsy or nod but stopped myself in time. I began to feel like Eloise at the Plaza but worried also that even the bellman knew about my predicament and how nervous I was about this whole major situation.

I continued on the path to the outside where there were three or four shops nestled in a row along a walk lined with hibiscus, brightly colored impatiens, and glossy green bushes. The air smelled orange sweet and the sun was shining. In one of the windows a display of women's apparel and adornments sparkled and winked at me. This must be the place, I thought. It was cool and dim inside and there was soft music playing. A kindly saleslady whispered, "Can I help you, dear?" I assumed whispering was the order of the day so I whispered back, "Yes, please" as she guided me to some "lovely cocktail wear."

Now, in the land where I come from we always look at the price tag first, which is what I did; I gasped. The items she was showing me cost more than the amount mentioned earlier for the entire contents of my suitcase. I got scared. Furtively looking around, I spotted a corner that had a Special Sale sign above it and excused myself with "I'll just look around if I may."

Fortunately, I found an off-white crepe dress with a little beading that was half price, but still by far the most expensive dress I had ever tried on. The hem was pinned and I was told that it would be delivered to my room by five o'clock; all I had to do was sign my name.

"Are you any relation to James Mason?" the saleslady whispered breathlessly.

"No," I volunteered, "but my father's name is James and we've acted together at my school. I'm going to be an actress."

"Well, the best of luck to you. You will enjoy San Francisco." I waltzed out of the cool, dim shop and into the blinding California sun. Back in my room I called Olive to tell her what I had spent for the dress, but that I had gotten it on sale.

"You saved me some money, I hear," Mr. Hilton said later with a grin as he stood and walked from behind his very large, very handsome mahogany desk. Placed around his impressively large, mahogany-paneled office, there were important people's pictures in silver and brass frames, and various plaques.

"Come, I'll show you around," he said and introduced me to several people, including his son Barron whose office was almost as big as his. Everyone smiled and everyone seemed happy.

"They must like their jobs," I said as we headed back to Olive's pretty office.

Mr. Hilton turned and raised his eyebrows and laughed. "No sense working where you're not happy," he said.

"Hmm," I answered, thinking of my father.

Olive gave Mr. Hilton some letters to sign and I noticed he used a fountain pen that was part of a beautiful desk set. His desk was spotless; not a single paper. I was surprised by this; I thought all busy peo-

ple had busy desks. Barron's desk was quite busy and so was Olive's,
although she had two secretary-typists under her.

I wondered about this and decided to ask Mr. Hilton. Again he
looked surprised, and he laughed. "Well, first of all, call me Connie."

"All right . . . Connie."

"I do like a clean, uncluttered desk," he continued. "But it's really
Olive and her two assistants who help me keep it that way. I can't
work with a lot of clutter. I don't know how Barron does it. But he's
very smart and knows what he's doing. Are you neat and organized
too?"

I blushed. "Well, I'm not terribly neat, but I know where everything is. My sister is always drawing a line down the middle of the
dresser we share so our parents won't think she's as messy as I am, but
our desk is always pretty neat. We take turns using it."

"I came from a poor but hardworking family," he said. "We didn't
have a desk." He looked back at his office with appreciation and his
satisfaction was clearly visible. He scrunched up his face, gritted his
capped teeth in a funny kind of embarrassed smile, took my hand in
his, and said, "Let's eat."

"I'll meet you at the house, Mr. Hilton." Olive was to join us for
dinner at Casa Encantada, which was the name he'd given his home.

Back in the limousine, we drove down Sunset Boulevard and
turned right onto a wide road with a small island of densely planted
flowers. We passed through two large, white stucco pillars with a
wrought-iron top piece. On one of the pillars was a wrought-iron
sign that said Bel-Air and under that East Gate. The gate house to the
right was as big as my family's house in St. Louis. There were several
patrol cars parked outside with Bel-Air Patrol emblazoned on the
side, and the men inside wore uniforms. The afternoon sun slanted
through the abundant green foliage, casting sharply slanting shadows
everywhere, and there was a sudden quiet. The road forked at the gate
house and we took the bend to the right, following a lazy turn on
Bellagio Road. We passed stately driveways with huge gates, gargantuan homes with dense, luxuriant shrubbery and high walls. This was

clearly a hugely expensive and private place to live. On the left, as we drove round another bend, I saw a buff-colored wall that seemed to go on forever. It finally stopped at a large buff-colored pillared gate. We pulled in, and as the chauffeur reached out his window and pressed a button, I noticed the wrought-iron detail on one of the pillars. It said Casa Encantada. The great iron gates slowly opened to lush wide borders of red, white, and orange impatiens that ran along both sides of the drive. There were manicured lawns with great tall trees and everywhere flowers and plants growing in healthy profusion. He must have an army of gardeners, I thought. The grounds were meticulously cared for, as though they had been tended with manicure scissors!

Connie loved Casa Encantada. I could tell by the way his face changed as he spoke, pointing out the various sights he wanted me to see.

"Casa Encantada means House of Enchantment," he said, "and over there, to the left side, is a grand rose garden where my picture was taken sitting on a white horse. Presidents have been photographed there. Maybe you will be photographed there." He smiled teasingly.

The car *finally* came to a stop at the front door of the house. Well, house isn't really an accurate term—villa or palace or very big mansion is more like it. I'd never before seen anything like it except for the Art Museum in St. Louis, but this was a home that someone lived in. And it was all for one person! Inside was a kind of personal museum, terribly formal and sparely beautiful and very large, although in all that space there were only two bedrooms! It also had quite a history and Connie became quite animated as he told me the story of how he came to acquire it.

It was built by a woman who'd been the nurse to a very wealthy elderly man. Upon his death she received the majority of his assets. She built the mansion with the dream that she would become a socially accepted doyenne of Los Angeles society. Marble columns were brought from Italy and artisans from all over the world were hired. First-edition books filled the library shelves and one room had large oval paintings of beautiful birds, which had been specially commissioned. They were truly beautiful paintings and Connie knew the details of each one. They matched perfectly with the specially made pale blond Art Deco furniture.

We had drinks in this room. A nice man in a white coat served us and brought out Connie's favorite nuts, shiny peeled almonds. I'd never seen them before. My soda was served in a heavy crystal glass and I was given a small delicate linen napkin to go with it. I'd never before seen this kind of napkin either. After each taking a handful of nuts we went on a tour. We munched and sipped away as he told me he would probably give the bird paintings to the Audubon Society. He said the house was so special he wasn't sure what he would do with it. Barron couldn't use it because he had lots of kids and it had only two bedrooms.

Next stop, the music room. Of course, I'd never seen a music room in a person's house before. I'd read of them in some of the plays, but his was my first in real life. The whole room was the color of the dusky pink satin fabric that covered the chairs and sofa, and in the center was a collector's harpsichord or pianoforte or baby grand.

"A room for Miss H., wouldn't you say?"

Definitely, G.A. Both Miss Havisham and Glinda would feel perfectly at home in that room.

As we moved through the house I tentatively started asking him questions about the paintings he had and the books and the art objects, and I asked him about the hotel business—what it was like, how he got started; and I also asked him what it was like to come from a very poor background and wind up living like a king. He smiled at all my questions and seemed pleased that I took such an interest in his business and his background. As he recounted his life story I realized he was a living example of the American dream, and I told him so. "Yes," he said, "America is the best country in the world. I'll tell you my philosophy: Dream big dreams, the biggest you can imagine. The only fear is that they will come true!"

Repeating his words over in my mind as we came back to the

room where Olive was waiting, I wondered out loud what he meant exactly when he said, "The only fear is that they will come true."

"Come, we'll discuss it at dinner." The dining room had a very long black walnut table with at least twenty-four chairs and at the center was an inset piece of thick frosted glass that was lit from below. In the bay window that went from floor to ceiling, a lovely round table proportioned to sit four or six was set for three. We were to sit there, thank God. The candles were lit and the crystal and china and silver sparkled. There was a bowl with water and a floating flower at each setting and I wondered what it was for. The napkins were soft and big and folded in an intricate way. All I could think of was dinner at my house in Crestwood. Ever since my mother started working, my sister and I always fixed dinner. As I looked at the elegant table I thought of me fixing Chef Boyardee from a box for my sister and me at our kitchen table, using paper napkins and plastic plates and stainless steel utensils. But here in Bel-Air dinner was very different and tonight wasn't even special. My eyes were glazed and my mind was on serious overload; so I was grateful that Olive had arrived for dinner. She lived in a guest house somewhere on the grounds but I think she drove up to the main house to join us.

"Is this the way you eat every night you don't go out?"

"Yes," he replied. "Sometimes I have dinner on a tray if I want to watch the news." I thought of my parents and how they sometimes had their dinner on a tray in front of the television down in the basement.

Dinner was elegantly served by the same man who had brought us our drinks, although he had changed his coat. I think his name was Igor or Ivan, and even though he was smiling and very, very nice, I was scared. Watching him coming toward us with a silver tray and serving utensils, I shuddered and silently prayed. "Dear God, please let him serve Mr. Hilton first. I promise I'll visit chapel every day." Fortunately, he served Olive first. What a relief! I watched carefully and waited until one of them picked up a fork or spoon and then I would do the same. I remember the food being tasty and beautifully prepared, and I sipped from my glass only after they had sipped from theirs.

When dinner was finally over, I was "in overwhelm" and glad that Mr. Hilton was taking me back to the hotel.

As we stood in front of the door to my rooms, I thanked him for the lovely dinner, the tour of his home, and, most important, our conversation, although I still wasn't sure what he meant when he said the only fear is that your dreams will come true. It would take me another ten years to experience the truth of those words. Remembering my manners I also thanked him for the plane ticket and the dress and, well, just about everything so far.

"Aren't you going to let me in to your room to say goodnight?" he asked.

I suddenly became flustered and stuttered a reply.

"Oh! I'm sorry. I c-c-c-can't . . . do that because I have all my clothes and my underwear laying out ready to pack for San Francisco. I can't let you see them!" I didn't want to see myself either. My face was probably bright red.

"Well," he answered and paused. Then with a smile he said, "You are the first person to kick me out of my own hotel!"

I laughed nervously and pathetically replied, "I'm sorry."

He laughed and put a big bony hand into his pocket, drew it out, and presented me with a wad of bills.

"Here is a little tip money for you to use here at the hotel," he said.

"How much should I give them?" I stammered.

"Whatever you think is fair," he replied. "And now I must go since you've kicked me out of my own hotel. But don't I, at least, get a kiss goodnight?"

I kissed him quickly on the cheek and he took my hand, bowed and kissed it, then said goodnight. I quickly slipped into my room and locked the door. I then pressed my ear to it, listening to his muffled steps on the carpet as he walked away. I took my first deep breath since arriving at the hotel and slid to the floor where I stared at the roll of bills in my hand. "Thank you, God, for getting me through this day," I murmured. Sitting there on the floor of my huge suite I tried to collect my thoughts. Finding I couldn't, I did the next best thing: I ran to the bedroom and plopped myself in the center of the king-size bed and counted out the money Connie had given me.

My parents had given me some money before I left, and I already had some money of my own that I had been saving; but this was a sizable roll of ones, fives, and tens. I stopped counting after one hundred and just spread the bills out on the bed, lay down on them, and thought about the day. I could get used to this, I decided. Yes, I definitely could get used to this! I got up, put the money away, and tried to calm down. It had been a very heady but in some ways difficult day, and if today was any indication, the trip wasn't going to get easier.

"But for now," I announced, "I'm going to play!" My bathroom had everything in it a woman could want: shampoos and bubble bath and fluffy big towels and a huge tub. Afterward I sleepily crawled between the sheets and felt that luxurious soft coolness of clean pressed cotton against my skin. There was lots of room to stretch my legs as I ate the gold-covered chocolate that the maid had left on my pillow.

"WEREN'T YOU SCARED at all?" Anna asked incredulously.

"Oh Anna, I'd been scared by all the beautiful and frightening things that had happened to me that day. But I also felt excited by my exposure to all the elegance that life offered. I thought about Mr. Hilton's home, the story of his life, the lovely people around him, and dinner with the china bowl and the floating flower for dipping and cleaning your fingers. And I thought about his valet/butler and the pleasant woman in the kitchen preparing dinner. I thought about the woman who had built the villa in the first place, just so she would be accepted into society.

"What happened to her? Do you know?"

Yes, Ed, she married the chauffeur, I think, and never was accepted by society. She eventually sold her mansion and everything in it to Mr. Hilton for a million dollars and wound up sick and infirm, living in a tiny apartment in the San Fernando Valley.

My mind drifted back through the day as my eyes closed, trying to collect all the sights and impressions into some kind of mental basket. I didn't want to forget any of it. Of course I couldn't know then, in 1964, that just ten years later I too would live in Bel-Air, passing by Casa Encantada every day on my way to and from my own beautiful home.

"And now here you are with no home! A vagabond, a nomad, traveling life's highway as you dream up your next abode." G.A.'s voice brought me crashing down to earth.

It was hot outside as we galloped toward Gallup.

"I wonder if my stuff is okay in those trucks. Only a portion of the truck is climate controlled," I muttered to myself, but out loud.

"Don't worry," Gary responded. "It's too late now anyway."

I smirked and thought about all my furniture and books and stuff inside those huge vans. Mr. Hilton had given me three books: a limited edition of a book that told the story of the building of Casa Encantada; an autobiography of his life; and a special edition of a book about the beginnings of his career. They were numbered and given as gifts to important people. My book was numbered too. I think a pope had the copy before mine and a president had the copy after mine.

Now these books and the rest of my entire fifty-year-old life was in those trucks. I glanced at Gary and said, "I wonder where the trucks are now."

In answering, Gary automatically looked out to the side view mirror. "I don't know for sure but they must be somewhere behind us."

"Why?"

"Because they arrive at the house tomorrow morning. They're gonna spend the night in Albuquerque, pick up a couple of men, and call for directions to the house in the morning."

"I can't remember the house I rented. I hope we can stay there tonight."

"Sure we can. We can sleep on the floor."

Oh well, what's one more night on a floor, I thought. Maybe there was carpeting. I sort of remember carpeting.

"Mind if I turn on the radio?" Gary asked.

"Be my guest," I answered. Funny, I thought. That was the name of Conrad Hilton's autobiography: *Be My Guest*. Well, being his guest at the Beverly Hills Hilton was one thing; being his guest for the opening of the San Francisco Hilton proved to be something else again.

FOR STARTERS, THE building looked odd to me. The windows weren't in rows, but were in a pattern whereby they skipped a place and then the next row down started where there wasn't one in the row above. Also, the building was by no means finished. Construction was still going on but we all had our own rooms on the fourteenth floor, which had been especially prepared for our arrival. My room faced the inside of the square building with sliding doors to the outdoor pool and sun deck. Mr. Hilton was put someplace else. The pool was complete with water and a lifeguard.

Here on the fourteenth floor of an incomplete hotel in downtown San Francisco, a young man was sitting in his high chair, wearing red swimming trunks, overlooking a completely deserted pool and deck that looked to be barely finished. For some reason this picture made me laugh and also made me feel lonely. Suddenly the trip overwhelmed me. I felt sad, lonely, and isolated. Everyone who had flown with us on the chartered plane was practically Mr. Hilton's age, and if they weren't that old, they still were older than me. Suddenly I wanted to be with people my own age. Everyone was so very different from my own life and experience.

The wives of the board members made me nervous. One of them had come up to me at the cocktail party, complimented me on my dress, and asked me what airlines I worked for! When I became flustered and confused she drew herself up and said imperiously, "Well, aren't you a stewardess?"

"No," I replied, "I'm representing Webster College. Mr. Hilton graciously invited me to the opening of his hotel. I'm going to be an actress." Apparently, Mr. Hilton had quite a reputation with stewardesses.

When I told Olive what the woman had said, she patted my shoulder and told me not to worry about what other people said and confided that she was given the formal title "executive assistant" and a formal place at board meetings because people assumed too much about her and her place in Mr. Hilton's life.

As I looked out the sliding doors onto the concrete deck and this lone figure sitting quietly and still in his lifeguard's chair, I longed to have a conversation with someone I could relate to. He appeared to be about my age, and as I slid open the door he smiled and looked my way. I went out to talk to him but kept glancing around, wondering if Mr. Hilton was watching and would be embarrassed. I certainly didn't want to embarrass him, but I also wanted to talk to someone my own age. The lifeguard and I chatted awhile and I told him I was graduating college and going to New York to be an actress. Then I just said, "Would you like to have breakfast with me tomorrow?" He hesitated a moment, not speaking, so I continued, "I just wanted to have a conversation with someone my own age. Mr. Hilton is nice and so are the other people, it's just . . . I don't know . . . it's a little lonely."

I'm not sure we got to have breakfast the next morning but I do remember he gave me a single, long-stemmed red rose.

CHAPTER TEN

SAGES, SAINTS, AND
SCALAWAGS

G ary?"

"Umm?" Gary's mind was on the road and the traffic. He was anxious to get there now that we'd passed Gallup. That meant we finally were on our way to Albuquerque and then the house.

"Gary, can I grow roses in Santa Fe? I mean, Abiquiu?"

"Oh sure! My Aunt Vi grows 'em. You can grow lots of different kinds of flowers."

"I want to grow roses. Red roses. Well, all kinds of roses. I had done well with roses in L.A., and trees too. Maybe we could grow flowers and trees on the farm for a cash crop?"

"Aren't we gonna grow organic vegetables?"

"Sure, we'll grow everything. Everything we need. I want to become totally self-sufficient. Comes the revolution, I want to be totally . . . self-sufficient." Holy-moly, a farmer, me, a farmer—who would have thought it? "Gary Dale?"

"Ummm?" He still wasn't really with me. I could tell by the look on his face. I noticed his posture too; he was concentrating on driving, lost in his thoughts. It was okay. I was in another kind of space myself, just rambling around in it. This was a quiet space for a change.

The view outside looked harsh and unforgiving. I sighed audibly and closed my eyes. I was in the car but I wasn't. I was without feeling, but I wasn't. Is this what is meant by "limbo"? I wondered. Perhaps. My physical self felt heavy mostly because of lack of sleep and exercise.

"Not to mention the sheer drain of one's emotions," G.A. volunteered.

I may be drained right now, G.A., but I'm sure that'll change when we get there.

Just the thought of arriving and having to unpack all my stuff from those huge vans makes my mind go numb, hence this disquieting state of "quiet." No sense of turmoil. I surrender, G.A., I'm not going to think about tomorrow today. I don't want to think about anything for a while.

SURRENDER—A SCARY word. A very scary word. Terror used to be my response to that word, manifesting itself as a chilling shudder that shot from my neck to my tailbone. After all, surrender meant giving up, failure, being beaten, as in war. When you lose you must surrender, putting yourself into the power of an adversary. Surrender meant acknowledging defeat, giving up, or signing away one's rights, having to give up something precious to someone or something in power, especially under compulsion. That was my understanding of surrender anyway, and I determined early on that I would not surrender to anyone or anything. Then I met Neil Simon and Swami Muktananda. A double whammy. I didn't know back in 1973–74 that, ultimately, both men would become my greatest teachers of life, love, surrender, and the pursuit of happiness. I unwittingly embarked on a serious journey of maturation and expansion during the ten years that I was involved with both of them.

My first lesson in "surrender" came one morning shortly after Neil and I were married. Neil announced to me that he didn't want to be married to an actress. My immediate but unvoiced response was, gee, I wish you had mentioned that *before* we got married, and *before* I was in rehearsals playing Lady Anne to Michael Moriarty's *Richard III* at Lincoln Center! I didn't say it because I'd made a commitment to him and to Ellen and Nancy and was determined to do right by them and, hopefully, myself. I'd decided that work was work, but family was paramount. My mistake was I thought you could do both, that you could have a family *and* work as an actress. But here was Neil, saying family was more important, that my effort to combine a career and a family wouldn't work. My father had said the same thing many moons before. Him I hadn't believed, but this was Neil.

"Okay, I'll try. . . . I've *always* worked, and I think of myself as a working actress; but I'll try." At first that decision caused me pain and disappointment. But I hid my feelings from my new family by crying into pillows and towels when no one was around. And then Swami Muktananda came into my life.

There are two old sayings in spiritual studies: "When the student is ready, the teacher will appear," and "You're never given more than you can handle." The second one often tested my mettle, haunting me during those first two years of marriage. I was willing to "give up" what I passionately loved, acting, for my new family whom I loved passionately as well, thereby experiencing my first major lesson in surrender.

I MET SWAMI Muktananda in New York City on a cold January day in 1974. My friend and fellow actor in *Richard III,* Barbara Colby, arranged a meeting—a darshan as she called it—with an Indian man who was something called a Siddha Master.

Barbara was a wild woman in the pure and best sense of the word, a kind spirit with great energy and strength, my touchstone. She was someone I wanted to be like. She was a serious seeker of art and God. She was also a strict vegetarian who carried blenders and juicers with her wherever she went, hauling them about in brightly colored cloth bags. She wore only natural fibers next to her skin, including her shoes—no leather for her. I was very impressed and in awe of the level of commitment she applied to whatever she did.

When we first had met a couple of years earlier, she'd been responsible for introducing Bill Ball, and the rest of the company at A.C.T., to Transcendental Meditation. Everyone was doing it, and since I wanted to be part of the group, I signed up for it too. Bill arranged for an instructor to come and teach. I'd meditated before so it wasn't something totally whoo-woo to me. Besides, The Beatles were doing it so why shouldn't I?

Barbara and I became reacquainted in 1974 in New York with the *Richard III* production at Lincoln Center. She'd met this Swami Muktananda fellow shortly after leaving A.C.T. in 1972 and had become a devotee, as those followers of gurus were called. The word "guru" used to make me wince a bit. It brought up unpleasant connotations of cults, slaves, and mind robbers, of followers who did as they were told, having no mind of their own. But if Barbara was into it, I wanted to be into it too. She was a no-nonsense kind of gal with a strong mind who was very smart, well read, and wise. I was thrilled that we were sharing another dressing room together. Barbara was the epitome of "artist" in my mind, and as an artist she kept me spiritually and philosophically on track and honest in our discussions and our work. She had a keen eye for the truth and consequently I trusted her opinions. As a woman she was an original. Her laugh was distinctive, her physical presence was extraordinary, and she walked from the hip with a stride that was music in motion. She exuded animal sensuality as those loose, long shirts and shawls draping her body moved with her. She stood tall without self-consciousness, and when she spoke she was sharp, funny, and insightful. God, I miss her.

The day the company moved into the dressing rooms in the bowels of Lincoln Center, she surprised me by taping up a picture of this Swami Muktananda fellow on the mirror in front of us. He was an exotic-looking, dark-skinned fellow dressed in bright orange robes, wearing tinted aviator glasses that shaded mischievous eyes hovering over a great smile. Perched on his head was a colorful knitted wool cap. She then set out a small card with some foreign language on it, an incense holder, and another picture, this one in a small silver frame. It was of a pair of feet. I was curious.

"Who's this guy, and whose feet are those?" I asked, looking at the picture.

"Baba," she answered with a great smile. "Swami Muktananda, but everyone calls him Baba. It means "father" in Sanskrit. He's a great teacher and saint, the head of the Siddha lineage of great yogis in India. His . . ."

"Whoa, what happened to TM?" I asked, somewhat surprised.

"I've finally found what I've been searching for," she responded, and then detailed her first meeting with this fellow, followed by her spiritual odyssey and commitment. As she talked, she was animated and excited and smiled with such radiance that I found myself wanting to feel like she looked. She told me how this man had profoundly changed her life, recalling her problems and difficulties when she was at A.C.T.

"But why feet?" I asked as I picked up the picture in the silver frame.

"A great saint's feet are considered holy as is his touch. He gives Shaktipat when he touches you.

"Shakti—wha?"

"He awakens the dormant divine energy in his devotees. Some people have gotten it just by looking at his picture."

"Really," was all I could say. "And this writing on this card?" I picked up the small blue and white sign with the words "Om Namah Shivaya" printed on it. She slowly pronounced them for me.

"Om Namah Shivaya, huh? What does it mean?" I asked.

"I bow to my inner Self who is God."

"Really?! I bow to myself?!"

"God exists within you as you. That's the mantra you use when meditating. "Om" is the great sound of the "One," and the mantra means "I bow to Shiva, my inner Self who is God." She explained that this was the mantra that Baba was giving publicly at his evening programs and she had been told by others that this was the mantra that the maharishi supposedly gave secretly to those TMers who had reached a high level of meditational instruction.

"Can I use this mantra while I'm meditating?" I asked.

"Of course," she said.

I was intrigued. I'd never thought of God as existing *in* me, let alone God *being* me. I'd always assumed he was a he, and someone quite separate, outside of me, someone with whom I, hopefully, would get in touch one day. So there we were, meditating in the caverns of Lincoln Center on matinee days, with a meditation sign that Barbara had made hung on the knob of our closed dressing room door. Insidious ribbons of musky-smelling "Blue Pearl" incense lazily coiled out from under the door and wafted into the hallway. Michael Moriarty, the star of this production, was curious as to what we were doing in there. He liked the incense so Barbara gave him some.

I liked meditating with Barbara because I wasn't as disciplined as she; and I found it easier when she was there.

Then one day she asked, "Would you like to meet him? He's coming to New York soon, on his second world tour."

"Sure . . . okay." The truth is, at that point, I wasn't excited at the prospect of meeting him, but I was curious.

SO THERE I was on my one day off, sitting uncomfortably on the carpeted floor of a bare living room in a brownstone on the Upper West Side of New York City waiting for this Indian guy to come in. Looking about the room, I surreptitiously studied a young man with a brown bag in front of him. The way he held on to it, rolling and unrolling it as his head hung low and his long brown hair hung limply at the sides of his face, gave him a nervous melancholy air. Looking around at the faces of the others, five in all, I couldn't tell if they had been here before or were, like me, here for the first time. Not that it really mattered; I just felt awkward, wondering what on earth I was doing here anyway.

"Why is everyone so quiet?" I whispered into Barbara's ear. "This isn't a church, is it?" She smiled and shook her head and shrugged. She seemed to be thinking about something, probably the question she was going to ask this swami fellow. She'd told me I could ask him about anything, or not say anything at all—it didn't matter. I thought about a question but felt ambivalent about what to ask.

"Tell me again what happens when this guy comes into the room?"

"He'll sit down over there," she said, pointing to a chair at the end of the room. It was a lanai kind of chair, something you'd typically see on an enclosed porch in California.

"We'll go up when they tell us to. Usually we bow down—a *pranam*—at his feet, and then I'll introduce you."

"Bow down?!" I interjected hoarsely. "Do I have to?"

"No, of course not. Do whatever feels comfortable for you. Relax, everything will be fine."

Bow down! Me? Bow down to another human being? I'd never heard of such a thing. Was this like having false gods before you? I wondered.

Boom. The door to the room suddenly opened and in he came. I could swear there was a wind machine behind him, causing the edges of his wild outfit to lift as he made his way to his chair. I mean, the energy all around him palpably moved the air. I definitely felt a shift. Boy, this man knew how to enter a room!

He looked just like his picture: a jazz musician who wore gold aviator tinted glasses and funny bright orange clothes. Instead of a musical instrument he carried dark red worry beads in his right hand and continuously plied his fingers over the beads as he lowered himself into a lotus position. The others in the room got on their knees and bowed their heads to the floor. The melancholy fellow across from me laid himself out flat on his stomach. I watched with wide eyes.

"Respect is one thing, but this bowing nonsense is quite another!" My inner Critic was on full-tilt indignation.

This jazz musician fellow didn't seem to notice or care who was in the room. He just looked serious and confident as he made himself comfortable, issuing quiet instructions to a bald-headed young man who was with him. Then we were called forward.

Barbara got up and motioned me to go with her. I suddenly felt excited, nervous, panicked, and shy all at the same time. Barbara knelt down in front of him, offering him flowers, then bowing her head to the ground. Bam! I was right there with her, down on my knees. I couldn't believe myself! As she presented her gargantuan bouquet she looked adoringly into Muktananda's face. I was afraid to look at him, so I shuffled my paltry pears and apple and stared at the floor, trying to control the flush in my cheeks. While Barbara explained through the interpreter who I was, I watched only her profile. She looked positively beatific. She loved and adored this man. Then the interpreter, a nice-looking man with a shaved head, asked if I had a question.

Barbara had told me that if I felt like it, I should ask something that might be troubling me. Suddenly my heart felt like it was going to crack open and jump out of my chest. My armpits became minifountains sending trickles of water down the inside of my arms and ribs.

"What do I do with my anger?" I asked as I looked up into Muktananda's eyes. I was glued to them, right through the tinted glasses. His eyes were big, brown, friendly, and inviting. I can see them to this day. I didn't hear anything; I just looked at those eyes. Then I felt Barbara nudge me.

"What?" I asked quizzically, still looking at him. Baba broke into a great grin and chuckled, his shoulders shaking up and down. His mirth, his joy really, was contagious. I blinked and came to, wondering how long I had been staring at him and not hearing a thing.

"I'm sorry," I said to him, "what did you say?" From the response of the people in the room I seemed to have landed a very funny joke. Baba looked at me and smiled.

"Get rid of it; you don't need it," the interpreter said with a smile as Baba put his hand on my head, stroking my hair and my cheek, his gesture so friendly, so compassionate, so understanding. The next thing I knew, I was being hugged, my face cradled in the folds of his orange silk outfit.

Intuitively, he appeared to know exactly what anger I was referring to, and at that moment, I suddenly realized I didn't feel any of the anger or disappointment about giving my notice—on opening night, no less, of *Richard III*—because of Neil's unhappiness with me working, and the feeling of having to give up the career I had worked so hard to build.

I went home that afternoon and said nothing to Neil or the girls about this strange man and my extraordinary meeting. I knew something major had happened, something important, but I hadn't a clue where it was going to take me over the next ten years. I only knew my heart had been cracked open and that I wanted to see this Baba Muktananda again.

Barbara told me that there were evening programs I could go to, and that he was also giving what was called an "Intensive" on certain weekends before leaving the New York area. The chances of me being able to get away in the evenings or a weekend were nil—Neil wanted me home. In the end, I signed up, but I didn't go. Still, something kept nudging me toward him.

I started to meditate at home using the mantra Barbara had taught me in the dressing room, Om Namah Shivaya. Meanwhile, Barbara continued to work at Lincoln Center in *Richard III* and the following production, *A Doll's House* with Liv Ullmann. I went about the business of being Mrs. Neil Simon and a new mother to Ellen and Nancy.

Shortly after that first meeting with Muktananda, Neil surprised me and wrote a movie for us to do together, *Bogart Slept Here*. We also made the decision to move from New York City to Los Angeles. The moving part was precipitated by a trip to Los Angeles for my first Academy Awards appearance. Neil and I appeared together to present the award for best screenplay; it went to *Butch Cassidy and the Sundance Kid*. I'd been nominated for best actress in *Cinderella Liberty*. I didn't win and didn't expect to. I didn't expect to move to Los Angeles either.

We spent Easter vacation with the girls in Palm Springs around that time as well, and we all enjoyed California. It was time for a change. How one knows that fact is a mystery, but somehow you do. Just like this enormous change I've made moving to New Mexico—I knew it was time quite a while ago; I just didn't know the specifics. Neil knew it was time for a change as well. He was scared about it, but he knew we needed to start our life together in our own home, not his home with Joan. What I didn't know was that I would meet up with Baba Muktananda in California as well.

"YOU KNOW, IT'S funny how life unfolds, Gary. Starting out in St. Louis and then going to Webster and meeting Mr. Hilton, and here we are so many years later passing through his state. I meet you, a New Mexican native, and get married way back when, and here we are some thirty years later. I married Neil and moved into the house on Sixty-second Street...."

"Yeah, in three weeks ... try using your signal, lady!"

"Yeah ... three weeks. But think of it—I didn't know I'd be moving to California when we got married...."

"Or that I'd move there before you ..."

"Yeah, and live in a big house up the road from Mr. Hilton's. And when I was at A.C.T. with Barbara Colby, I didn't know I'd be doing *Richard III* with her in New York and be introduced to a guru. Neither of us knew that we'd become devotees of Baba. And neither of us knew that she'd be dead within a year or so of that meeting."

Barbara was shot down and killed outside her acting studio one night, along with her boyfriend. They never found the people responsible for their deaths. It was a supposed robbery gone bad.

"Look at that guy! His truck is gonna fall apart in front of us!"

We were close now. Very close. Albuquerque lay dead ahead. I glanced around at my new home state. There were some tall buildings and there was traffic, but nothing really registered. Maybe it was the lack of sleep.

"Maybe denial," intoned G.A. Maybe, I allowed. Or maybe just too much change right now. It's enough that I'm here. I haven't a clue what the house looks like even though I saw it briefly on the day I signed the rental papers. I hope it'll be okay.

"Only forty minutes or so. We're almost there!" Ed was getting excited.

"But where exactly is 'there'?" Miss H. harumphed. Conrad Hilton country, Miss Havisham. Conrad Hilton, Indians, pueblos, the Spanish language, and farming, Miss H., farming. Some road trip, huh.

Tears came and I let them flow. I didn't care why; it wasn't really important. I didn't hide them from Gary, although he wouldn't have noticed anyway. He was concentrating on traffic and all the bad drivers.

"Bernalillo up ahead, Marsha May. That's where we had the Diamond Tail Ranch. I'll point it out when we get to it . . . you okay?"

"Yeah, just tired. I'm okay. I wonder if there's a Siddha Yoga center here or in Santa Fe."

"Why do you wonder that?" came the chilling, accusatory voice of my inner killer Critic. "You won't go. You always have good intentions, but you don't follow through and *actually* do it. You'll follow anybody! You'll talk to anybody! Astrologer, psychic, madman! You talk disrespectfully to God and you make fun of the Catholic Church!"

Now hold it right there. What on earth are you talking about? Whether mental or verbal, my conversations with God, as well as with His mother and the various saints, were colloquial as I recall. I like the idea of talking rather than formally praying, but that isn't disrespectful. Sometimes I'd lapse into a "Thou" or a "Thine," but more often than not, it felt most comfortable saying, "Hello, God," or "Hi, Jesus, how's it goin' with you?"

When I spoke with the Virgin Mary, I always addressed her as "Dear" or "Blessed." With God it was always a little confusing because He was three people, for heaven's sake: a Father, a Son, and a Holy Ghost or Spirit. Since I was a kid, my understanding of God the Father was that He's the Big Cheese—mythical, ancient, and, as often viewed by me, the Grand Punisher. In fact, I never met such a hellish punisher as that guy. He damned people to Hell if they weren't good. He was superior and separate and not really accessible to us poor, earthy, earthly folks.

But I happen to believe that man made *that* god, and if you think man's definition of God is accurate, you are mistaken, and so are all those poor souls who do what they are told and hate those who aren't exactly like them. It's shameful how we treat each other, all in the name of that god.

Baba was aware of all religions and spoke of Mohammed and Buddha and Jesus as great saints and masters like his beloved guru, Bhagwan Nityananda. It was encouraging to me that Siddha Yoga never spoke of false gods like the Catholic Church does. "Thou shalt not have false gods before me," and all that. Baba always spoke lovingly and respectfully of Confucius, Buddha, Mohammed, and Jesus as well as Mirabai and other Indian yogis and yoginis. He gave me a new understanding, a broader and better understanding of what these men and women accomplished. Consequently, my appreciation of some of what I'd been taught as a child and young adult was reestablished through him. I began to have a greater understanding of the mystery of the Trinity as well. It was interesting to listen to some of his devotees who were nuns speak about how Baba's teachings and meditation enhanced their own religious disciplines.

Now, Baba was never much for psychology. It didn't make a lot of sense to him, especially when you had Siddha Yoga. However, he liked the idea of open dialogue. We had a special program one weekend for everyone who was a practitioner in the mental and physical health fields. Marilyn Hershenson was a speaker, and my therapist Roger Gould came. His willingness to come and sit on the floor in a crowded hall and listen to Baba and our honored guests and speakers meant a great deal to me.

I've heard other masters from different disciplines speak to this subject, like Llama Sogyal Rinpoche, a Tibetan Buddhist, and they too are somewhat bewildered by the West's interest in therapy, analysis,

and psychology; but like Baba they want to create an open dialogue
to see where these separate fields can come together. There was one
psychiatrist, however, who just didn't get it, and his name was Christ.

I've never known a man named Jesus, either. I've heard of a few, but
their name is usually pronounced with a Spanish *H*.

However, I have known a man named Christ, he was a psychiatrist,
and I did "study" with him for a short period of time. It fascinated me
that his mother would give him that name, Christ. Thankfully, he
called himself Chris.

He was the technical adviser on a television movie I starred in, *The
Clinic*. The movie was written by Jay Presson Allen, a formidable
writer and woman who is perhaps best known for the successful
adaptation of the book *The Prime of Miss Jean Brodie*. The movie of
The Clinic, which was originally titled *Hothouse*, I think, was to be a
pilot for a projected network television series. The clinic was a place
where a special kind of "in your face" therapy was used to rid one of
whatever was bothering him or her at the moment. This did not in-
clude serious mental illness like schizophrenia, but I think Dr. Christ
Z., the therapeutic magician, with his partner and associates, promised
that you would be "cured" of whatever it was that brought you there,
in twenty to thirty hours of this intense therapy. Each session was two
to three hours long, it was videotaped, and you had as many sessions a
week as you felt you could handle until the twenty or thirty hours
were completed. As I remember it, these sessions took place twice a
week.

I decided that I would go through this "in your face" process for
real, since I had to portray a famous actress who goes through it and
comes out a better person in the end. I was playing a movie star, married to a famous head of a studio, who goes bonkers in the middle of
shooting a picture. The husband slash producer, wonderfully played by
Ed Herrmann, gets me to this clinic, by helicopter, and deposits me
on the lawn and into the hands of my therapist, artfully played by Art
Malik, Jr. My husband slash studio bigshot gives the clinic a promise

of mucho buckos if they can cure me in time to finish the picture.

The shooting schedule of *The Clinic* fortuitously allowed me to experience the therapy firsthand while I was shooting. I dutifully showed up for my first session with our technical adviser. I sat practically knee to knee with Christ. I was instructed never to look away from his eyes, not at any time during the session, not even for an instant. If I did, he would point it out and back my eyes would go. There were small video cameras on tripods in each corner of the small room. You were videotaped for the entire session from several angles. This unique therapy tool was used in real life with real patients, providing a teaching tool to the associates who were to spread the work of Christ and his partner.

This video device was a great tool in the film, helping tell the story of my character in *The Clinic*. Dr. Christ Z. and I, though, had an agreement that the tapes of my real sessions would never be used or shown.

Despite my initial misgivings, Dr. Z. was instrumental in helping me move through a rite of passage by asking me a question that no other therapist or psychiatrist had even thought to ask: "When was the last time you visited your father's grave?"

I sat there dumbfounded, totally stunned, mouth ajar, and just stared at him until I probably started to drool. At least I don't think I looked away. Finally coming to, I told him that I couldn't remember my last visit.

"It's quite possible I've never *ever* been to my father's grave."

As soon as I left his office, I called my mother in St. Louis and asked her if I'd ever gone to the gravesite where Dad was buried. I hadn't. Nor had she, ever! Also, there was no marker on his grave. This revelation was stunning and telling. My mind reeled with the implications. I had to do something about this right away.

Frank Wallis, one of my lawyers, lived in St. Louis, so I asked him to get me the name of a stonecutter who would inscribe my father's marker for his grave and help locate the gravesite in Calvary Cemetery. I wasn't at all sure that my mother would know where it was, even though she was to be buried with him when she died.

I went home after the completion of *The Clinic,* having arranged for the stone to be placed. I was going to my father's gravesite, bringing my mother, somewhat reluctantly, and my sister and brother-in-law with me. Before going out to the cemetery, we all had lunch with Frank downtown, near his office. As we were saying good-bye to him I noticed a newly opened flower shop across the street, with Grand Opening signs waving. I turned to my family and said I was going to buy some flowers. No one else came or asked me to get some for them.

"How odd," I thought as I went to the shop across the street. As it happened, I was its first customer. I felt this was serendipitous that the flower shop just happened to be there, just happened to have opened a couple of hours before, and that I, or rather my father, was its first customer. There wasn't much of a selection, but I put together a nice bouquet and wished the owner a happy opening. Marv, my brother-in-law, had brought the car round and we piled in. I had a map with me and instructions on how to get to the cemetery. Once there, we would be provided with a map to my father's grave. The conversation in the car was odd as well, nothing about where we were headed. When we arrived at the cemetery, my mother behaved strangely. She walked ahead of us and appeared to be angry. As we continued walking through the cemetery grounds, studying the map given us, I looked ahead, studying my mother's back and the way she carried herself.

Without warning, my perception altered, an experience not unlike déjà vu. I suddenly saw her with my nine-year-old eyes, viscerally experiencing what it was like to be with her then. My feelings were also those of a nine-year-old: mystified, confused, and afraid of my mother's behavior and attitude. Why was she angry? She looked angry. Returning to my present reality, I realized that what I had back then thought to be anger, disapproval, something bad was perhaps her pain. I now understood why I always felt we never bonded as mother and child: she didn't share her emotions. She didn't understand her own emotions and consequently didn't realize how she appeared to me. Mixed messages. Misunderstandings.

I'd known that her mother wasn't a happy woman and had treated her coldly, but that experience in the cemetery, that realization, resonated and answered a profound and lifelong question in my grown woman's psyche.

Life is extraordinary. I thought that trip home was about me and my father, which it was, but it also turned out to be a most important lesson in my maturation, and another piece of the puzzle about me and my mother fell into place.

We found my father's grave right after that moment. My mother was unaware of my experience, as were my sister and her husband. My mother was still ahead of us, her body language still strong as we walked up to the newly planted stone that lay flat with the grass. She didn't come near it, but instead stood off to the side. I swept the new stone clean and laid the flowers on it as the rest of my family stood back. Talk about your awkward moments. It amazes me still that life really is a series of pictures, mental snapshots, and scenes. And if I can detach myself, I see clearly what is taking place, what is going on in the "photograph" just by studying the physical behavior of the subjects. When I'm "in" the picture I can't always see what is taking place; I can only act or react. That mental snapshot of my small family, standing at my father's grave for the first time, showed me a family emotionally disconnected. And in turn, I realized, or rather experienced, the difference between emotional disconnectedness and detachment.

Gently arranging the flowers around my father's simple stone, I asked myself, How do I begin? Innocuous thoughts came: How long had it been since he'd died (over twenty years)? I hoped he was happy wherever he was, which again brought to mind the disconnectedness of my family. I told him I didn't feel angry anymore, that I forgave him for his physical abuse, his prejudices, his weakness. I told him I hoped he had gone on to a better life than the one he'd had on earth, and that I was leaving for California the next day. Neither my mother nor my sister ventured closer to me as I carried on this mental communication. Standing up, I mentally told him I now understood his deep unhappiness as a child and young man. He'd had no skills for a successful life, having gotten no support or self-esteem from his father and mother. As I stood there looking down on his grave, I felt connected to him with a healthy sense of detachment, as though I'd known him and yet didn't know him. The same applied to my mother. I knew her, but I didn't *really* know her, because neither she nor my father really knew themselves enough to be able to share themselves with me. My prayer is that somehow they shared themselves with each other.

We remained quiet in the car on the way home. As we drove, I felt my anger building at this silence. What a missed opportunity for us, I thought. Why couldn't we have joined hands and shared our feelings around his grave? If that was too much for them, why couldn't we have had some kind of connection as we looked upon the simple flat stone? Do I let this go? Do I say nothing? What *do* I say? I struggled for appropriateness, but the longer no one said anything, the stronger my anger became. Finally, looking at the back of my mother's head, I said, "Did you at least like the stone, Mother?" She didn't turn her head.

"I told you, it was fine." Her tone was hard, edgy. When we reached her place I got out of the car as did Lyn and Marv. I told her I was going to stay with Lyn and Marv that night. I knew she'd say good-bye the way she always did, suddenly smiling, putting her face out for a kiss, careful not to bring her body forward. Was I going to let this go? Was I going to comply and not be truthful to my feelings? But was this moment an appropriate one for the truth? I felt it was. I didn't automatically kiss her, tell her I loved her, yah-de-yah-de-yah. I said good-bye and got back in the car.

As Lyn and Marv and I drove to their home, I shared my impressions and feelings.

"It's incredibly sad to me that we couldn't gather at Dad's grave as a family joined in feeling. Would it have been so terrible for her, for any of us, to admit our sadness out loud, our uncomfortableness, to join hands, to—God forbid—hug each other in real feeling at that moment?"

Marv said, "Well, you know your mother." Lyn then said that she felt uncomfortable and I told her that I did too. I felt awkward. I felt handicapped. Why didn't I ask them to join hands and be together? I knew that the moment was important for me. I'm glad that I came, that I put the marker there, that I paid my respects. I was just sorry that the moment couldn't have been "more."

Shortly after we got to their house the phone rang and I said, "I'll bet that's Mom." It was. She felt bad the way we'd said good-bye. I told her I felt bad that we couldn't have been more connected at Dad's grave, that she appeared angry at having to be there. She started to cry and say how much she missed "Jimbo." I told her that perhaps the pain was still great because she'd never let him go, never made her peace through grieving, that she'd never really acknowledged that he was dead. Her being cut off from her feelings cut her off from the rest of her family, I said quietly, without anger. My hope was that she might visit his grave on her own some day, but I don't think she ever has gone back. But thank you, Dr. Christ.

"Scalawag, scalawag, scalawag!" Ed and Anna chanted. "Is Chris a scalawag?.

"Oric Bovar certainly was!" G.A. crowed. Oric Bovar. What a strange name. What a strange man!

"So why the heck did you believe in that guy?" Ed pleaded.

Good question, Ed. Who was he really? A guru? A master? He thought himself to be. He professed to have the gift of being able to see the past and the future of people he had never met and didn't know. His gift was accessed by sending him your astrological information: your name, date, place and time of birth, and eventually he sent back your "Life Path." He lived in Italy, outside Genoa, but he was an American. He was somehow involved in the opera and music world.

He was supposedly uncannily accurate about your parents and your childhood. He even told you what the children you never had looked like!

"Jeezzzz," Ed sneered.

Thinking about it now, I marvel at some of the experiences I got myself into. But at the time, everything "new agey" appealed to me and the idea of knowing the future part of my so-called Life Path sounded exciting to me and to my friends. A lot of people wrote to Oric, including the Garys.

I received a double-spaced, typewritten letter. He told me I was a bundle of fire and water. An Aries with a Scorpio personality that had a lot of Sagittarius in it. If I wasn't careful my life could go up in wasted steam. He did, in fact, describe me pretty accurately and he was dead-on when he described my childhood. He said he would send me a meditation that I was to do every day for fifteen minutes. He felt that this concentration work was invaluable in overcoming the difficulties I had chosen to work out in this life. I wrote back immediately and told him to send the meditation because, he wrote, I had to be careful or I might mess up a fantastically successful life.

The Garys were "hooked" too, especially Dontzig. We loved sharing and comparing all our Oric info. What I did do, though, was go to Genoa, Italy, to meet Oric Bovar.

"Yeah, and on your honeymoon. No wonder Neil worried about who he married."

That's unfair, G.A. But true. Neil graciously arranged for us to be driven to Genoa, to have lunch with the much sought after Oric Bovar. I brought letters and greetings for him from a growing contingent in New York City. We arrived in Genoa the night before and stayed at a hotel that Oric recommended. The next morning we drove out of the city to our appointed lunch date at a restaurant that Oric had chosen. Now, even if my perceptions were exaggerated or, at the least, influenced by Neil's presence, I still remember to this day the visceral reaction I had upon meeting this man.

I met the devil. That is exactly what I thought. As we ate and listened to his catty and unkind remarks—everything he said sounded negative—all I kept thinking was, *What on earth must Neil be thinking?*

When we got back into the car and drove away, I told him what I thought and how strongly I reacted to that man. He was visibly relieved. I think he thought my devil reference was just a matter of speech.

When I returned to New York I took Gary and Gary aside and explained what I had experienced, that I was no longer interested in keeping up a correspondence with Oric Bovar and certainly wasn't going to keep up the concentration work. I wanted nothing to do with his energy and, as far as everyone else was concerned, they could do what they wanted. I thought that was that. I was mistaken.

On a trip to New York some time after we'd made the move to Los Angeles in 1975, I had dinner with new friends I'd met through Swami Muktananda, Uma Berliner Patel, her husband, and Raul Julia and his wife, Meryl. We had dinner at Nirvana on Central Park South one evening and as they walked me back to the Park Lane Hotel, Uma pulled me aside and asked me if I had seen the *Daily News* that day. Oric Bovar jumped out of a twenty-third-story window claiming he was Jesus and could fly!

I was embarrassed about Oric Bovar back then. I worried that other people would think me "a flake."

"Weeeellllll."

"Okay, okay, G.A. I'm not embarrassed about it now, although I can't imagine myself doing a lot of things I've done. It amazes me sometimes when I think of some of the characters I've met on this journey.

"You're an adventurer, lovey! Enjoy." Yikes!

WITHOUT WARNING I was pitched forward and brought back to the present by the screeching of brakes and the smell of burned rubber. We were inches from plowing into the back of what looked like a moving junk heap.

"You better get used to this, Marsha. That's the way it is out here. Plus, there are a lot of drunk drivers on the road."

Great, just great. Hello, new life. Hello, New Mexico.

"You better look at the directions to the house too; we're almost there."

As I reached into my big bag for the map and direction sheet, I pulled out Nancy's artwork for a Mother's Day long ago, my Filofax, and other sundry necessities. At the bottom was the tiny silver travel frame pictures of Baba and Nityananda and Gurumayi. I opened it and smiled at them.

"What a trip I'm on, Gary Dale. What a trip."

"This trip won't be over if we miss the exit."

"No, I know, I've got the directions. I mean the whole thing, my past. What a trip. I was just thinking about some of the crazy experiences I've had, with some pretty crazy people, and all the momentous change that went on while I was married to Neil, and just now, looking at Baba's picture, I am reminded of the seemingly accidental fact that both Neil and Baba came into my life at the same time, and then roughly ten years later, would leave it. Neil divorced me and Swami Muktananda died, all within a year or so, 1982–83. You talk about all known structures crumbling! Whoooeee!"

"When did Baba die?"

"Baba took *mahasamahadi* on October 2, 1982; he left his body on the full moon."

"Wait till you see a full moon here!" Gary was so happy, he was downright excited. I just felt tired.

"We've been together a long time, Gary Dale."

"Yep," was his only reply.

Neil and I separated in February 1983 and were divorced by the following April. And both men had a profound effect on me. They still do for that matter but in a different way now. I'll probably always be linked to Neil in the minds of some people, and certainly I am linked through my stepdaughters and their children—my grandchildren—and through the work Neil and I did together; and I suppose through Neil's plays *Chapter Two* and *Jake's Women* . . .

"Oh my gosh! This is the exit, Gary, the driveway is right up there. We're here! Can you believe it? I hope the house is okay."

"What does it look like?"

"Honestly? I don't remember!"

CHAPTER ELEVEN

THE MOVIE THAT NEVER GOT MADE (AND THE ONES THAT DID)

hat? I can't hear you!" the banshee screamed, "I'm out in the office!" The banshee was me, of course. I had lost it again, but felt entitled because my back ached and samba drums were pounding between my ears. Plus, the right side of my neck hurt with that constant killer migraine pain. My hands and fingers were clenching and unclenching in rhythm to the samba beat, so I stopped tearing at the invincible cardboard and assessed the damage. What used to be presentable hands were now petrified claws; my nails looked like The Gatekeeper's in *Tales from the Crypt*.

It hadn't helped that sleep eluded me four nights in a row. Perhaps the first night was to be expected because the night before you drastically change your life can be anxiety-making; and perhaps the second night was inevitable because we were on the road and sleep was never going to come; and again, the past two nights because Max is worse, the new house is strange, and even though there's carpeting, a sleeping bag is no fun when the temperature is above seventy degrees at three in the morning.

Gary and I opted to sleep on the carpeted floor of one of the bedrooms—there are five in all—because Max, not feeling well at all, had retired to the bathroom of this particular wing (the beige wing as opposed to the blue wing) and wouldn't come out. We decided we'd better be near him through his first night. Besides, it was the coolest of all the bedrooms.

Unfortunately, I found out the first night that the master bedroom was unbelievably hot. Windows that only opened on one side of the large room gave no cross ventilation because the window on the opposite wall was sealed glass. Great view but no air. I wouldn't let myself think about what it was going to be like in there for the rest of the summer. This was only June 30, and the worst of the summer was yet to come. I took solace in the fact that the house was very nice, and overall it was cool.

"Let's get a handsome carpenter out here, knock out the small section of that big picture window and put in a real window! Waddyah say?"

Good idea, G.A. Meanwhile, Chris and Gary Da Silva were running around town taking care of purchasing electric dryers (as opposed to gas, which I schlepped with me), sheets for the beds that we found when we arrived, food and wine (thank God for wine), plus a big fan for me.

It was only mid-morning, but already it was in the nineties. The moving men had arrived at 7:30 A.M. the day before and they had finally finished unloading everything an hour ago. Thank God some of the artwork was staying in the truck to be unloaded later in insured rental space. When they had cleaned everything up and were ready for me to sign off on all the papers, the nice man looked at the long list.

"Well, this is a first for me. I've never unloaded this many boxes of books on a single delivery. You must like to read a lot."

"Yes, I do. I hope the job wasn't too difficult."

"Naw," came the reply, "but you sure do have a lot of heavy stuff. Pretty but heavy."

GARY DA SILVA and Chris had decided to try out the guest house and they were happy campers. It had a king-size bed in the

bedroom and felt pretty cool on first inspection. There were five bedrooms in the main house, some with ceiling fans. Of course the master bedroom had no ceiling fan. Great. Just great.

"My God!" cried a voice in my head. It was the Martyr's voice. She
was in the snake pit, up on her crucifix, and she was wailing. I slowly
tried to stretch out my fingers while painfully struggling to stand upright from my field-hand position. I felt like a 104-year-old crone.

"Hell, I am a one-hundred-four-year-old crone!" I stated out loud.
"But without the wisdom!"

Staring out the big glass windows that make up one corner of the
office, I definitely feel like all of Southwest nature is gunning for me.
That majestic, CinemaScope nature view of New Mexico now seems
like a terrible psychedelic nightmare. I've never taken an LSD trip, but
this must be what it's like when you wind up on a bad one and can't
come down. The dry oppressive heat is palpably shimmering around
the juniper and chamisa, and the high, viselike altitude seems to press
in on the windows as the flies, mosquitoes, and vicious wasps the size
of birds go on about their day, taunting me, just waiting for me to step
outside.

My introduction to the "wildlife" of New Mexico has been daunting. There are these three-inch-long black, creepy, crawly beetle
things that seem to be everywhere, raising their backsides and spray-
ing if you come too close. The two-inch red "killer" ants scurry
around, pissed that I'm invading their territory. I've been told you
could get sick and die if they attack, so be on the lookout. And let's
not forget the major stars of the welcoming party, a four-foot-long
bull snake at the back door, and the fabulous five-foot rattler at the
front! Fuck the fact that bull snakes won't hurt you and rattlers just
want to be left alone. All this godforsaken nature has conspired to
drive me ragingly mad.

Oh! And let's not forget the infamously cute little creature critters
running around everywhere—Hunta Mice! Just the mention of them
on national television has kept the sane tourists away in droves, but
not me. Oh no, I had to leave that barbarous town called Hollywood

and strike out on the path not taken. I've decided to be a farmer. In the *desert*. At fifty!

I hope Gary Dale didn't detect my bitch-edged tone, because he's been so irritatingly great. He moves as if his feet were wheels, getting furniture in the right rooms, making jokes with the phalanx of moving men and woman, the latter for unpacking my more personal items. He's making sure all the beds are dressed and ready for the throng of eleven friends due in from L.A. just days from now, to help celebrate this momentous Fourth of July. He slides mattresses from one room to another, setting up each bedroom with a specific person in mind. I can't even think, let alone create pleasant spaces. He's already hung a couple of his paintings in his and Dontzig's bedroom (the coolest one!) while I'm still awash in Styrofoam and cardboard.

"Yeeeessss?" he croons as he stands at the doorway, looking at me with the sweet, weary patience of a parent. There's just a hint of mischief in those pretty, gray-blue eyes.

"Sorry," is my only reply as I gingerly begin to lower my tortured body down to the cool hard floor.

"Now, Marsha May," he admonishes as he surveys my flailing ship of a body surrendering to the foaming sea of Styrofoam, packing paper, and cardboard that is spread all around me. I point in the general direction of still more unopened boxes. He marches over my supine body and begins scooping up the foamy refuse, pitching it toward the door. I care not that I am in the way. Painfully, because my neck won't swivel, I try turning my head to watch Gary Dale, "Wonder Man." Grateful tears spring to my eyes.

"Oh, Gary," I tearfully begin, "thank you . . . Gary." I scream, "Don't Do That!"

He has attempted to pick up a large cumbersome box, straining to lift and balance it with the help of his knee as he careens precariously toward me on his way to the door.

"'Crushed by the Weight of Her Past.' That will be my epitaph."

"Testy, testy," he cautions as one of my first smiles of the day creeps across my face.

"Where do you want all these leather-bound scripts?" he asks, gri-
macing under the strain and weight.

"Just drop it on me, Gary. I might as well be buried by my past."

"Break time!" he announces as he drops the box with a thud right
next to my body, stomping over me and heading out the door.

I hate when I get so hopelessly bitchy and full of bad-tempered
self-pity.

"Come on, old girl, you can do it." Even G.A. sounds tired. Encouraging myself to rise to the occasion, and using the box as my
leverage, I manage to rise to my knees and slowly stretch from side to
side and then, finally, painfully try to get on my feet. Grunting and
panting I come nose to nose with a brown leather cover bearing the
title, *Bogart Slept Here* embossed in gold.

"The best job you'll ever have!" That's what everybody said. On
paper it did sound like the best job I could ever have: *Bogart Slept
Here,* written by Neil Simon, directed by Mike Nichols, and starring
Robert De Niro and moi. Anthea Silbert was doing costumes and a
slew of talented actors and a great creative team had been hired. On
paper it sounded great, only the movie never got made. Well, two
weeks of rehearsal and two weeks of shooting were "made," but the
picture was never finished. John Calley was head of Warner Bros. Studio at the time and I suppose he made the final decision. I remember
a figure of around $2 million having been spent or owed.

I was especially excited about the project because I was going to be
able to work again. After my limited time in *The Good Doctor,* due to
marriage and a surprise gall bladder attack that put me in the hospital
and my subsequent recoupment on a delayed honeymoon in Jamaica,
I had the very short stint in Lincoln Center's production of *Richard III*
starring Michael Moriarty, the shortness being due to handing in my
notice on opening night.

"Bad form, old girl." I realize that now, G.A. In the play I was cast
as Lady Anne, who is wooed to marry by Richard III after he kills her
husband and her father-in-law. And she accepts! Michael and Mel
Shapiro, the director, decided that Richard *shouldn't* woo Lady Anne

in the famous "wooing scene" because that's the way Laurence Olivier did it in the movie. How this is a valid choice for an actor to make remains a mystery to me. It is one of the most complicated scenes in all of Shakespeare because Anne is wooed by Richard. Evil is erotic. Isn't that complicated enough?

Exactly what I was supposed to do in that situation was never clearly explained, other than allow Anne to appear to be a complete idiot. Talk about trying to find "the truth" of the moment. When I asked the director what *exactly* he thought my first scene was about, since it takes place over the casket of my father-in-law, he had a re-markable response, "Necrophilia."

I tried to be a good camper about it all but I got tired of being backed upstage with a sword, ignored, despised, and sneered at, and I got tired of not being able to understand just what kind of production I was in. However, the pressure at home was the major contributing factor to my handing in my notice.

Sometimes, out of pain and hardship, humor rises to overcome all. That was the case with *Richard III* and Neil Simon on opening night. He sat in the audience that evening and waited for the play to start. Michael appeared and began his speech, "Now is the winter of . . ."

"Nope." That was exactly what Neil thought at that moment. He told me so after the performance.

"That quick?" I asked, astounded.

"I can generally tell the minute the curtain starts to rise if it's going to work or not." Amazing. An amazing man!

He was intrigued by the "wrongness" of the production and Michael's characterization and subsequently wrote wonderful scenes for another Richard in *The Goodbye Girl*. In that case Richard Drey-fuss played the infamous Richard III.

Because I was willing to surrender to Neil's wishes that I give up acting, at least for now, he felt more secure about my commitment to him and his daughters. He was, after all, still in a tailspin of grief and guilt, as were the girls, but we all managed to come together through that rough time in our own ways.

Neil called to me from his office one day; it was a room on the same floor as the bedroom. When I came in he was sitting behind his desk with an impish grin spread across his face. He always looked so delectable to me, but when this particular grin washed over his face he was irresistible.

"How'd you like to be in a movie?" he asked.

I was dumbstruck. "What happened to me not working?" I asked. He explained that we would be working together, and that I was talented and should work, and that a film commitment takes a shorter length of time than a play usually does. My mind whirled with the realization that Baba was accurate. I didn't hold on to my anger; I surrendered and wound up where I wanted to be in the first place. I'd honored my commitment to our marriage and consequently Neil honored me with a change of heart. He showed me some of the first pages of what would be our first film together.

THE STORY OF *Bogart Slept Here* was inspired by a conversation Neil and Dustin Hoffman had about what it was like having been a struggling, unknown actor in an Off-Broadway play, and having the great director Mike Nichols single him out for the starring role in his film *The Graduate*. It was also about what happens to you and your family when you become an overnight sensation. At the time, Dustin was married to a beautiful dancer, Anne, and they lived across the street from us in Manhattan with their two children. The film was about the vagaries of Hollywood as seen through the eyes of a talented New York actor with his bright and supportive wife and their two small children. The title came from the opening scene when the New York actor goes to Hollywood to be the lead in his first movie and the bellboy from the Chateau Marmont Hotel tells him that Humphrey Bogart once slept in his room.

The script was sent to Dustin first, but he took too long getting back to Neil and Ray Stark, the producer. Ray liked to get things going. He was a brilliant producer and extremely loyal and protective of

Neil. He knew how to produce a movie for a reasonable amount of money, which is what Warner Bros. was willing to do. Dustin, after all, was a big star and his fee would be big as well. Mike Nichols was also very expensive, but Neil was excited to work with him again. They had periodically tried to find a project together but hadn't been a team since *Plaza Suite* and *Prisoner of Second Avenue.*

Mike, Neil, and Ray decided next on a relatively unknown actor who had scored a big success in an early film of Brian De Palma's and the Martin Scorsese film *Mean Streets.* He was very talented and considered "hot," on the brink of major stardom. His name was Robert De Niro. He signed on and everybody was thrilled, especially me. There was just one small problem. He wanted to squeeze in a picture for the director of *Mean Streets,* before starting ours, which made his schedule very tight, literally. He would finish *Taxi Driver* on a Saturday in New York and be in Los Angeles for rehearsals on *Bogart Slept Here* on Monday. Faithful to his word, he arrived for rehearsal on the day promised.

We were pretty busy ourselves. Between the time Neil wrote those first pages and the first day of rehearsal, we moved to California. When I wasn't house hunting or house fixing or house moving, we were helping Ellen decide what college to go to, and trying to figure out what school Nancy would go to as well. When I came up for air and told friends about the project, everyone had a positive and sometimes envious response: "You are so lucky!" "What a fabulous opportunity!" "Robert De Niro!" "What a dream come true!"

Actually, it turned out to be a nightmare come true for all concerned. Neil came home one day from a preproduction meeting with Mike, his thumb sporting a bandage. He had gotten angry during a meeting and clenched a soda can so tightly he drew blood. By the time we went into rehearsal he and Mike were barely speaking.

Then several days before shooting was to begin while we were rehearsing, Mike's latest picture premiered at the Filmex extravaganza in Century City. Neil, Mike, and I stood at the back of the floor section and watched *The Fortune,* starring Jack Nicholson and Warren Beatty and Stockard Channing. Mike looked ashen. It was clear from the audience's response—or nonresponse—that the picture was a failure. The terrible part for Mike was that he didn't understand why it wasn't working. Neil put his arm around him. I just stood there watching these two incredibly gifted and successful men, not saying anything. Mike's confidence was deeply shaken. I know what that feels like. It was especially devastating because he was in the throes of our picture and had no time to himself, for his feelings, his thoughts, anything.

Then to make matters worse, Robert De Niro's body was still Travis Bickle's body. He too had no "down time," no space for himself before leaving one kind of character and inhabiting another. He seemed a bit at sea when he tried to connect to the funny, sunny, upbeat, and ebullient nature of his character in our movie. He needed time to "live" the character he was to play. When he asked me to move into the set with him I was flummoxed. Neil would have loved that. Living on the set with Mr. De Niro was definitely out of the question. I could feel the tension coming from Mike, from Neil, and from Robert. So there we all were, trying valiantly to have a good time, when a good time was not being had by anybody. The tension from both home and work was wearing on me. Mike came to my trailer and called me "Mason." I hated it and told him please not to call me that. He was taken aback and explained he had a nickname for everyone. For example, Anthea Sylbert was called "Bells," so what would I like to be called? With no humor left, my body as tight as a coil, I became Travis Bickle. Through clenched teeth I told Mike Nichols not to call me Mason, my name was Marsha, and I didn't want any nickname. Everything went downhill from there.

One morning we shot a very difficult breakfast scene. In it, I was cooking breakfast, for real, while my two small children were at the kitchen table eating cereal. Bobby comes to the door of the kitchen having just gotten up and asks a single question, which I answer while completing what I am cooking, dealing with business and dialogue at the kitchen table with the girls, and answering the phone and speaking with my mother who gives me an ulcer in the first place. To handle the phone call with all the dialogue, travel the length and breadth of the kitchen, and cook bacon and eggs for real required enormous concentration and choreography as to what goes where when because microphones were everywhere—behind cereal boxes, by the stove, and on me, picking up the dialogue as well as the ambient sound. We rehearsed with all the props for real, including the spitting bacon grease, along with the dialogue. Then we began to shoot.

Through all this action Robert had one line. We attempted several takes but when he couldn't get the timing right for his line, I'm ashamed to say I cracked. I lost it. I was pissed and blew it. Totally frustrated by all the men in my life at that moment, not to mention what the scene was about, I left the set and went to my trailer. Mike appeared a few minutes later and told me I should apologize to Bobby. Then I really lost it.

"*I should apologize?!*" came my measured clenched-jaw reply. I could barely contain the array of feelings roiling in my body. Unfortunately, I couldn't tell anyone why I was feeling the way I was. It wouldn't be right to tell Mike about the letter Neil had left me, knowing that he and Neil had conflicts. All I kept thinking was, This is the greatest job I'll ever have and I am majorly miserable. Unfortunately, because of my own conflicts and nervous tension, I couldn't recognize anybody else's problems. I felt like I was totally alone on that set amidst all that complicated male energy. Neil wasn't there, he refused to come to the set. He was at home, sleeping in another room, taking the girls out and telling them the marriage may not last. Mike was somewhere that I definitely wasn't and didn't or couldn't get to, and Robert was working the way he knew best. I felt beat up by all the men and everything around me.

The truth was that *I* was uncomfortable and intimidated around all that testosterone, and that wasn't their fault. I didn't realize then that the whole first year of my marriage and all that it entailed had taken up so much of my energy that by the time I came to work on *Bogart Slept Here* I had little clarity or energy or understanding left in reserve. The job of trying, all alone, to fulfill all my responsibilities to my family, to make Neil feel secure and happy while being available and sensitive in my career, all created a major overload.

What helped me to be able to move through the situation was meditation and Baba. Whenever I had feelings of anger and resentment toward Neil or Mike or the milkman, I'd put Baba's face between me and the other person, and all the difficult emotions would ease—at least, most of the time—and I could find the air to breathe and be able to step back and try to see the larger picture: Neil's anxiety about being abandoned, Mike's anxiety about failure, Robert's anxiety about the character he was trying to create. But there were nights and days, like the one I blew, when I couldn't or wouldn't put Baba's face between me and the problem. Sometimes I just didn't have the stamina and I let loose, generally inappropriately. And there were those times when I remembered the chilling words of my father: "A marriage and a career won't work."

My conscious mind fought that belief, but my subconscious mind held that belief to be true. It scared me when my reality seemed to be bearing out my father's dictum, echoed and reinforced by Neil.

I did go and dutifully apologize to Bobby, but underneath I wanted someone to come and apologize to me, to hug me and tell me it was all going to be okay. But I didn't have anyone around who could help me with this struggle. We'd just moved to Los Angeles, and although Gary and Gary had moved to L.A. before us, Neil was insecure about my relationship with them. It was difficult for him to understand, in great part because of his generation, that "exes" could be close friends. That's just the way most men of his generation were brought up, I suppose, and I was brought up to be scared and dutiful, with little room allowed for my beliefs. In later years, with the larger perspective that comes with time, I understood that I should have explained my position clearly, asked for the support of my friends, and helped Neil to learn to be more flexible.

In these later years I've come to understand that Neil represented the patriarch in my life. I was scared of him, the way I was scared of

My favorite shot of Neil and me during shooting of *The Goodbye Girl.*

17.

(left to right) My brother-in-law, Marv Candido; mom; my sister, Linda; and my best friend, Sally Dooling.

16.

19.

Lady Anne in *Richard III* at Lincoln Center

18.

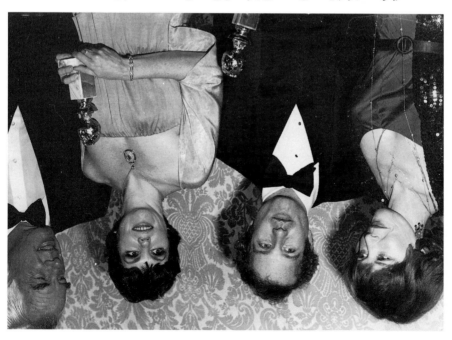

(left to right) Lee Grant, Richard Dreyfuss, me, and Lee Marvin.
He must be looking at my eye makeup!

20.

Robert Wise and Tony Hopkins during shooting
of *Audrey Rose.*

21.

Oscar de la Renta, who taught me how to dress in *Chapter Two*

My brief foray into racing with the Newman
Sharp Team. One day to be exact.

(left to right) Jimmy Coco, me, and Joan Hackett
during shooting of *Only When I Laugh.*

24.

Another killer smiler, Clint Eastwood.

25.

Nancy and Ellen.
What a fabulous duo.

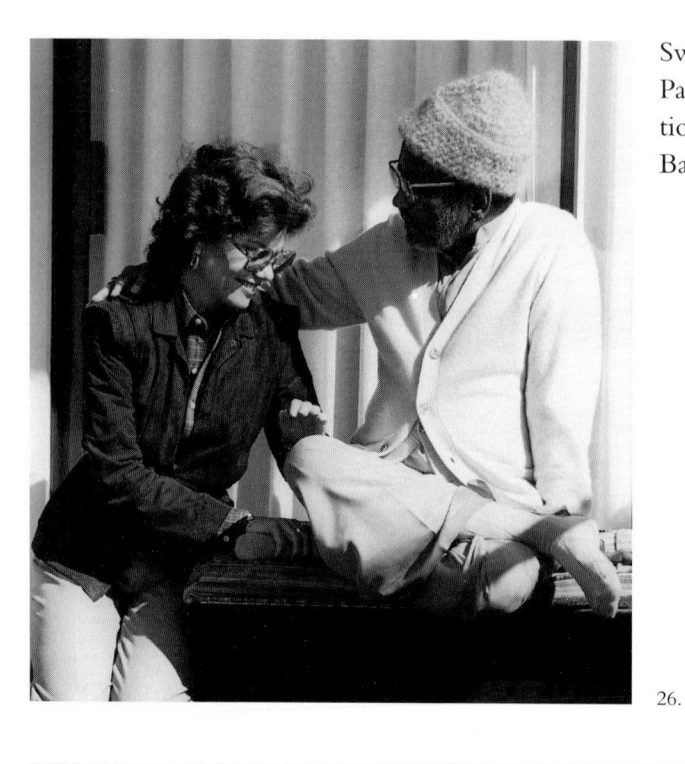

Swami Muktananda
Paramahansa. Affec-
tionately known as
Baba!

26.

27.

(left to right) Me, Kathy Baker, Robert Cooper, and Swoosie
Kurtz at the premier of *The Image*.

28.

John Erman, the director of *Stella*, Gary, and me.

29.

Carolyn Wright took this photo of Buddy, Dulcie, and Max resting that gorgeous head on Dulcie's tush.

Gary and Gary. That's Donzig on the left.

my father. In many ways I married my father, the patriarch, while I remained the child. Unfortunately, as the child, I always felt responsible for his happiness and terribly guilty when he wasn't.

At a private screening of *Cinderella Liberty* Neil watched the film with great discomfort. I immediately felt like I had done something wrong. Neil hated to see me nude and playing a prostitute, with an African-American ten-year-old son, who picks up sailors in a bar while shooting pool. We left the screening room and all I wanted to do was run down the middle of Broadway and never come back. I couldn't do that because I had to show up for the evening performance of *The Good Doctor*, so I walked slowly down Broadway to the theater and wondered what was going to happen when I got home after the performance. All my good work went right out the window and in its place came guilt, all because he was upset.

Consequently, I never allowed myself to enjoy my work in that movie. When it was generally released we finally took the girls to see it. They liked it and said so, and by that time Neil was able to see the work in it for what it was—very good. Unfortunately, Ellen and Nancy each received anonymous letters saying terrible things about their father and me because he had "married that whore," a reference to my character in the film, and stating how disrespectful it was to the memory of their dead mother—"Shame, shame, shame." All chances for me to enjoy my first real success in film were banished. Guilt, guilt, guilt. I had so much guilt I may as well have been Jewish.

ANYWAY, DURING THE shooting of *Bogart Slept Here* we went on location to an all yellow house. Literally. That, of course, was the joke. In the story, me and my two little ones arrive in Los Angeles. The studio has provided us with first-class travel and accommodations. The accommodations just happen to be all yellow. The house was yellow all over, down to a piece of porcelain, a head of Nefertiti, which just happened to be fired all yellow. I loved the scene because as an actor all that had to be done was to react to this house with all

its yellowness. We shot somewhere in the Hollywood Hills in a real
house that had been prepared by an ace designing team. Everyone was
in good spirits because the house looked great. By the next day
everything hit the fan.

The powers that be didn't think Bobby understood the humor in
the script. Worse, they were worried he might *not* have a sense of humor. It was an agonizing situation that I tried to stay out of because I
was a wimp and wasn't feeling any too funny myself. Gratefully, a
weekend came. Neil, Mike, and Ray Stark were all on the phone with
one another. I knew Neil was concerned and, frankly, I was concerned
because he was concerned; but I behaved like a coward in the situation.

The decision to fire Robert was made. Then came his phone call
asking me for help, asking that I come and rehearse with him. He said
he knew he could do it, he just needed another chance. I was still the
coward. I should have fought for Bobby, but I didn't know how. The
dailies had not been good and Neil was seriously worried about the
humor and tone of the whole movie and didn't agree with the slant
that Mike was bringing to the scenes. For his part, Mike seemed unsure about Bobby's ability to find the humor. I was in the middle, my
work on one end and my home life on the other. The pressure of the
situation was enormous but I should have fought for Bobby. What had
started out to be such a wonderful project had become a tense and
unhappy one for everybody involved. What had started out as an opportunity for me to continue to work and have a marriage at the
same time had become doubtful on all counts. And, finally, all that
male energy just plain overwhelmed me and I capitulated. I put my
tail between my legs and my head in the sand. I was no warrior then.
I wouldn't find my Warrior Self for some eight years more, and I
wouldn't bring closure to the whole situation of *Bogart Slept Here* for
another fifteen. But some kind of closure did take place.

ONE SUMMER, LONG after the picture folded and several years
after my divorce from Neil, I was on my way to London to record a

play for the BBC. Right before I left, I went on an interview for a movie that Danny DeVito was directing, *The War of the Roses.* I loved the script and begged my agents to get me a meeting. Danny was terrific and made the arduous task of interviewing easy, but he asked me a troubling question. He asked me if the reference in *The Goodbye Girl* to my ex-boyfriend, Tony DeForrest, was a slap at Robert De Niro. He cited the scene at the beginning of the film where I throw several bottles at a large picture of the infamous Tony, and he referred to the fact that the character's name had a "De" in it. I was stunned. None of these connections had ever occurred to me during the shooting of that picture, nor during all the years after, but now I was troubled by Danny's association. If he had made it, had Robert made it too?

I left for London and met up with my producer and friend Susan Loewenberg. She and I had been working together, through her production company L.A. Theatre Works, on a wonderful array of live recorded radio pieces. She was producing a series of radio plays for the BBC and I was over there to do, of all things, *Plaza Suite.* One night after work we went to the movies. She wanted to see *Midnight Run,* starring Robert De Niro and Chuck Grodin, with whom she used to live. The picture was wonderful. Chuck was wonderful. Robert De Niro was wonderful and *funny.* Yes, he could do comedy, in spades. As we left the theater I thought about what Danny DeVito had asked and couldn't stop thinking about it that whole time. As soon as I returned to New York, I checked into a hotel on Central Park South, and since I was still on European time I went to the movies. Down the street, *Jackknife* had just opened, starring Robert De Niro. He played a Vietnam vet who is trying desperately to find his way back from that horrible experience. I cried through most of it because Bobby was so incredible, playing a remarkably different character than the one in *Midnight Run;* and I was beside myself with the guilt of the *Bogart* experience and the weight of Danny's query. As soon as I got back to the hotel, I called my office and asked them to get an address for Robert in New York. I then sat down and wrote him a letter. The words just flowed out. The letter was painful to write because I had to own up; but it did come easily. I told him everything: about Danny DeVito's association, about my cowardice and guilt, about my denial of any responsibility for all those years, and about my enormous respect and admiration for him and his talent. Plus, I apologized for not being the strong person I should have been, for not fighting for him when I should have. I sent the letter as soon as I finished writing it. Robert called me as soon as he received it.

His voice was soft and sweet and gentle. He thanked me for the letter and told me that he hadn't made the Tony De Forrest connection at all, and that he well understood what the difficulties were when you worked with the person you were married to. I couldn't help it; I cried and thanked him for responding and told him what an inspiration he was. I also told him how sorry I was that I wasn't a warrior when I should have been. After I got off the phone I realized that I had been carrying that heavy baggage for a long, long time. I felt lighter having confessed my weaknesses, and after making amends and asking for forgiveness. I closed the drapes on Central Park South that day, crawled into bed, and lay there thinking.

My running from pain, conflict, and confrontation came from my childhood—my parents ran from theirs as well. Most of us do at one time or another I suppose. It's taken me a very long time, too long I sometimes feel, to stop and plant my feet and say, "Now, wait just a minute." I used to be so afraid of my faults, my weaknesses. Afraid that I couldn't possibly be loved if I revealed my foibles. It took being divorced by the most important man in my life to wake me up and begin the very painful, but ultimately rewarding, process of being fully responsible for all of myself, not just the easy or acceptable parts. I buckled under pressure because I was intimidated by all that successful energy. Men had something I didn't grant myself: permission to be who I am. I didn't have a "real" sense of myself: I thought I needed to get that from others. I didn't think I had any personal power.

When I was younger, during my thirties, I saw myself and my success only through Neil. I wanted to be as talented and as special as he and Mike and Robert are, but obviously I didn't think I had the right to an equal place. Entitlement. I didn't think I was entitled to success because I believed the greatest part of my success came from Neil. That's why, after the marriage, I tried to hold on to *Cinderella Liberty* and my earlier work, but the real problem was that my identity came *only* from my work.

Thankfully, that's changed, and I now see the path of entitlement clearly. There's always work to do, but I'm armed with all the knowledge, experience, education, and understanding I got from all my coaches, and my teachers. Sure, it smarts and sometimes feels painful to have regrets, especially since I promised myself as a young girl that I was determined to have none.

"The arrogance of ignorance, old girl." That's G.A. talking.

I suppose I was arrogant in thinking I'd never regret anything, but that day that I wrote Robert De Niro changed all that—that and the divorce.

As I drifted into a peaceful sleep that afternoon in New York City, I thought of Mike. He had tried valiantly to carry on after Bobby was let go so that the picture could move forward, but his confidence was critically undermined, and trying to make clear decisions when you are in that state is unbelievably difficult.

I've failed and not really known why, like in the production of *The Indian Wants the Bronx* in the late sixties, and would again in the Roundabout Theatre's production of *Night of the Iguana* in 1996. When I lose confidence in myself and my talent, fear clutches my heart and tears me apart. I wish I had realized that then; perhaps many things might have been different. At the very least, I could have comforted my fellow artists and shown some compassion instead of avoiding the situation.

Mike tried to forge ahead with *Bogart* for a while, and thought about who to cast. He thought of my friend Raul Julia, and a couple of others, but in the end he bowed out of the picture. Ray and Neil and the studio then hired Howard Zieff for about two weeks. One afternoon during that short time we had a reading of the script at Ray's office at Columbia, with Richard Dreyfuss.

Neil, Ray, Howard, and myself were in the room. The door opened and this bundle of sexy energy came through the door. I'd seen Richard in *American Graffiti* and thought he was nice. As soon as he reached out to shake my hand, I felt something. Chemistry was afoot. We all said hello and then sat down and began to read. And it was chemistry, pure and simple. He was wired with intelligence and rhythm and the quickness of response that made Neil's script crackle with wit. Richard and I were a match. We read as if we'd known each other for years. Our timing was in tune. We didn't have to question; we didn't falter. We just flew through the material. When we stopped, we spontaneously hugged each other and got downright giddy. To this day, whenever I see Richard, we just break into big smiles and I hug'm and kiss'm till he laughs. I was so excited after the reading. Everyone was excited—except Neil.

"You two are great," he said. "It's the script. But I know what's wrong with it. Give me three to four weeks and I can fix it." And that's how *The Goodbye Girl* was born.

The Goodbye Girl was a wonderful movie and wonderfully received. Herbert Ross directed it, David Walsh shot it, and Al Brenner was the art director. And oh my, what a great time we had! Richard was unstoppable—full of energy, barely containable. He was so cocky and so sure of himself. I, of course, was my usual earnest, insecure, frightened self.

Richard was fast and funny. I was thoughtful and more serious. Richard was wild and free. I was a responsible wife and mother and an actress. I wanted so much to be like him. He was so sure of himself, so sure of his place and space, and he moves forward accordingly. He's bright, bright, bright, incredibly well read, and comfortable with his intelligence. Sometimes he's pompous and self-involved, but beneath all that lurks a good heart and a fine brain.

Our chemistry was a special electricity that was apparent to both of us the first time we met and it continued through the shooting of the picture, except once when he reeked of fish. We were in the middle of shooting and Richard was obsessed with his weight and how he looked on-screen. He decided that he was too fat and needed to diet instantly. His diet of choice was sushi. Day in and day out the man ate nothing but sushi. He had sushi brought to his trailer; he had sushi brought to the set. He had sushi sent to his home. The man lived and breathed—and reeked—sushi. I think he even slept with it. Unfortunately, I don't think he lost much weight. I adored everything about him—his quickness, his wit, his imaginative choices. The manic chimpanzee jumps at the door of his room, the way he pulled my panties off the shower rod in the bathroom. Everything about Elliot Garfield was Richard Dreyfuss. He loved that character. They were perfectly suited to each other.

Acting with him was so easy—at least, once he stopped eating raw fish—there was so much to react to. We were in sync without even trying. We even had the same thoughts about the work without even knowing. An example of this telepathic trait was in the bathroom scene, when I'm wearing a white moisture mask and he's trying to wear me down with his affectionate energy and make me admit we are definitely attracted to each other and should pursue this new relationship into a romance. My character wants none of it (but, of course, she does) and has decided that she is definitely off the idea of romantic relationships.

Herbert wanted to shoot the scene in one take and maybe "go in" for a close-up at the mirror. I loved the idea because movies don't often give you a chance to play a scene through to the end all in one take and leave it that way. There are some independent directors like Gus Van Sant and Robert Altman who like to work that way, but it's not done on a regular basis. We rehearsed with the camera operator working out some tiny moves, necessary because the bathroom was small. And then we shot it. We did it fast and wild and funny without a lot of rehearsal because Richard and I connected so well. We finished the scene and went home for the day.

The following morning we both arrived on the set.

"Where's Herb?" Richard asked me, walking onto the set.

"I'm looking for him too," I responded. "I want to talk to him about the sce . . ."

"I want to reshoot it," Richard interjected. "It was too fast, it . . ."

"Me too!" I interrupted. "I mean, I want to too. He'll have to listen, we both . . ." We didn't finish the conversation. We went in search of Herb.

Herbert Ross is a droll fellow and very much the benevolent dictator, which I think all great directors probably are. They have to be. How else to keep the production in line, on budget, and on time? There are so many decisions that have to be made and so many people waiting for an answer. A picture has to have a vision that's communicated clearly and concisely to everyone who is involved. And then there is the actor. Herb had a simple law or dictum when it came to doing a scene successfully, and he stated it simply, elegantly, and quietly: "Do I believe it? That's what I ask myself. Do I believe what I'm seeing? I believed what you two did yesterday. I think it was a great scene beautifully done. It's the right tone and the right energy, but if you want to reshoot, we'll reshoot. Show me what you want to do. We'll look at the dailies this afternoon, at lunch, of what you did yesterday and then decide. Okay?"

All my bluster energy dissipated. Richard and I sheepishly grinned at each other and said okay. We looked at dailies, then looked at each other, shrugged our shoulders, and that was that. We didn't reshoot the scene and it's still one of my all-time favorites.

One of my favorite actresses to work with was nine years old going on twenty-seven. She made "precocious" a wonderful word. Quinn Cummings was a little girl with a very big intelligence. She knew her lines, was as quick and almost as smart as Richard, could land a joke with the best of them, and she was a professional. I suppose her mother was partly responsible for that.

We were rehearsing a scene together one day and she was to say her line and move to a chair and sit down. I noticed that she did it exactly the same way every time. Acting that way shows good discipline, but the freshness can go away pretty quickly. I spoke with Herbert about it and told him I wanted to try something. Quinn and I started the scene again and when it came time for her to move to the chair, I sat in it instead. Naturally, she was thrown by this and looked to Herb. He carefully and quietly explained to Quinn that in life we never know what another person is going to do and we don't always know how we are going to respond to someone or something. She listened intently, nodded her head, and said, "I got it." She was extraordinary in her ability to go with it. At nine!

Her father had a sudden heart attack during the shooting and died before we finished. He was a very nice man, only forty-four or so at the time, as I recall. I wonder if she experienced her father's death in any way like Nancy experienced her mother's? Quinn went on to be a regular on a television series where Kristy McNichol got her start. Kristy was another daughter of mine, in *Only When I Laugh*. Another natural.

"WELL, I DON'T feel so natural right now, I'll tell you that!" I spoke out loud to no one in particular. Or rather, to no dog in particular. Max was still in his bathroom and not about to come out. Blood and serum was still oozing from his surgery wound. I knew I'd have to take him to a new vet on Saturday. Warren says the vet has a good reputation, but I'm nervous. Dulcie and Buddy are lounging on all the cardboard and filler that surrounds me, sound asleep.

Slowly I leaned down to pick up another leather-bound script. The next one was royal blue with gold embossed letters: *Only When I Laugh*.

"Now there's a good movie and a good performance, old girl." Thanks, G.A.

That was another terrific working experience. I was in my prime, a well oiled machine cooking away. One of the unique experiences of that movie was ensemble performing. Neil wrote the script that way deliberately. He wanted to have the experience of the play *The Gingerbread Lady* up on the screen and this was his adaptation. I am particularly fond of it because I feel my work in it is good, very good. I was particularly right for it too, although Neil didn't know that at the time. He said to me before we began shooting that I was going to have to work hard to "get" this character. He didn't think "Georgia" was close to me at all. I knew she was. She existed before our marriage and after my marriage to Gary. The movie and the play are about an alcoholic actress trying her damnedest to make her life with her friends and daughter work. I could relate. I could relate to the alcoholic aspect of the character as well. Although I'd never been to an AA meeting until I started the research, I could relate because of my experience at home while growing up. I thought about it a lot and decided that what was important was to reveal the character of Georgia in as honest and truthful a way as possible. My relationship with my mother helped me to do that.

Way back in 1980 I hadn't seen a drunk woman played any other way than what would be considered generic. What had always confused me as a child about my parents' behavior when they drank was that they didn't act like people in movies or on television. They were "glow drinkers," people who behaved in a socially acceptable manner in front of other people, but sometimes, like Jekyll and Hyde, when they were in their own home their personalities changed remarkably. Georgia's behavior in *Only When I Laugh* was often unacceptable, although sometimes acceptable. She'd lost the right to her child and had lost her marriage and her latest lover. My parents didn't act like Georgia but it was sometimes difficult to understand their change of temperament and seesaw behavior. It was that hyper, strained, "turn-on-a-dime" quality I wanted to put on the screen. One of my favorite scenes from that movie is the telephone scene between me and my doctor's office.

"WHAT ARE YOU doing Marsha May?" Gary's break time was over and he was at the door with a plate and a sandwich in his hand. "You should be finished in here by now. Guests are coming." The last sentence was sung in a slightly irritating singsong manner. Part of me wanted to scream, "I *know* guests are coming!" But I didn't.

"Sorry I've been so bitchy. I just hurt all over and I'm not at all sure I'm gonna be up for all the festivities."

"I know, I know," he answered sweetly. "Here, eat this. You're probably just hyperglyseeik." I laughed and continued to laugh until I had to sit down on the floor again. Mr. Malaprop.

"Hypoglycemic, Gary Dale, not 'hyperseemia' or 'hyperglyseeik.' Hypoglycemic. And thank you for the food. I was just about to put these scripts up there on the top shelf," I said, pointing to the wall next to where the desk had been positioned earlier.

"Eat," he ordered, handing me the sandwich, and hauling away some scripts.

"I was just thinking about *Only When I Laugh*."

"Some of your best work. Well, all your work's good, I think."

"Thanks, Gare."

He continued on, heaving the scripts with the focus of a missionary and I was grateful. I was grateful for the sandwich as well.

"Where are you gonna put your nominations and stuff?" he asked as he opened another box.

"I don't know, wherever."

"Hey, there's two of these blue leather binders for *Only When I Laugh*. One's Neil's, but it doesn't have anything in it."

"Yeah, I know," I said, munching away. "I wanted to keep it though, something of his. But now, I don't know, maybe I'll send it back to him. When is everyone showing up?"

"Tomorrow, Marsha May. I told you before. Let's get a move on. You still have to unpack the books from your bedroom." He was starting to sound like Chuck Moses, the Pusher.

"Okay, okay! Tell you what, I'll do this box. You open that one. It's the plaques and stuff." I emptied the box of all the scripts and inched the ladder over.

Max Dugan Returns. September 21, 1981. Property of Twentieth Century-Fox. Screenplay by Neil Simon. Second Draft. This script mustn't be the final one, no leather binding. Then I find the final: *Max Dugan Returns*. Revised Final Script dated February 19, 1982. This one was the working script. All my scribbles are there, faded now, in pencil. Inside the binder, loose green pages marked "Revised

May 18, 1982" were on top. Gently turning the loose pages, a three-holed, heavy paper slips out to the floor. "Debbie Evans" is printed in black boldface type and the insignia of the Society of Professional Stuntwomen is printed above a black-and-white picture of a very pretty young woman holding a cat. There are several pictures of her on the flip side, three of them in very dangerous situations on a motorcycle. In one she's airborne on a bike, in another she's just airborne! Ah yes, motorcycles.

IN THE MOVIE I had to ride a small motor bike on Venice Boulevard so they needed a stunt double. She would probably be used for a scene where I'm riding on the back of a motorcycle with Donald Sutherland when he chases some bad guys in the act of robbery. It was a night scene where we pull into a convenience store in my neighborhood—rather, "Nora Dugan's" neighborhood—Venice, California. Donald played a police detective and I was a schoolteacher. He was after me romantically and after my father Max Dugan, played by Jason Robards, who was a criminal and a philosopher.

I'd never been on a motorcycle before (this was before my racing days). Donald on the other hand was an "old hat" when it came to motor bikes and race cars. The producers arranged for a stunt coordinator to be my teacher. We'd meet across the street from the studio, in the large parking lot of a community park on Motor Avenue. By the third or fourth lesson I was feeling pretty confident. I'd ride behind him feeling what the bike was doing when he shifted and then I'd get on it by myself. I'm a good student and can pick up stuff pretty well.

One of my first scenes on the bike was the night shooting of the convenience store robbery. We are coming back from our first date and we're using the motorcycle as transportation. We rehearsed the action of Donald to the rescue a number of times "by the numbers" as they say. Finally, someone yells, "Picture's up." My makeup is checked, which wasn't really necessary considering I had a helmet on and it was totally dark. We all take our places, Donald driving, me straddling and holding. I felt wonderfully relaxed. I didn't have much to do, just hold on to Donald while he does his "cop to the rescue" thing.

Herbert Ross, our director, yells "Action!" and Donald "Lone Ranger" Sutherland suddenly becomes a knight on a metallic horse. Fortunately, reflexes took hold and I grabbed tight as Donald peels rubber with the back wheel, which I'm sitting on. I watch the front wheel appear above our heads with the Venice Beach moonlit sky facing me. I was parallel to the asphalt instead of perpendicular and mesmerized by the slow-motion action I was experiencing. It all happened so fast and was over so quickly, but somewhere in the middle, everything went into slow motion. I have the picture in my head to this day, the top of the front wheel of the motorcycle, a moon with twinkling stars, and the sensation of momentarily lying down taking it all in and then Bump! I'm upright again. Fortunately, no one behind the camera yelled cut and they got it on film. To say that everyone's face was a bit gray is an understatement, but the guys loved it. I was mesmerized by the whole thing. I felt lightheaded, having kept my cool and following through with whatever the rest of the action was. Everyone was thrilled we hadn't landed on our backs. A few days later, however, there was another motorcycle incident; I was not at all cool and no one was thrilled.

That day the motorcycles were outside the soundstage, right by our trailers. Everyone was just "hang'n'" around waiting for Davey Walsh and his crew to finish lighting the next set-up. Herbert asked if my motorcycle lessons were going well, and I piped up and said, "Here, I'll show you."

I had quite an audience: Herbert, Neil, Jason, Roger Rothstein our producer, Donald, and my teacher. Donald got on one of the bikes to cruise around while Miss Harley here decided to show hubbie how she was doin' on the bike. I got on, without a helmet, started the dear little thing, picked up some speed, and then turned around for home. I was within a few feet of the group and shifted gears. The bike surged ahead, headed squarely for the side of my trailer. Everything happened so fast I thought I was on "fast forward." The front wheel rammed the trailer, fitting right between the back tire and side frame. I slammed into the handle bars and my head came just inches from hitting the aluminum siding. I was still standing, but I couldn't breathe.

I looked at the grown men running toward me. Neil was truly the color of gray. It was then that I felt I needed to lie down, which is what I did, but I still couldn't get my breath. While grown men tried not to cry, I kept wondering what happened to the slow-motion part.

I wasn't hurt, thank God. I'd suffered just a skinned knee, a few bruises, and a bruised ego. But I was forever impressed with the scary feeling of not being able to breathe. I also felt bad because I wanted to do well, make my teacher proud. He too was ashen, peering down at me. He never regained his sexy confidence with me, but he did get me back up on that little kritter, right away, and I did drive in regular traffic a few days later with Matthew Broderick, who played my son, sitting on the back. I considered it a major triumph that I could say my lines and drive at the same time. Granted, we went thirty-five miles an hour, but by God, I got us there without mishap or a ticket.

Since then I've driven race cars 150 miles an hour on a racetrack, finished second or third in my division several times, and raced the Valvoline National Runoffs three years in a row. I've spun out tons of times, sometimes saving it, sometimes not; I've been rear-ended, punted off the track, and T-boned by crazed male drivers who lost their cool, but I've retired from motorcycles, thank you very much.

"MARSHA MAY!" GARY was losing his patience.

"Sorry. I know . . . I was just thinking about shooting *Max Dugan Returns*. I loved making that film. One of my favorite moments was the baseball sequence between Matthew and Charlie Lau, the White Sox batting coach . . ."

"Never mind that. You have guests coming."

"We have. We have guests. I know. Just let me do this in my own way. Don't make me any more crazy than I already am." He heard me but grunted and went on unpacking.

"I'll be back in a minute," I said, heading outside. The hot air didn't make me feel any better. I went and sat down under the big old Russian olive. There was nowhere to go to get away from the uncomfortableness or myself. I hate not feeling good, and I especially hate not feeling good when I'm working. Mostly I do feel good when I'm working, but if I don't, I'd rather be working because then my mind is off my problems. Unfortunately, my problems were apparent while I was shooting *Max Dugan Returns*.

We were shooting the baseball game scenes at a school field in Venice one day. I was standing by the bleachers as Donald Sutherland walked over to me. He had the irritating habit of standing too close to me, or so I thought. I remember that his proximity really bothered me at the time so I'd back away a bit, but he'd adjust and move in a bit. This particular time as I sat down on the bleachers he plopped down next to me, leaving no space between our bodies. I became so irritated I moved and put my purse down between us.

"Rather belligerently you must admit." Yes, I made a moment of it, G.A. Naturally he was taken aback by this gesture and asked me why I had done it. I said something about his being six feet five inches and his presence being somewhat overbearing. I also charged that he seemed to have no awareness of how he invaded a person's "space." I think that's the word I used. "After all," I said rather huffily, "he was a big man, and not to be aware of how he was invading another person's space was irritating and occasionally upsetting." I seem to remember feeling rather righteous about it all, but a bit embarrassed by my use of the phrase "personal space." He immediately shifted his body away from me, cocked his head with a quizzical air, and seemed to be looking at me with new eyes.

He looked at me rather compassionately and said that I had to be careful about becoming more and more isolated. I remember that term distinctly—"isolated." Hearing it scared me, but also made me curious. Then he asked me if I'd ever read *The Outsider* by Colin Wilcox. When I replied that I hadn't as I reached for some paper and a pen to write the title down, he stopped me, insisting he wanted to get it for me. And in fact, he presented me with the book a couple of days after that.

He was right. I was isolated. I'd been moving in that direction for some time by then. I felt I had no personal space left and was becoming desperate for it. I was also protecting myself; something deep was afoot but I didn't want to look at it. I admitted that I was scared. The gnawing feeling in the pit of my stomach became specific. I was losing myself.

What Donald's gift did was bring me out of myself a bit. His interest helped me feel not so alone. I started making an effort at conversation with Donald, sincerely interested in what he had to say. I admired his sense of adventure. He led an interesting life, definitely out of the ordinary. He was an activist during the protest era of the Vietnam War; he was obsessed with the Toronto baseball team; he worked with terrific European directors; he loved cars and racing; and he had a beautiful "wife" and family. Donald is, by my definition, a Renaissance man. On top of everything else, he spoke French and was the first man I knew to wear Armani. He loved clothes and looked fabulous in them. The man has style.

He was also a father. His oldest son, Kiefer Sutherland, played a small part in the movie. He was around fifteen years old at the time and very intense. I think he and Donald were in the throes of teenager-parent stuff then. Several years later I would work with Kiefer again in a movie titled *Trapped in Silence*. It was about a young man who wouldn't or couldn't speak and the therapist who helps him. He's a wonderful actor both to work with and to watch.

"Back to work," ordered Chuck Moses.

I MOSEYED ON down to the guest house to find Gary barreling out the door.

"Do you ever just stop and take a breath?" I asked.

"Haven't got time. Where's the hammer and stuff to put up pictures?"

"I don't know," I replied as he bounded toward the house. When I looked in, Gary had placed all my plaques and stuff out on the floor, arranged in a neat pattern. I stared down at my past. The top row consisted of the white, gray, and black plaques for the four Academy Award nominations in chronological order. The second row started with the British Academy Award nomination for *The Goodbye Girl* and then came a certificate of appreciation from the city of Los Angeles and the Emmy plaques for the program I produced for the *Pioneer Women* series. Then came the American Film Institute and various other acknowledgments. Two of them I hadn't seen in a really long time: one was for work on the Equal Rights Amendment and the other was for setting a fine example of "Liberated Motherhood." I had to smile. That one actually belongs to Nancy and Ellen and all the characters I've played who had children.

CHAPTER TWELVE

JOURNEY TO RECOVERY

W hat are ya doin', Marsha May?" Gary Dale's question was garbled by the handful of popcorn he was stuffing into his mouth as he sauntered into my new, albeit rented, bedroom, holding a Diet Pepsi and a huge bowl of what was his favorite food.

"I can't believe you made it in here without spilling something or killing yourself. This house is a minefield of packing refuse and supine animals. How on earth did you do that?"

"Years of practice," he answered, then abruptly changed the subject. "I don't see any books on the shelves. I felt books under my feet but see no books on the shelves. You don't get any popcorn. That was the deal."

"Give me a break, will you?" I said rather peevishly.

"I've been giving you breaks, haven't I?" he crowed. "But *I've* finished . . . on time and under budget!" He graciously gave the dogs some popcorn, but still offered none to me.

"Hand over that bowl," I growled. "I'm working on it. I'm trying to decide what books I want to have in here. I want everything in this room to help me feel good. I want to put my favorite things around me. This pile is what I've chosen so far. I know I want to make a puja table out of the next to last shelf and I want all my Siddha Yoga books to be in here . . ."

"What are these?" Gary asked, turning the two books over in his hand. I recognized them instantly.

"Oh, one of them was a gift and the other I found some years later. They are beautifully written. . . ."

"Who gave them to you?"

"Well, one was a gift—*Joy of Man's Desiring.* It's a novel written by a French writer who died in 1970, Jean Giono. The other, *Blue Boy,* I found in a bookstore. I've had them a very long time. . . ."

"Who gave you the book?"

"The Shadow Man."

"The what?" The look on Gary's face made me laugh.

"Oh, it's a name I gave someone because he showed up in my dreams a lot, dressed like Humphrey Bogart in *Casablanca.* He was always in the shadows of my dreams."

"Is he real or did you make him up?"

"Oh, he's real. Very real. He was perhaps one of the most real men in my life, although I haven't a clue what I mean by that." I laughed again and wanted to change the subject but I knew he'd now be in my mind for the rest of the night. That's always the way it is with him. Long periods of time will go by and I won't think of him. Then suddenly I'll see him on television or something will remind me of him and boom, I'll think of those fleeting moments. . . .

I first saw him on a New York City street in the late sixties. I was waiting to board a chartered bus that was taking me and several others to the Eugene O'Neill Playwrights Conference up in Connecticut. He walked down the street toward the rest of us accompanied by a man and a woman. I was instantly dumbstruck, as well as stricken by a piercing pain in my chest that felt both exciting and depressing. It was exciting because he was going to be at the conference and he was gorgeous; Adonis came to mind. It was depressing because as I watched him say good-bye to his girlfriend, who was beautiful, I knew that he'd never be interested in me.

As the days passed, I'd watch him carefully, hoping no one would notice. When he was rehearsing, I'd try to sneak a peek. I watched him make friends with some of the other actresses. Women adored him; he was hot. His girlfriend came up to see him and stayed. She was a beautiful, long-legged dancer who thought nothing of doing cartwheels while conversing with others on the steps of Eugene O'Neill's old house. They were a physically striking couple without a single ounce of fat anywhere. A beautiful couple.

I'd watch from a distance, feeling disappointment and sadness because I couldn't hope to be noticed. I had long hair too, and I tried to make it look like hers, but it always curled when it was dry. Hers was long and straight and shiny. I had nice-looking legs but that was about all.

Years went by and I didn't see him. Then I'd notice his name in the paper, about to open in a show. I'd go and watch him work and wish that I could be as good. Sometimes I'd see him come out of the theater and I'd say hello and tell him how wonderful he was. He was always courteous and would thank me as he took off down the street. More years went by.

And then an odd thing happened. I was able to recommend him for a play and he was wonderful in it. One night, in New York, I accepted an invitation to meet him for a drink. We were to meet up on a corner on the East Side. As I walked to the appointment I felt my heart beating so fast that it hurt, pounding with excitement and happiness. I couldn't wait to see him. After all those years of secret longing my feelings for him blossomed on that walk, and I felt as if I would burst apart. The crowds going home after work were scurrying past when suddenly there was an opening and I caught a glimpse of him standing and waiting for me. He was looking around; he wanted to see me. I started running, laughing and breathing hard. He quickly turned in my direction just as I was approaching, and without hesitation he scooped me up in his arms and twirled me around. We laughed and hugged each other. I held on tight and felt the warmth of his neck and the cold of his ear and the softness of his hair while I breathed in his scent, memorizing all of it.

He was born in another country and came to the United States to be an actor. He's also a writer, and a good one, but extremely shy about it. I encouraged him to put his stories on paper, and finally one afternoon in bright warm sunshine we sat and he began to read his story aloud. His hands shook and his voice was low. He was born in the wild and lived in a harsh environment with his family. His father was blind and would take his glass eyes out before he went to bed. His mother was a quiet woman, kind and strong. They lived in a cabin in the woods, a place without electricity.

He wrote about his first day at school and how he ran away and hid because he was so fearfully shy. I felt fortunate that he allowed me to see who he really was. He was still Adonis to me, but he was also a frightened child. He was so very real and I loved him. He brought out something hidden in me, something that had become unfamiliar during the years with Neil. I wasn't afraid of him. I didn't worry about his approval. I was looking at someone I wanted to be and to be with. But the circumstances conspired against us. It wasn't right to jump into someone else's life while mine was in shambles. I didn't want to hurt him. I didn't want to hurt anyone anymore.

He also brought out the child and the young woman in me. He was grounded, with his heart wide open, rooted to the center of the earth like the great giant trees that live on high mountains, just like the stranger in Jean Giono's book. I wanted to be like him but he was much more courageous than I.

I wrote all kinds of letters, all unsent. They filled several journal books. I'd write to him as if I were speaking to him, telling him my feelings. I finally sent a letter to his agent's address. He wrote back and gave me an address I could use while he was out of the country. Shortly after that a reporter called me while I was in New York, working out the details of my divorce from Neil, arranging the division of furniture and belongings. He said he was from a London

paper I'd never heard of and wanted to verify a story that I was running away with—and he used his name—the Shadow Man. The reporter said he'd heard that he was the reason Neil and I had divorced.
A chill clutched my heart.

It was so creepy that someone knew something so private about my
life and that an innocent person could be dragged into false gossip
about my divorce. And then life became truly surreal. I went to a play
a couple of evenings later, by myself. As I looked around at the crowd
waiting for the play to begin, I looked up to the top rows of the steeply
raked seating, and there he was, Shadow Man, sitting with a beautiful,
dark-haired woman. The divorce, the reporter, him—everything conspired against me. I started to shake all over and couldn't stop. I didn't
know why I felt so scared. The lights went down and the play began. I
was grateful for the dark. I haven't a clue what play I saw or why I was
there. When the play was over I was determined to get out of the theater. Wild thoughts flew in my mind. What if that reporter was in the
theater? What if he'd followed me? What if, what if, what if? I knew I'd
fall apart if I had to have a conversation with anyone.

It was raining as I ran from the theater, heart pounding, breath
coming in gasps. Spotting a cab with his light on, I ran down the middle of the street, giving rise to a chorus of horns. The cabby didn't see
me so I slammed my hand hard against the closed window and
screamed, "Stop!" The poor cabby was so shaken by my sudden presence that he practically had a heart attack and told me so in no uncer-
tain terms, for which I apologized. As we drove through the summer
rain, I tried to understand what was happening to me. I was terribly,
terribly scared.

"Your fear of intimacy, old girl. The Shadow Man had opened the
sluices of your soul."

It's such a strange struggle, intimacy. Something I craved and yet
something I feared. It came so easily with him, that first and only
time.

"Okay. What's next?"

"What?" I stared at Gary. How long had I been "gone"? I wondered.

"I've got Baba's books and stuff on this shelf here, and I put the books that were in that stack over there on the shelf above. What's next?"

"A soda. Do you mind?"

"Okay, I'll get you one, but start on that pile over there," he said, pointing to still another stack of books, which fell over as if on cue, sending brightly colored journals all over the floor.

"I haven't looked through those journals in years," I said as I reached for popcorn.

"No reading! Read later, after July Fourth!"

"Okay, okay, but hurry! I'm liable to choke if I don't get something to drink." As Gary went off to the kitchen I sat down again on the floor. My journals looked like variously colored stepping-stones leading nowhere. My favorites were the shiny fire-engine red ones and the periwinkle blue ones. They were French. They didn't hold any of those unsent letters to the Shadow Man. None of them did. I tore them up after the last time I saw him.

I went to see him one afternoon at Circle in the Square, the Manhattan Theater Company on West Fifty-first Street. This time he was alone as he came out of the stage door after the performance. I wanted to explain my erratic behavior, the fear of lost privacy, but I just made small talk as we walked to the corner. He ran into the street and hailed a cab. For a brief moment I thought he was going to get into it with me. Instead he opened the door for me then closed it quickly, saying good-bye. It felt like I'd had the biggest brushoff of my life.

Gary returned and handed me the soda, looking balefully at the sea of books and journals scattered around me.

"It's 10:30 Marsha May. I'm . . ."

"Yes, go on. I'm not tired. I'm gonna finish this up. Thanks for the soda."

"Don't stay up too late. We have to get up early and get everything done."

"When is Dontzig coming?"

"In the afternoon." He yawned. "Tom, Steve, and I think Todd will be with him. Amy's coming later that night or in the morning and . . . I can't remember the rest. See ya in the morning."

I was grateful to be alone. It's odd that I've kept the Shadow Man alive in my memory all these years. I'm not even sure I know today who he really is.

Sighing deeply, I picked up the oddly rectangular-shaped journal next to me. The beautiful, slick white paper opened at the matching ribbon marker inside. These particular journals marked the beginning of my love affair with fine quality, heavy, shiny paper, and broad-tipped fountain pens filled with all kinds of colors of ink. I smiled as I ran my hand across the smooth paper surface, remembering how the pen would literally move across the shining page like a beautiful skater gliding on virgin ice. I'd purchased them on one of several trips I took to Paris, traveling the Concorde no less. I opened one and read the date aloud. "Oklahoma City, September 9, 1984." I must have been shooting *Surviving*. Yes, the story of two families and how they dealt with the suicide of their children. I played an unsympathetic mother who didn't understand her daughter at all. Molly Ringwald was my daughter and Paul Sorvino played my tortured husband. Ellen Burstyn played the other mother and Len Cariou played her husband. Zach Galligan played their son. River Phoenix was also in it and the little girl from *Poltergeist*. Gosh, River is gone and so is that lovely little girl.

Sighing deeply, I am reminded of just how transitory life really is.

"All the more reason to enjoy it while we're here, old girl." Yes, G.A., enough of this "mooning" about.

THE RITUAL OF journal writing in these lovely diaries, on this sensual paper, was far more satisfying than what I wrote, I'm afraid. I'm disappointed. These are unbelievably vague entries, nothing remotely specific, not even marking down the year. My recollection of some of the entries is much more vivid and specific than what I chose to write down. Why is that?

Here, in another one, with a periwinkle blue cover, I wrote, "What does it matter what I write on these pages! Who cares! To what end! Perhaps it is worthwhile if I find some creative use for them (all these half-finished journals) when I'm older." Turning the shiny pages with my vague scribbling, I ran my fingers back and forth over the smooth, cool surface of the paper as I continued to read aloud.

"Virginia Woolf wrote in her diary at a prescribed time, after tea, knowing it stands a better chance of fattening if it has a prescribed mealtime. And she enjoyed rereading her diaries. She believed she got closer to her feelings and even closer by leaving them to be read later. I'm not sure I *want* to get any closer to any of my feelings at this point in my life. I'm not sure I even wrote about my feelings in these diaries." I tossed the shiny blue journal aside, lay my tired back to the floor, and ate more popcorn.

"I couldn't sleep. Want me to help?" Gary reappeared, looking cute in his T-shirt and shorts. He sat and I lay down as we munched in silence. It was nice having him by my side. He, of course, couldn't sit quietly for long. Crawling over to a box, he started to transfer the books and diaries to the shelves behind him.

"Oh wow, my Journey to Recovery journal!" I exclaimed, reaching for it as Gary continued to empty the box. I recognized the green border and the beige paisley and gilt paper center.

"Oh, and this book is here too," I said, grabbing a volume from him: "*An Unknown Woman: A Journey to Self-Discovery* by Alice Koller. Neil gave me this book. I remember thinking at the time that he was trying to tell me something." Gary paid me no mind as he continued to empty the box onto the few shelves.

"I remember him coming into our bedroom on Chalon Road in Bel-Air one afternoon and giving me the book, saying something like, 'I thought you might be interested in this.' He hadn't read it, but the title caught his eye. I guess he thought I was an 'unknown' woman in search of herself and might find the book helpful. I remember feeling guilty when he handed it to me."

"Guilty about what?" Gary grunted as he opened another box.

"I felt guilty about my oh-so-earnest struggle to know myself, wanting to get a handle on all those 'messy' feelings. 'An unknown woman,' that was me all right, back then, I mean."

"You were never unknown, Marsha May. Not to me," Gary mumbled as he stopped with the books and rearranged himself on the carpeted floor, leaning against the side of my big wooden bed. He dipped into the popcorn next to me. The bed we were leaning against was huge and heavy. It was the bed from the guest room in the Palisades house that had originally been in the master bedroom of the Santa Fe house that Neil and I owned when we were married, and now here it was, back in Santa Fe.

"When I think of the furniture I gave away when Neil and I got divorced," I said between munches.

"I'm glad you *did*! You'd just have *more* stuff to haul and unpack!"

I burst out laughing, spitting popcorn and causing myself to cough and choke. Gary slapped me on the back and sent a soda can rolling. Dulcie started to bark and for a few moments everything was mayhem. I just let myself go, rolling and holding my stomach, hoping I'd be able to breathe easier. It felt so good to just let go and be silly and stupid. After calming Dulcie down and pushing Buddy away from the bowl, I took a deep breath.

"Well, I learned a valuable lesson. Never trust your judgment when you are in the middle of a divorce or in the middle of a major move like this and always, for certain, never take your life so seriously that you can't fall apart and laugh until you cry."

"I love this bed," Gary said as he patted the foot of one of the posts. His non sequitur shifts were fascinating. "If you don't want it, I'll take it."

"I'll live with it a while and see how I feel," I answered. Turning the pages of the green and gilt paper-covered journal, my eyes resting on the top of the first page.

Huh. I thought I started this journal with the first of those eight meetings, but I guess I didn't because the first entry is dated 3/16/91 and below that I wrote, "A life worth living is a life worth recording."

Anthony Robbins said that. And below that I wrote "en route, N.Y. to L.A.," and then, "My One Year Goals." My eyes skimmed the page.

"You want to hear this?" I asked Gary.

"Sure," he answered, as he began to feed the dogs the remainder of the popcorn. "Go on, read. I'm listening," Gary said as he dropped a handful of popcorn onto the floor.

"Well, I'm not sure I want to share everything that may be . . ."

"You couldn't say anything I don't already know about. You sure that's the journal from the Recovery . . . thing?"

"Yep," I replied, as I thumbed the pages.

Gary had taken the "Journey to Recovery" course after I did. It surprised me, actually. He didn't usually want to do that kind of thing—the therapy, self-knowledge kind of thing.

I began to read aloud: "'My one year goals. Number one: the presence of real magic in my professional and personal life. . . .' I'm still waiting for that one," I said with a smirk and continued. "'Number two: a vibrantly sexual, loving, intimate relationship with a wonderfully exciting, healthy, bright, talented, and available man who loves women and enjoys his successful life . . .' I'm still waiting for that one too! Sure was in love with adjectives then . . . Uh-oh, it gets worse. 'My Soulmate' is at the top of the next page. Are you sure you want to hear this?"

"Go on," he said, laughing, "this should be interesting. You took the course because you hated your choices in men."

"Really?"

"Umm-hmm. I think it was after that weird actor guy," he responded.

"Which one!" I asked and laughed. "I didn't remember that until you said it just now." I shook my head. "It amazes me sometimes what I remember and what I don't remember."

"It amazes me I remember anything!" he guffawed. The phone suddenly rang, startling us all. I screamed out of sheer stress, Gary coughed all the harder, and the dogs started barking again.

"Jiminee!" was the only reaction I could muster as Gary wheezed and managed a choked whisper.

"Dontzig . . . phone . . . water . . ." he mumbled as he careened to his feet. "Be back . . ." was thrown over his shoulder as he managed to navigate between dogs, popcorn, and books, taking in gulps of air and letting out bronchial coughs that sounded life-threatening as he headed for the kitchen. The dogs became vacuum cleaners and proceeded to clean up the remaining bits of popcorn. Looking around at the mess I started to chuckle, again spreading myself out on the carpet.

I had taken this . . . what? . . . course? . . . or seminar? or series of meetings? called "Journey to Recovery" every Monday evening for a period of eight weeks. The course was held at a Jewish Center on Olympic Boulevard in Los Angeles. Gary was right; I'd signed up because of the frustrating and debilitating relationships I'd gotten myself into following the divorce from Neil. That Gary remembered the reason while I hadn't, left me with the sinking feeling that I'm always trying to remember what I've already learned.

Finally hitting the proverbial wall unleashed feelings that erupted like a volcano. "I've hit a few walls in my years of car racing haven't I, old girl," I said to Dulcie, who had come over and lay down next to me. She looked up at me adoringly, giving me the impression that she understood it all. It felt good to nuzzle her and lovingly stroke her pretty head. Buddy was too busy sniffing bits of popcorn out of the carpet to notice, otherwise he'd be standing on my stomach licking my face till it hurt.

I've been soundly T-boned by crazed drivers and hit physical walls hard, but hitting this particular wall, being emotionally T-boned by my choices in men following my divorce had left me enraged, upset, and totally frustrated. I had had it! No more! I told myself. Being pissed and fed up with my decidedly dubious series of choices in the love-life department, I finally saw them all as one long, slow buildup to a very big breakdown.

The beginning of the end started with the divorce in 1984, which led to relationships with Bob, the actor; Jack, the actor; then Ron, the businessman.

"Some business!" G.A. chided, "the man was an international weapons merchant!"

Quiet, I'm trying to think. Then there was Alexander, the cinematographer, a wonderful man and lover, a serious relationship that came at the wrong time. Then John, the "Creature from the Black Lagoon" actor, truly messed up. Then Lewis, another actor and my first "serious" relationship in that we tried living together. Then Keith Hernandez, my one and only foray into the world of professional jocks, and finally Narcissus himself, Robert, the weird actor Gary referred to. Please God, save me from any more actors! That line from *The Goodbye Girl,* when I first meet Elliot Garfield, "Actors!" resounded in my head.

Starting with the divorce and ending with Robert, I skied a downward spiral that was subtle and treacherous. The problem was, I had no perspective. I was too busy racing out of control to notice where I was headed.

Men did that to me for some reason. I love them. I adore them. I got into such trouble with them. And I had no idea why. They'd be attracted and pursue me and I would be flattered and instantly fall for them. The addiction of love and obsession. Wow, what a trip!

Then they'd be distant, and suddenly an old girlfriend of theirs would show up or was already lurking in the back bedroom; or a new girlfriend suddenly appeared, and there I was being "let down." Then I'd be off and running, trying to "unhook," but generally being obsessive and compulsive and trying to remain friends for some strange, weird reason.

There were times when I would be immensely attracted and pursue them, desperately needing them to love me, and if they did, then *I'd* suddenly feel I had to run in the other direction!

"Ah yes, that old 'fear of intimacy' two-step," chimes in G.A.

THAT FIRST YEAR following my divorce, the winter of 1984–85, while performing Off-Broadway at the Roundabout Theatre in *Old Times* by Harold Pinter, Tony Hopkins told me—when I was loosely involved with John, the Creature from the Black Lagoon—that an alcoholic has to hit rock bottom before he can climb back up. Tony had been sober for some time by then so I sought his advice concerning how to help my alcoholic creature friend. He told me I couldn't help, that I shouldn't even try.

"He has to do it himself," he said. "He has to seek help himself and you can't help him; it won't work until he hits rock bottom and wants to climb out himself and seek the light." So on Valentine's Day I delivered an eight-page letter to the Broadway theater where John was performing, wherein I described him as that creature from the black lagoon, who decides to come to the surface only to find the rest of the world, and me, standing on the edge of the pond with a hand outstretched and smiling. This sight so unnerves him that he retreats back to the muck and mire, where he burrows down deep in his black lagoon and stays there.

I seemed always to feel the need to save men even if they didn't need or want saving. I hadn't heard the word "co-dependent" then but I might as well have been a founding member of Co-dependents Anonymous. Years later, Lady Life caused us to meet up again, and I saw that John was trying valiantly to live the 12-Step Program. He apologized, made amends, and went on his tortured way.

Continuing on my tortured way as well, I realized how I had tortured Alexander, the cinematographer. It was in the waters of Barbados that I'd warned him to be careful. We went on a very romantic and incredibly sex-filled vacation, an effort to get to know each other better. I knew I was spinning with my divorce from Neil and afraid of getting "involved" in a major way. I told him I didn't want to run after relationships to fill the void left by my divorce. Alexander had a relationship with someone in Denmark or Sweden, but he was sure of his feelings for me, he said. I didn't want to hurt him, I said, which is precisely what I proceeded to do.

He went to Sweden or Denmark to work and break off his relationship there. We talked by phone every day and missed each other madly. We decided to meet in Paris. I booked the Ritz and fantasized an unbelievably romantic and fabulous stay in my favorite European city. I got off the plane in Paris and took one look at him as he stood there waiting for me. A clear voice in my head said, "Nope."

Thinking it was the fact that I hadn't slept on the plane even though I took several Valium, I tried to make the voice wrong, but it didn't work. I found everything about him bothered me, irritated me, made me want to scream. I had no idea why. I just knew I had to get out of "it."

Having spent a ton of time and money and emotional energy in therapy, dealing with all my feelings and the men in my life, there I was, some thirty years and two divorces later, still seemingly bereft of any helpful understanding as to why I was either picking men who were all active members of the "Love Me but You Can't Have Me Club" or running from the ones who cared for me. I raised myself up on my wobbly legs and announced to myself, "No! No More!"

NEIL WAS THE great love of my somewhat undeveloped self. I lavishly gave him total control of our relationship and our life together, including my career. I did it willingly and lovingly. I thought that was what marriage was all about.

What I also wanted was to be an equal, to sit at the kitchen table and discuss what was best for *both* of us and for the marriage. It's natural for a man raised when Neil was, and abandoned as a child like he was, to want to always keep his family around him. But sometimes Lady Life has another point of view.

"Remember what old Rudy said: 'We must learn in a new way how to become old, and we can only do so through spiritual deepening.'"

Well, G.A.! Aren't you the intellectual. Who's Rudy?

"Good heavens, child!" trills Glinda the Good Witch. "Even I know of whom she is speaking! The great man, Rudolf Steiner."

Gee, I wonder if I have that book here. It definitely belongs on my bedroom shelf. The truth is, Glinda dear, Neil and I didn't grow together because we decided we wanted other things from our marriage.

"You were good for him and he was good for you, old girl."

Fortunately, we lived fully, G.A.. Neil and I loved and fought and ultimately challenged each other, and while we were married we supported each other in the work we shared and had a great time doing it. Our time together was a great experience for me. I did grow up. And there is, always, that special chemistry between us whenever we see each other now. Our time together was quite an accomplishment after all: my rite of passage to adulthood, the work we did together, and my continuing relationship with Ellen and Nancy and their families. Neil will always have a special place in my heart.

"Not bad, old girl, not bad at all. You've done a remarkable job of growing up and no matter what the outcome, you are a winner." Thank you, G.A.

"Now, now, don't cry." I know, G.A., I know. My tears are tears of gratitude and thanks. I'm grateful to and for all the men and women in my life, especially the ones who gave me a hard time!

"That's right, let's see that smile get bigger!" Laughing out loud, I suddenly came back to the present, becoming aware of how quiet the bedroom was. My neck and shoulders loosened and, shifting my weight off my right arm, I shook the ache out of my wrist. All this musing and remembering had taken me away from my tired body and the disheveled room and the diaries and books scattered around me.

"Was Shadow Man like all the others?" Wow, Ed, where did that come from? He didn't respond. Was he like the others? No, not really. He held my shadow side. He was guarded, yet I knew him to be other than that. He knew the world was dangerous, but he was a warrior. I wasn't. I'm grateful and happy that he too has a place in my heart. Perhaps he represents some unfinished business. Perhaps my feelings for him are karmic; perhaps it's just my romantic nature. Whatever it is, he's been an important person in my life, like Neil and Gary.

"Hah, and he doesn't even know it!" G.A. said, laughing. I laughed right along with her as my eyes scanned the bookshelves across the room. And there, on a shelf, was the picture of Baba, seeming to smile just for me. His picture always affects me that way, his eyes looking at me with total unconditional love and his smile causing my heart to leap. Next to his picture is a picture of Bhagawan Nityananda, his guru, and next to him is a picture of Gurumayi. Three generations of Siddha Yoga lineage. I move to the shelf and assemble my *puja*, my meditation altar.

As I placed each article on the shelf I mentally said the mantra Guru Om and, as usual, my mind quieted down, my breath slowed and became fuller. All the stuff of life seemed to recede and in its place a quiet space formed. I love this space; I wish I went to it more often, although I do experience it more often than when I first started to practice Siddha Yoga.

"Patience, Marsha," Grace quietly admonished. So I sat there and did nothing except observe my breath and look at their pictures. I thanked each of them for helping me, for being who they are, and for my very existence. The quiet of the room enveloped me and I closed my eyes and remembered Baba's message: "Love your Self, Honor your Self, Worship your Self, Understand your Self because God exists within you as you."

To think that I used to be petrified of being alone and now . . . I'm alone and never lonely. In fact, I love being alone. My life is very full right now and I'm very happy. Sure, I'm scared about this move. Will New Mexico work for me? I honestly don't know. I think so. And there's the farm. I love the land and I can't wait to grow things. Maybe there will be a man in my life here. I hope so, but for right now I am very happy all by myself, knowing that Baba is with me, Nityananda is with me, and Gurumayi is with me. That is the grace of the guru.

I SUDDENLY CAME to as I heard Gary's voice.

"That was Dontzig on the phone. He sends his love. Were you

meditating?" Gary asked as he reappeared, plopping down next to me.

"Sort of. How's Dontzig?"

"Okay. But he still tries to punish me for leaving him alone. He sends his love and misses you."

"Maybe it's a Jewish thing, the abandonment thing," I said smiling, as I began to put some of Baba's books on the shelf above his picture.

"Maybe," he said as he reached for my journal from the Journey to Recovery course.

"Why did you take the Journey to Recovery course, Gary?" I asked as I propped a pillow under my head.

"You."

"Me?" I sputtered. "What . . . what do you mean?"

"Well, if you took it, it must be a good thing," he explained and started to laugh. "I gotta go to bed, Sweet Pea. See you in the morning. Up early. There's lots of unpacking to do yet!"

Gary dragged himself out of the room. Dulcie looked up to see if I was leaving. Satisfied that I was staying, she put her sweet head back down, heaved a deep sigh, and started snoring immediately. Buddy was already comatose. Max was probably still in Gary's bathroom. I turned the diary over in my hand and started leafing through it.

A Course in Recovery. First meeting. "Alcoholic parents are dependent on kids. We are there to take care of them. 'When the lead horse leaves the train . . .'" My mother said that to me when I returned home from running away . . . at twenty-one.

"One of the first things ACAs (Adult Children of Alcoholics) learn: Hide your feelings. ACAs look aloof and hostile to non-ACAs because we learned to hide our feelings. No crows feet around our eyes, no deep laugh lines, etc." People have often complimented me: "You have no lines!" they say and I respond, "I get it from my mother." I always tell them I'm lucky. My mother has great skin.

"We are waiting for someone to love us so much we will finally be acceptable to ourselves. We need to begin with Self-Tolerance, then

Self-Acceptance, Self-Like, and Self-Love. Exercise: Two times a day, morning and evening, look in the bathroom mirror. Make eye contact for twenty seconds. Smile gently, not seductively, no grin. Say, 'Hi, Honey' or 'Hello, Sweetheart.'"

The first time I tried this exercise, I burst into tears, couldn't look at myself, and hid my face in my hands. Each time, for weeks, the same thing happened. Jael Greenleaf, the creator of the course, said the tears are about grief. We grieve for the loss of what we should have had but didn't. We have to gain compassion for ourselves and the situation. The grief is finite and will eventually pass, but it's imperative that we do allow ourselves to grieve. Death and grieving, however, is not accepted in dysfunctional families. My mother never grieved or accepted my father's death, that's for sure. And neither did I, until some fifteen years later.

In the second session I learned that the harder the "Hi Honey" exercise is to do, the more forbidden compassion was in your family. Eventually I was able to make contact with myself in the mirror and actually smile and gently pat myself on the face and say, "It'll be okay, Honey." Eventually I got to the place where I could say, "I love you. You are terrific. I'm so proud of you," without crying. But boy, that was some exercise.

"It is very important that you *not isolate when hurt.*" Well, of course, that's exactly what I want to do when feeling depressed. I don't even feel the hurt, I feel nothing. Like Max, I go into a dark corner and can't talk to anybody. Neil did the opposite. He talked to everybody, even people he barely knew.

Divorce also brought back "The Rolling Fog Depression." In alcoholic families the depressed child is tacitly rewarded for not making waves, and my situation was exacerbated by my mother's rule, "Children are to be seen and not heard." Kids deal with the stress by going numb or by retreating, like a child who reads all the time, alone in her room.

I lived in this depression when I divorced, lost a job, did badly on an audition, or was rejected by someone I liked. It would just come over me, often seconds after awaking or sometimes not until late afternoon as night was coming on. I'll always be grateful to Jael Greenleaf for finally giving me some tools to overcome it.

The first tool was, "Waking Up Intervention." Get up immediately! Get up earlier than you normally might and walk immediately. Jog to that coffee pot or that toilet with your hands over your head! You can't stay depressed jumping up and down with your hands over your head first thing in the morning. Check yourself out in the mirror as you go jumping by. It's pretty weird, but hey, it works.

Secondly, change your routine. When coming home from work, stop off somewhere for twenty minutes or so and read the paper and have a cup of coffee or a soda. Pick someplace nice, someplace you haven't been. This simple idea helped me enormously, if I could get myself to do it. Sometimes I couldn't. Sometimes The Rolling Fog Depression just rolled right over and flattened me. I ended up crawling into bed and pulling the covers over my head. Depression can also be a safe haven, it's comforting. Depression can also be compulsive behavior. It puts a lid on anxiety. It blurs our vision and then we think maybe the anxiety will go away.

What I managed to do as I grew up was talk to myself. When I was a child, I had internal conversations reminding myself that I was okay, that I wasn't crazy, that I was surviving. I took long walks, talked to the saints, and tried to find secret places to play and be by myself. When I got a little older I discovered *acting!* I could get lost in the plays, the scene shop, my imagination. I got to express my feelings safely. Then I met Gary and could finally talk to him. He sent me to therapy. And then I met my Baba. When things got tough, I would think of him, see him in my mind's eye, and remember what he taught me, putting myself in that witness state and watching myself like I was watching a movie.

Unfortunately, adult children of alcoholics love people who often try to make them feel crazy, who try to make us feel like there's something seriously wrong with us. It's a familiar situation. To a kid, there is nothing crazier than trying to figure out what that glow drinker parent is talking about or why he's behaving the way he does or why his responses are so erratic. To a kid, this is a life-and-death situation because we depend on parents for our survival.

Fortunately, for most of us, learning those survival techniques at the knees of that crazy-making parent helps us get to adulthood. As a kid we intuitively or subconsciously understand that we can't know or be fully conscious or aware in a dysfunctional family because we would wind up being psychotic ourselves or dead before we reach our teens. It's impossible to take the level of loneliness, fear, and chaos that comes from a lack of structure and constancy in our lives, so we become profoundly creative in order to survive.

Sometimes I just want to scream at our schools and our government, "Put a paintbrush, a story, a toe shoe, a tap shoe, a soft shoe, clay, a play, music, an instrument, something artistic, something creative in a child's hand for God's sake!" There are so many children out there who need the help of such an outlet.

"Be actively grateful that you survived." I am grateful for my creativity. I figured out how to be a pleaser; how to stay hypervigilant; how to read behavior. I solved the problem of my exploding universe and I survived. But what about winning, not just surviving?

"If I win. I'll destroy that low ceiling of self-esteem and prove that Dad is a failure. I'll also be a target for other people's resentment and jealousy and therefore I'll be anxious and depressed. If I win, I'll have to leave behind the people I love. So don't win! It's much easier, much nicer that way." Wow!

Suddenly, there's that voice in my head, "Oh! This is all so much a cliché, cliché, cliché, cliché! You are ridiculous; do you know that? You are a failure, a has-been, a "second-rate" at best! You're a fool, a fool! Bemoaning your oh-so-tragic past!"

Wooooh. Well, so there's my malevolent inner Critic. Interesting you should shout your way in now. Why do you say all that? Tell me why? I want to know.

"What difference does it make?" comes the answer. "Who cares!"

There's something familiar about this question. What is it? I began to flip through the pages of the journal. Somewhere there was something about this . . . yes, here it is.

"What we learn at birth and actually before is very powerful. Dysfunctional families teach: Give up. Why waste your energy. There's no point. I have no control." We have to recondition ourselves to recover this powerful learning. In healthy families, kids learn by imitation and association, by naming things, asking parents what they're feeling. In healthy families, they are told the truth; the parent doesn't lie or try to hide her feelings. For a kid, being able to name a feeling is very often a cure *for* the feeling.

"In a dysfunctional family, the parent isn't there or is there intermittently, and when asked what's wrong, the parent says, "Nothing's wrong," or "I'm fine." Kids *know* when parents are lying and learn from them that feelings must be dangerous and therefore shouldn't be expressed. Kids learn they can't look at feelings, can't talk about them, and as a result don't really know what feelings are.

"Kids also know that parents can read their minds. Therefore, in dysfunctional families, kids learn they cannot even think about their feelings. So what we do is put our feelings in a place where there are no words. All our feelings go in a "fog bank." To talk about feelings destabilizes my universe, so it's too dangerous to talk; therefore I don't learn the vocabulary.

"Little kids do not have an Observer self. Aware Ego develops around eleven years of age. In dysfunctional families the Observer self becomes the inner Critic. It doesn't get a chance to observe, but rather it becomes hypervigilant. When we talk to ourselves, we talk in harsh and dramatic terms."

Well, my inner Critic was certainly harsh and dramatic just now.

"Learn new words to express yourself: comfortable, mid-range words like 'annoyed, disappointed, sad, pleasant, irritated, uncomfortable.' Remember, drama is about victim. The word 'abandoned'—drop it forever. Don't use 'safe' and 'unsafe' either. Dysfunctional families allow words like 'disgusted, nasty, depressed, nice, or not nice.' The most illegal feeling in a dysfunctional family is fear. It's the most destabilizing. Remember, a wonderful life is a collection of small pleasantries." Gee, I'm glad I'm rereading this.

"Well, your life is far from a collection of small pleasantries, old girl, and look how great you came out!" G.A.'s laugh sounds great, suddenly making me laugh out loud. Dulcie looks up at me to see what is so funny.

"It's okay, girl," I tell her, "I was just laughing at myself. And now I need something to drink." Just like Nick Nolte in *North Dallas Forty*, I slowly made my way toward the kitchen.

The foyer was dark and so was the rest of the house. I tiptoed past the boxes and padded softly toward Gary's room. He was sound asleep. I looked in on sweet Max, still curled in the corner of the bathroom where he'd been since we arrived. At least he was sleeping and not in pain. I picked up his water bowl and headed on to the kitchen. I passed the pictures on the wall I had hung last night.

I paused and stared at the wall of pictures that encompassed my life to this point. Pictures of the girls and pictures from the various movies and theatrical productions I'd appeared in. Not bad, old girl. Moonlight caught the glass of one of them and drew me to it. It was of Clint Eastwood and myself from *Heartbreak Ridge*.

"What a guy," G.A. sighed. I'll say. My favorite recollection from that film was the night we shot a dance sequence. We were dancing to slow music on a small dance floor outside under the stars. There were colorful paper lanterns strung across the floor and couples of extras moving to the music. We had dialogue to say to each other, so Clint decided the cinematographer, Jack Green, should use a handheld camera and move around us. So, there we were, acting and dancing as Clint moved me around the floor, smooth as silk. After we had done the scene a couple of times, I asked Clint why he had changed direction the way he did as we danced.

"I was watching the play of light across your face to make sure everything was good." I was so impressed. There he was, directing, acting, and dancing—all at the same time.

I stepped back and took in all the pictures of my life and breathed a deep sigh of . . . what? Contentment, satisfaction? Yes, they all looked like they belonged there.

Buddy and Dulcie, quietly padding along with me, glanced back, then went to see Max. I watched them stand at the door to the bath-room and sniff the ground, wondering if they should go in. Buddy looked at me and then back at Max.

"Oh, Buddy boy, he's gonna be okay," I softly muttered. "We're all gonna be okay."

"Come on you two," I whispered, "let's see what night looks like, shall we?" I grabbed a big glass of water and drank it down. The water from the kitchen tap tasted clean and refreshing. Wonder of wonders, no bottled water required.

The full moon seemed brighter than I had ever seen it. The sky, sparkling with stars, was reflected in the swimming pool, and the big old junipers were black against the moonlit sky. Everything stood out in sharp relief. It was quiet and the air felt cool and comforting on my skin. In the distance, to my left, were the blinking lights of Santa Fe. Somewhere between there and here coyotes began howling to each other and the great cottonwoods rustled. Buddy and Dulcie pricked their ears, looking out toward town. After waiting a bit, they both gracefully settled themselves down on the black-green grass.

Like the weary traveler I was, I lowered myself onto the chaise. The sweet breeze came by and ruffled the scalloped edges of the awning, and somewhere close by night birds shared their secrets before settling down to sleep. I watched the black junipers gracefully wave to the stars and thought of those cowboys long ago who slept under this grand sky accompanied only by their trusty horse and six-gun to keep them safe. Laying my head back I felt my neck ache ease as I slowly breathed in a deep drink of pure night air, letting it wash through me, releasing tension and tiredness. Just watching the night, which looked almost like a blue day because of the bright moon, my mind slowed, my shoulders dropped, and peace began to settle as if the journey was done, the first part anyway. This is nice. This is good. This is beautiful.

CHAPTER THIRTEEN

RESTING IN THE RIVER

My friends came and we put the rest of my stuff in order, celebrating the Fourth of July 1993 with fireworks, fun, and lots of good cheer. Gary Dale went back to Los Angeles to be with Dontzig until it was time for them to begin building their house. I settled into my new life in New Mexico and began dreaming about the house I would build (I didn't know then I would stay at La Bajada Ranch for five years before moving permanently to the farm in Abiquiu, New Mexico). Max was operated on and came through it just fine. He and Buddy and Dulcie became friends with Ruby, a pit bull terrier, who eventually came to live with us, as well as Misha, a Border collie mix, found on the highway, and Billy and Red, Australian cow dogs who showed up at the farm one Christmas looking poorly.

I finally built my dream house and moved in Labor Day of last year. We coexist with blue herons, ducks, eagles, hawks, bobcats, coyotes, geese, cattle that live next door, and creature critters of all kinds. Gary Dale lives next door permanently and Gary Dontzig comes out from L.A. whenever he's free from his television writing obligations.

As I write this, all's quiet on the southwestern front this February 14, Valentine's Day, in the year 2000. The sky is a riot of winter sunset color: all red-orange, pink-magenta, and blue-gray. If you painted it, it wouldn't look real, but that's the way it is out here in the Southwest. Mother Nature provides us with the greatest form of entertainment, weather. Weather is an ever present topic in my life since the farm is now beginning its third year of production. Resting in the River is a certified organic/biodynamic medicinal herb farm with our own Web site, www.riverherbs.com. And my library has grown even larger with the addition of many books and periodicals on medicinal herbs, soil amendments, lunar calendars, the work of Rudolf Steiner, and all kinds of books on organic farming. I didn't know back then, in the summer of 1993, that this journey would take me into the compost business and medicinal herbs but it all feels very good, very right, and positive. I certainly don't lack for anything to do!

When I began this journey in 1993, I said I hoped I'd find a new existence, a completely different life that makes sense to me and brings with it some kind of sustained peace and enjoyment. Well, I have.

Meanwhile, I've continued to work in theater and television, traveling to Los Angeles, New York, and even London, England, where Richard Dreyfuss and I starred in the West End in Neil Simon's *Prisoner of Second Avenue* to great success. My next "gig" is in Anaheim, California, for a guest appearance at probably the biggest expo of natural health products in North America. Go figure!

ABOUT THE AUTHOR

A four-time Academy Award® nominee and a two-time winner of the Golden Globe award, Marsha Mason has starred in movies such as *The Goodbye Girl*, *Cinderella Liberty*, and *Nick of Time*. Most recently she appeared opposite Richard Dreyfuss in a stage revival of *The Prisoner of Second Avenue* in London, in *The Vagina Monologues* in New York, and as Sherry on TV's *Frasier*. She now lives in Abiquiu, New Mexico, where she owns a successful medicinal herb farm. *Journey* is her first book.